The Study of Language

This best-selling textbook provides an engaging and user-friendly introduction to the study of language. Assuming no prior knowledge of the subject, Yule presents information in short, bite-sized sections, introducing the major concepts in language study – from how children learn language to why men and women speak differently, through all the key elements of language. This fourth edition has been revised and updated with twenty new sections, covering new accounts of language origins, the key properties of language, text messaging, kinship terms and more than twenty new word etymologies. To increase student engagement with the text, Yule has also included more than fifty new tasks, including thirty involving data analysis, enabling students to apply what they have learned. The online study guide offers students further resources when working on the tasks, while encouraging lively and proactive learning. This is the most fundamental and easy-to-use introduction to the study of language.

George Yule has taught Linguistics at the Universities of Edinburgh, Hawai'i, Louisiana State and Minnesota. He is the author of a number of books, including *Discourse Analysis* (with Gillian Brown, 1983) and *Pragmatics* (1996).

The Study of Language

Fourth edition

GEORGE YULE

CAMBRIDGE UNIVERSITY PRESS

Cambridge, New York, Melbourne, Madrid, Cape Town, Singapore, São Paulo,
Delhi, Tokyo, Mexico City

Cambridge University Press
The Edinburgh Building, Cambridge CB2 8RU, UK

Published in the United States of America by Cambridge University Press, New York

www.cambridge.org
Information on this title: www.cambridge.org/9780521749220

First and second editions © Cambridge University Press 1985, 1996

Third and fourth editions © George Yule 2006, 2010

First published 1985
Second edition 1996
Third edition 2006
Fourth edition 2010
4th printing 2011

Printed in the United Kingdom at the University Press, Cambridge

A catalogue record for this publication is available from the British Library

ISBN 978-0-521-76527-5 Hardback
ISBN 978-0-521-74922-0 Paperback

Additional resources for this publication at www.cambridge.org/yule

Contents

Preface

This new edition

Extensive feedback from instructors during the writing of the fourth edition of *The Study of Language* brought forth suggestions for improvements and some excellent advice – many thanks to all. These suggestions have resulted in:

- a change in the overall organization of the book, with *Writing* moving to Chapter 16.
- revision of the internal organization of some chapters, with a clearer division of the material into main topics and subtopics, with additional topics including new accounts of language origins, text messaging, kinship terms and more than twenty new word etymologies.
- over fifty new Tasks, including thirty that involve data analysis, so that students can apply what they've learned.
- a new online Study Guide www.cambridge.org/yule to help students with those Tasks.

I hope these revisions will make the book easier to read and generally more user-friendly.

To the student

In *The Study of Language* I have tried to present a comprehensive survey of what is known about language and also of the methods used by linguists in arriving at that knowledge. There have been many interesting developments in the study of language over the past two decades, but it is still a fact that any individual speaker of a language has a more comprehensive "unconscious" knowledge of how language works than any linguist has yet been able to describe. So, as you read the following chapters, take a critical view of the effectiveness of the descriptions, the analyses, and the generalizations by measuring them against your own intuitions about how your language works. By the end of the book, you should then feel that you do know quite a lot about both the internal structure of language (its form) and the varied uses of language in human life (its function), and also that you are ready to ask the kinds of questions that professional linguists ask when they conduct their research.

This revised edition is designed to make your learning task easier and more interesting:

- Topics are split into manageable subtopics.
- Learning is active with Study Questions at the end of each chapter, as a way for you to check that you have understood some of the main points or important terms introduced in that chapter. They should be answered without too much difficulty, but to support you a set of suggested answers is available in the Study Guide online.
- Tasks at the end of chapters give you an opportunity to explore related concepts and types of analysis that go beyond the material presented in the chapter. The online Study Guide again supports your learning with analysis, suggested answers and resources for all these tasks. The Discussion Topics and Projects found at the end of each topic provide an opportunity for you to consider some of the larger issues in the study of language, to think about some of the controversies that arise with certain topics and to try to focus your own opinions on different language-related issues.
- To help you find out more about the issues covered in this book, each chapter ends with a set of Further Readings that lead you to more detailed treatments than are possible in this introduction.

Origins of this book

This book can be traced back to introductory courses on language taught at the University of Edinburgh, the University of Minnesota and Louisiana State University, and to the suggestions and criticisms of hundreds of students who forced me to present what I had to say in a way they could understand. An early version of the written material was developed for Independent Study students at the University of Minnesota. Later versions have had the benefit of expert advice from a lot of teachers working with diverse groups in different situations. I am particularly indebted to Professor Hugh Buckingham, Louisiana State University, for sharing his expertise and enthusiasm over many years as a colleague and friend.

For help in creating the first and second editions, I would like to acknowledge my debt to Gill Brown, Keith Brown, Penny Carter, Feride Erkü, Diana Fritz, Kathleen Houlihan, Tom McArthur, Jim Miller, Rocky Miranda, Eric Nelson, Sandra Pinkerton, Rich Reardon, Gerald Sanders, Elaine Tarone and Michele Trufant.

For feedback and advice in the preparation of the third and fourth editions, I would like to thank Jean Aitchison (University of Oxford), Linda Blanton (University of New

Orleans), Hugh W. Buckingham (Louisiana State University), Karen Currie (Federal University of Espíritu Santo), Mary Anna Dimitrakopoulos (Indiana University, South Bend), Thomas Field (University of Maryland, Baltimore), Anthony Fox (University of Leeds), Luisa Garro (New York University), Gordon Gibson (University of Paisley), Katinka Hammerich (University of Florida), Raymond Hickey (Essen University), Richard Hirsch (Linköping University), Fiona Joseph (University of Wolverhampton), Eliza Kitis (Aristotle University), Terrie Mathis (California State University, Northridge), Stephen Matthews (University of Hong Kong), Jens Reinke (Christian Albrechts Universität zu Kiel), Philip Riley (Université de Nancy 2), Rick Santos (Fresno City College), Joanne Scheibman (Old Dominion University), Royal Skousen (Brigham Young University), Michael Stubbs (Universität Trier), Mary Talbot (University of Sunderland) and Sherman Wilcox (University of New Mexico).

In creating this new edition, I have also benefited from reader surveys conducted by Sarah Wightman and Andrew Winnard, as well as the work of many others in the excellent production team at Cambridge University Press.

For my own introductory course, I remain indebted to Willie and Annie Yule, and, for my continuing enlightenment, to Maryann Overstreet.

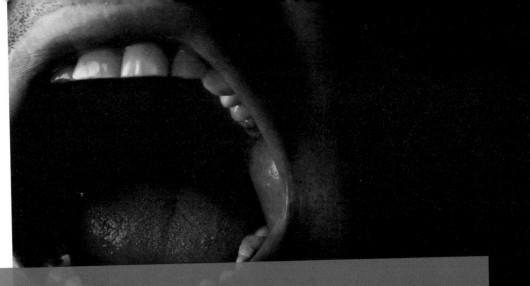

1 The origins of language

The suspicion does not appear improbable that the progenitors of man, either the males or females, or both sexes, before they had acquired the power of expressing their mutual love in articulate language, endeavoured to charm each other with musical notes and rhythm.

Darwin (1871)

In Charles Darwin's vision of the origins of language, early humans had already developed musical ability prior to language and were using it "to charm each other." This may not match the typical image that most of us have of our early ancestors as rather rough characters wearing animal skins and not very charming, but it is an interesting speculation about how language may have originated. It remains, however, a speculation.

We simply don't know how language originated. We do know that the ability to produce sound and simple vocal patterning (a hum versus a grunt, for example) appears to be in an ancient part of the brain that we share with all vertebrates, including fish, frogs, birds and other mammals. But that isn't human language. We suspect that some type of spoken language must have developed between 100,000 and 50,000 years ago, well before written language (about 5,000 years ago). Yet, among the traces of earlier periods of life on earth, we never find any direct evidence or artifacts relating to the speech of our distant ancestors that might tell us how language was back in the early stages. Perhaps because of this absence of direct physical evidence, there has been no shortage of speculation about the origins of human speech.

The divine source

In the biblical tradition, as described in the book of Genesis, God created Adam and "whatsoever Adam called every living creature, that was the name thereof." Alternatively, following a Hindu tradition, language came from Sarasvati, wife of Brahma, creator of the universe. In most religions, there appears to be a divine source who provides humans with language. In an attempt to rediscover this original divine language, a few experiments have been carried out, with rather conflicting results. The basic hypothesis seems to have been that, if human infants were allowed to grow up without hearing any language around them, then they would spontaneously begin using the original God-given language.

The Greek writer Herodotus reported the story of an Egyptian pharaoh named Psammetichus (or Psamtik) who tried the experiment with two newborn babies more than 2,500 years ago. After two years of isolation except for the company of goats and a mute shepherd, the children were reported to have spontaneously uttered, not an Egyptian word, but something that was identified as the Phrygian word *bekos*, meaning "bread." The pharaoh concluded that Phrygian, an older language spoken in part of what is modern Turkey, must be the original language. That seems very unlikely. The children may not have picked up this "word" from any human source, but as several commentators have pointed out, they must have heard what the goats were saying. (First remove the *-kos* ending, which was added in the Greek version of the story, then pronounce *be-* as you would the English word *bed* without *-d* at the end. Can you hear a goat?)

King James the Fourth of Scotland carried out a similar experiment around the year 1500 and the children were reported to have spontaneously started speaking Hebrew, confirming the King's belief that Hebrew had indeed been the language of the Garden of Eden. It is unfortunate that all other cases of children who have been discovered living in isolation, without coming into contact with human speech, tend not to confirm the results of these types of divine-source experiments. Very young children living without access to human language in their early years grow up with no language at all. (We will consider the case of one such child later in Chapter 12.) If human language did emanate from a divine source, we have no way of reconstructing that original language, especially given the events in a place called Babel, "because the Lord did there confound the language of all the earth," as described in the book of Genesis in the Bible (11: 9).

The natural sound source

A quite different view of the beginnings of language is based on the concept of natural sounds. The basic idea is that primitive words could have been imitations of the natural sounds which early men and women heard around them. When an object flew by, making a CAW-CAW sound, the early human tried to imitate the sound and used it to refer to the thing associated with the sound. And when another flying creature made a COO-COO sound, that natural sound was adopted to refer to that kind of object. The fact that all modern languages have some words with pronunciations that seem to echo naturally occurring sounds could be used to support this theory. In English, in addition to *cuckoo*, we have *splash, bang, boom, rattle, buzz, hiss, screech*, and forms such as *bow-wow*. In fact, this type of view has been called the "bow-wow theory" of language origin. Words that sound similar to the noises they describe are examples of **onomatopeia**. While it is true that a number of words in any language are onomatopoeic, it is hard to see how most of the soundless things as well as abstract concepts in our world could have been referred to in a language that simply echoed natural sounds. We might also be rather skeptical about a view that seems to assume that a language is only a set of words used as "names" for things.

It has also been suggested that the original sounds of language may have come from natural cries of emotion such as pain, anger and joy. By this route, presumably, *Ouch!* came to have its painful connotations. But *Ouch!* and other interjections such as *Ah!*, *Ooh!*, *Wow!* or *Yuck!*, are usually produced with sudden intakes of breath, which is the opposite of ordinary talk. We normally produce spoken language on exhaled breath. Basically, the expressive noises people make in emotional reactions contain sounds that are not otherwise used in speech production and consequently would seem to be rather unlikely candidates as source sounds for language.

The social interaction source

Another proposal involving natural sounds has been called the "yo-he-ho" theory. The idea is that the sounds of a person involved in physical effort could be the source of our language, especially when that physical effort involved several people and the interaction had to be coordinated. So, a group of early humans might develop a set of hums, grunts, groans and curses that were used when they were lifting and carrying large bits of trees or lifeless hairy mammoths.

The appeal of this proposal is that it places the development of human language in a social context. Early people must have lived in groups, if only because larger groups offered better protection from attack. Groups are necessarily social organizations and, to maintain those organizations, some form of communication is required, even if it is just grunts and curses. So, human sounds, however they were produced, must have had some principled use within the life and social interaction of early human groups. This is an important idea that may relate to the uses of humanly produced sounds. It does not, however, answer our question regarding the origins of the sounds produced.

Apes and other primates live in social groups and use grunts and social calls, but they do not seem to have developed the capacity for speech.

The physical adaptation source

Instead of looking at types of sounds as the source of human speech, we can look at the types of physical features humans possess, especially those that are distinct from other creatures, which may have been able to support speech production. We can start with the observation that, at some early stage, our ancestors made a very significant transition to an upright posture, with bipedal (on two feet) locomotion, and a revised role for the front limbs.

Some effects of this type of change can be seen in physical differences between the skull of a gorilla and that of a Neanderthal man from around 60,000 years ago. The reconstructed vocal tract of a Neanderthal suggests that some consonant-like sound distinctions would have been possible. We have to wait until about 35,000 years ago for features in reconstructions of fossilized skeletal structures that begin to resemble those of modern humans. In the study of evolutionary development, there are certain physical features, best thought of as partial adaptations, which appear to be relevant for speech. They are streamlined versions of features found in other primates. By themselves, such features would not necessarily lead to speech production, but they are good clues that a creature possessing such features probably has the capacity for speech.

Teeth, lips, mouth, larynx and pharynx

Human **teeth** are upright, not slanting outwards like those of apes, and they are roughly even in height. Such characteristics are not very useful for ripping or tearing food and seem better adapted for grinding and chewing. They are also very helpful in making sounds such as *f* or *v*. Human **lips** have much more intricate muscle interlacing than is found in other primates and their resulting flexibility certainly helps in making sounds like *p* or *b*. The human **mouth** is relatively small compared to other primates, can be opened and closed rapidly, and contains a smaller, thicker and more muscular **tongue** which can be used to shape a wide variety of sounds inside the oral cavity. In addition, unlike other primates, humans can close off the airway through the nose to create more air pressure in the mouth. The overall effect of these small differences taken together is a face with more intricate muscle interlacing in the lips and mouth, capable of a wider range of shapes and a more rapid and powerful delivery of sounds produced through these different shapes.

The human **larynx** or "voice box" (containing the vocal folds or vocal cords) differs significantly in position from the larynx of other primates such as monkeys. In the course of human physical development, the assumption of an upright posture moved the head more directly above the spinal column and the larynx dropped to a lower position. This created a longer cavity called the **pharynx**, above the vocal folds, which acts as a resonator for increased range and clarity of the sounds produced via the larynx and the vocal tract. One unfortunate consequence of this development is that the lower position of the human larynx makes it much more possible for the human to choke on pieces of food. Monkeys may not be able to use their larynx to produce speech sounds, but they do not suffer from the problem of getting food stuck in their windpipe. In evolutionary terms, there must have been a big advantage in getting this extra vocal power (i.e. a larger range of sound distinctions) to outweigh the potential disadvantage from an increased risk of choking to death.

The tool-making source

In the physical adaptation view, one function (producing speech sounds) must have been superimposed on existing anatomical features (teeth, lips) previously used for other purposes (chewing, sucking). A similar development is believed to have taken place with human hands and some believe that manual gestures may have been a precursor of language. By about two million years ago, there is evidence that humans had developed preferential right-handedness and had become capable of making stone tools. Wood tools and composite tools eventually followed. Tool-making, or the outcome of manipulating objects and changing them using both hands, is evidence of a brain at work.

The human **brain** is not only large relative to human body size, it is also **lateralized**, that is, it has specialized functions in each of the two hemispheres. (More details are presented in Chapter 12.) Those functions that control the motor movements involved in complex vocalization (speaking) and object manipulation (making or using tools) are very close to each other in the left hemisphere of the brain. It may be that there was an evolutionary connection between the language-using and tool-using abilities of humans and that both were involved in the development of the speaking brain. Most of the other speculative proposals concerning the origins of speech seem to be based on a picture of humans producing single noises to indicate objects in their environment. This activity may indeed have been a crucial stage in the development of language, but what it lacks is any structural organization. All languages, including sign language, require the organizing and combining of sounds or signs in specific arrangements. We seem to have developed a part of our brain that specializes in making these arrangements.

If we think in terms of the most basic process involved in primitive tool-making, it is not enough to be able to grasp one rock (make one sound); the human must also be able to bring another rock (other sounds) into proper contact with the first in order to develop a tool. In terms of language structure, the human may have first developed a naming ability by producing a specific and consistent noise (e.g. *bEEr*) for a specific object. The crucial additional step was to bring another specific noise (e.g. *gOOd*) into combination with the first to build a complex message (*bEEr gOOd*). Several thousand years of development later, humans have honed this message-building capacity to a point where, on Saturdays, watching a football game, they can drink a sustaining beverage and proclaim *This beer is good*. As far as we know, other primates are not doing this.

The genetic source

We can think of the human baby in its first few years as a living example of some of these physical changes taking place. At birth, the baby's brain is only a quarter of its eventual weight and the larynx is much higher in the throat, allowing babies, like chimpanzees, to breathe and drink at the same time. In a relatively short period of time, the larynx descends, the brain develops, the child assumes an upright posture and starts walking and talking.

This almost automatic set of developments and the complexity of the young child's language have led some scholars to look for something more powerful than small physical adaptations of the species over time as the source of language. Even children who are born deaf (and do not develop speech) become fluent sign language users, given appropriate circumstances, very early in life. This seems to indicate that human offspring are born with a special capacity for language. It is innate, no other creature seems to have it, and it isn't tied to a specific variety of language. Is it possible that this language capacity is genetically hard-wired in the newborn human?

As a solution to the puzzle of the origins of language, this **innateness hypothesis** would seem to point to something in human genetics, possibly a crucial mutation, as the source. This would not have been a gradual change, but something that happened rather quickly. We are not sure when this proposed genetic change might have taken place or how it might relate to the physical adaptations described earlier. However, as we consider this hypothesis, we find our speculations about the origins of language moving away from fossil evidence or the physical source of basic human sounds toward analogies with how computers work (e.g. being pre-programmed or hard-wired) and concepts taken from the study of genetics. The investigation of the origins of language then turns into a search for the special "language gene" that only humans possess.

If we are indeed the only creatures with this special capacity for language, then will it be completely impossible for any other creature to produce or understand language? We'll try to answer that question in Chapter 2.

Study questions

1 Why is it difficult to agree with Psammetichus that Phrygian must have been the original human language?

2 What is the basic idea behind the "bow-wow" theory of language origin?

3 Why are interjections such as *Ouch* considered to be unlikely sources of human speech sounds?

4 Where is the pharynx and how did it become an important part of human sound production?

5 Why do you think that young deaf children who become fluent in sign language would be cited in support of the innateness hypothesis?

6 With which of the six "sources" would you associate this quotation?

> Chewing, licking and sucking are extremely widespread mammalian activities, which, in terms of casual observation, have obvious similarities with speech.
>
> (MacNeilage, 1998)

Tasks

A What is the connection between the Heimlich maneuver and the development of human speech?

B What exactly happened at Babel and why is it used in explanations of language origins?

C What are the arguments for and against a teleological explanation of the origins of human language?

D The idea that "ontogeny recapitulates phylogeny" was first proposed by Ernst Haeckel in 1866 and is still frequently used in discussions of language origins.
Can you find a simpler or less technical way to express this idea?

E In his analysis of the beginnings of human language, William Foley comes to the conclusion that "language as we understand it was born about 200,000 years ago" (1997: 73). This is substantially earlier than the dates (between 100,000 and 50,000 years ago) that other scholars have proposed. What kinds of evidence and arguments are typically presented in order to choose a particular date "when language was born"?

F What is the connection between the innateness hypothesis, as described in this chapter, and the idea of a Universal Grammar?

Discussion topics/projects

I   In this chapter we didn't address the issue of whether language has developed as part of our general cognitive abilities or whether it has evolved as a separate component that can exist independently (and is unrelated to intelligence, for example). What kind of evidence do you think would be needed to resolve this question? (For background reading, see chapter 4 of Aitchison, 2000.)

II A connection has been proposed between language, tool-using and right-handedness in the majority of humans. Is it possible that freedom to use the hands, after assuming an upright bipedal posture, resulted in certain skills that led to the development of language? Why did we assume an upright posture? What kind of changes must have taken place in our hands? (For background reading, see chapter 5 of Beaken, 1996.)

Further reading

Basic treatments

Aitchison, J. (2000) *The Seeds of Speech* (Canto edition) Cambridge University Press

Kenneally, C. (2007) *The First Word* Viking Press

More detailed treatments

Beaken, M. (1996) *The Making of Language* Edinburgh University Press

Johannson, S. (2005) *Origins of Language* John Benjamins

Music before language

Mithen, S. (2006) *The Singing Neanderthals* Harvard University Press

A hum versus a grunt

Bass, A., E. Gilland and R. Baker (2008) "Evolutionary origins for social vocalization in a vertebrate hindbrain-spinal compartment" *Science* 321 (July 18): 417–421

"Bow-wow" theory, etc.

Jespersen, O. (1922) *Language: Its Nature, Development and Origin* Macmillan

Social interaction

Burling, R. (2005) *The Talking Ape* Oxford University Press

Physical development

Lieberman, P. (1998) *Eve Spoke: Human Language and Human Evolution* W. W. Norton

Gesture

Corballis, M. (2002) *From Hand to Mouth* Princeton University Press

Brain development

Loritz, D. (1999) *How the Brain Evolved Language* Oxford University Press

Tool-making

Gibson, K. and T. Ingold (eds.) (1993) *Tools, Language and Cognition in Human Evolution* Cambridge University Press

Innateness

Pinker, S. (1994) *The Language Instinct* William Morrow

Against innateness

Sampson, G. (2005) *The "Language Instinct" Debate* (Revised edition) Continuum

Other references

Foley, W. (1997) *Anthropological Linguistics* Blackwell

MacNeilage, P. (1998) "The frame/content theory of evolution of speech production" *Behavioral and Brain Sciences* 21: 499–546

2 Animals and human language

One evening in the mid-1980s my wife and I were returning from an evening cruise around Boston Harbor and decided to take a waterfront stroll. We were passing in front of the Boston Aquarium when a gravelly voice yelled out, "Hey! Hey! Get outa there!" Thinking we had mistakenly wandered somewhere we were not allowed, we stopped and looked around for a security guard or some other official, but saw no one, and no warning signs. Again the voice boomed, "Hey! Hey you!" As we tracked the voice we found ourselves approaching a large, glass-fenced pool in front of the aquarium where four harbor seals were lounging on display. Incredulous, I traced the source of the command to a large seal reclining vertically in the water, with his head extended back and up, his mouth slightly open, rotating slowly. A seal was talking, not to me, but to the air, and incidentally to anyone within earshot who cared to listen.

Deacon (1997)

There are a lot of stories about creatures that can talk. We usually assume that they are fantasy or fiction or that they involve birds or animals simply imitating something they have heard humans say (as Terrence Deacon discovered was the case with the loud seal in Boston Aquarium). Yet we think that creatures are capable of communicating, certainly with other members of their own species. Is it possible that a creature could learn to communicate with humans using language? Or does human language have properties that make it so unique that it is quite unlike any other communication system and hence unlearnable by any other creature? To answer these questions, we first look at some special properties of human language, then review a number of experiments in communication involving humans and animals.

Communication

We should first distinguish between specifically **communicative signals** and those which may be unintentionally **informative signals**. Someone listening to you may become informed about you through a number of signals that you have not intentionally sent. She may note that you have a cold (you sneezed), that you aren't at ease (you shifted around in your seat), that you are disorganized (non-matching socks) and that you are from somewhere else (you have a strange accent). However, when you use language to tell this person, *I'm one of the applicants for the vacant position of senior brain surgeon at the hospital*, you are normally considered to be intentionally communicating something.

Similarly, the blackbird is not normally taken to be communicating anything by having black feathers, sitting on a branch and looking down at the ground, but is considered to be sending a communicative signal with the loud squawking produced when a cat appears on the scene. So, when we talk about distinctions between human language and animal communication, we are considering both in terms of their potential as a means of intentional communication.

Properties of human language

While we tend to think of communication as the primary function of human language, it is not a distinguishing feature. All creatures communicate in some way. However, we suspect that other creatures are not reflecting on the way they create their communicative messages or reviewing how they work (or not). That is, one barking dog is probably not offering advice to another barking dog along the lines of "Hey, you should lower your bark to make it sound more menacing." They're not barking about barking. Humans are clearly able to reflect on language and its uses (e.g. "I wish he wouldn't use so many technical terms"). This is **reflexivity**. The property of reflexivity (or "reflexiveness") accounts for the fact that we can use language to think and talk about language itself, making it one of the distinguishing features of human language. Indeed, without this general ability, we wouldn't be able to reflect on or identify any of the other distinct properties of human language. We'll look in detail at another five of them: displacement, arbitrariness, productivity, cultural transmission and duality.

Displacement

When your pet cat comes home and stands at your feet calling *meow*, you are likely to understand this message as relating to that immediate time and place. If you ask your cat where it has been and what it was up to, you'll probably get the same *meow* response. Animal communication seems to be designed exclusively for this moment, here and now. It cannot effectively be used to relate events that are far removed in time and place. When your dog says *GRRR*, it means *GRRR, right now*, because dogs don't seem to be capable of communicating *GRRR, last night, over in the park*. In contrast, human language users are normally capable of producing messages equivalent to *GRRR, last night, over in the park*, and then going on to say *In fact, I'll be going back tomorrow for some more*. Humans can refer to past and future time. This property of human language is called **displacement**. It allows language users to talk about things and events not present in the immediate environment. Indeed, displacement allows us to talk about things and places (e.g. angels, fairies, Santa Claus, Superman, heaven, hell) whose existence we cannot even be sure of. Animal communication is generally considered to lack this property.

We could look at bee communication as a small exception because it seems to have some version of displacement. For example, when a honeybee finds a source of nectar and returns to the beehive, it can perform a complex dance routine to communicate to the other bees the location of this nectar. Depending on the type of dance (round dance for nearby and tail-wagging dance, with variable tempo, for further away and how far), the other bees can work out where this newly discovered feast can be found. Doesn't this ability of the bee to indicate a location some distance away mean that bee communication has at least some degree of displacement as a feature? Yes, but it is displacement of a very limited type. It just doesn't have the range of possibilities found in human language. Certainly, the bee can direct other bees to a food source. However, it must be the most recent food source. It cannot be *that delicious rose bush on the other side of town that we visited last weekend*, nor can it be, as far as we know, possible future nectar in bee heaven.

Arbitrariness

It is generally the case that there is no "natural" connection between a linguistic form and its meaning. The connection is quite arbitrary. We can't just look at the Arabic word كلب and, from its shape, for example, determine that it has a natural and obvious meaning any more than we can with its English translation form *dog*. The linguistic form has no natural or "iconic" relationship with that hairy four-legged barking object out in the world. This aspect of the relationship between linguistic signs and objects in the world is described as **arbitrariness**. Of course, you can play a game with words to make them appear to "fit" the idea or activity they indicate, as shown in these words from a child's game. However, this type of game only emphasizes the arbitrariness of the connection that normally exists between a word and its meaning.

Figure 2.1

There are some words in language with sounds that seem to "echo" the sounds of objects or activities and hence seem to have a less arbitrary connection. English examples are *cuckoo*, *crash*, *slurp*, *squelch* or *whirr*. However, these onomatopoeic words are relatively rare in human language.

For the majority of animal signals, there does appear to be a clear connection between the conveyed message and the signal used to convey it. This impression we have of the non-arbitrariness of animal signaling may be closely connected to the fact that, for any animal, the set of signals used in communication is finite. That is, each variety of animal communication consists of a fixed and limited set of vocal or gestural forms. Many of these forms are only used in specific situations (e.g. establishing territory) and at particular times (e.g. during the mating season).

Productivity

Humans are continually creating new expressions and novel utterances by manipulating their linguistic resources to describe new objects and situations. This property is described as **productivity** (or "creativity" or "open-endedness") and essentially means that the potential number of utterances in any human language is infinite.

The communication systems of other creatures are not like that. Cicadas have four signals to choose from and vervet monkeys have thirty-six vocal calls. Nor does it seem possible for creatures to produce new signals to communicate novel experiences or events. The honeybee, normally able to communicate the location of a nectar source to other bees, will fail to do so if the location is really "new." In one experiment, a hive of bees was placed at the foot of a radio tower and a food source placed at the top. Ten bees were taken to the top, given a taste of the delicious food, and sent off to tell the rest of the hive about their find. The message was conveyed via a bee dance and the whole gang buzzed off to get the free food. They flew around in all directions, but couldn't locate the food. (It's probably one way to make bees really mad.) The problem seems to be that bee communication has a fixed set of signals for communicating location and they all relate to horizontal distance. The bee cannot manipulate its communication system to create a "new" message indicating vertical distance. According to Karl von

Frisch, who conducted the experiment, "the bees have no word for *up* in their language" and they can't invent one.

This limiting feature of animal communication is described in terms of **fixed reference**. Each signal in the system is fixed as relating to a particular object or occasion. Among the vervet monkey's repertoire, there is one danger signal *CHUTTER*, which is used when a snake is around, and another *RRAUP*, used when an eagle is spotted nearby. These signals are fixed in terms of their reference and cannot be manipulated. What might count as evidence of productivity in the monkey's communication system would be an utterance of something like *CHUTT-RRAUP* when a flying creature that looked like a snake came by. Despite a lot of research involving snakes suddenly appearing in the air above them (among other unusual and terrifying experiences), the vervet monkeys didn't produce a new danger signal. The human, given similar circumstances, is quite capable of creating a "new" signal, after initial surprise perhaps, by saying something never said before, as in *Hey! Watch out for that flying snake!*

Cultural transmission

While we may inherit physical features such as brown eyes and dark hair from our parents, we do not inherit their language. We acquire a language in a culture with other speakers and not from parental genes. An infant born to Korean parents in Korea, but adopted and brought up from birth by English speakers in the United States, will have physical characteristics inherited from his or her natural parents, but will inevitably speak English. A kitten, given comparable early experiences, will produce *meow* regardless.

This process whereby a language is passed on from one generation to the next is described as **cultural transmission**. It is clear that humans are born with some kind of predisposition to acquire language in a general sense. However, we are not born with the ability to produce utterances in a specific language such as English. We acquire our first language as children in a culture.

The general pattern in animal communication is that creatures are born with a set of specific signals that are produced instinctively. There is some evidence from studies of birds as they develop their songs that instinct has to combine with learning (or exposure) in order for the right song to be produced. If those birds spend their first seven weeks without hearing other birds, they will instinctively produce songs or calls, but those songs will be abnormal in some way. Human infants, growing up in isolation, produce no "instinctive" language. Cultural transmission of a specific language is crucial in the human acquisition process.

Duality

Human language is organized at two levels or layers simultaneously. This property is called **duality** (or "double articulation"). In speech production, we have a physical level at which we can produce individual sounds, like *n*, *b* and *i*. As individual sounds, none of these discrete forms has any intrinsic meaning. In a particular combination such as *bin*, we have another level producing a meaning that is different from the meaning of the combination in *nib*. So, at one level, we have distinct sounds, and, at another level, we have distinct meanings. This duality of levels is, in fact, one of the most economical features of human language because, with a limited set of discrete sounds, we are capable of producing a very large number of sound combinations (e.g. words) which are distinct in meaning.

Among other creatures, each communicative signal appears to be a single fixed form that cannot be broken down into separate parts. Although your dog may be able to produce *woof* ("I'm happy to see you"), it does not seem to do so on the basis of a distinct level of production combining the separate elements of *w* + *oo* + *f*. If the dog was operating with the double level (i.e. duality), then we might expect to hear different combinations with different meanings, such as *oowf* ("I'm hungry") and *foow* ("I'm really bored").

Talking to animals

If these properties of human language make it such a unique communication system, quite different from the communication systems of other creatures, then it would seem extremely unlikely that other creatures would be able to understand it. Some humans, however, do not behave as if this is the case. There is, after all, a lot of spoken language directed by humans to animals, apparently under the impression that the animal follows what is being said. Riders can say *Whoa* to horses and they stop (or so it seems), we can say *Heel* to dogs and they will follow at heel (well, sometimes), and a variety of circus animals go *Up*, *Down* and *Roll over* in response to spoken commands. Should we treat these examples as evidence that non-humans can understand human language? Probably not. The standard explanation is that the animal produces a particular behavior in response to a particular sound-stimulus or noise, but does not actually "understand" what the words in the noise mean.

If it seems difficult to conceive of animals understanding human language, then it appears to be even less likely that an animal would be capable of producing human language. After all, we do not generally observe animals of one species learning to produce the signals of another species. You could keep your horse in a field of cows for years, but it still won't say *moo*. And, in some homes, a new baby and a puppy may arrive at the same time. Baby and puppy grow up in the same environment, hearing mostly the same things, but about two years later, the baby is making lots of human speech sounds and the puppy is not. But perhaps a puppy is a poor example. Wouldn't it be better to work with a closer relative such as a chimpanzee?

Chimpanzees and language

The idea of raising a chimp and a child together may seem like a nightmare, but this is basically what was done in an early attempt to teach a chimpanzee to use human language. In the 1930s, two scientists (Luella and Winthrop Kellogg) reported on their experience of raising an infant chimpanzee together with their baby son. The chimpanzee, called Gua, was reported to be able to understand about a hundred words, but did not "say" any of them. In the 1940s, a chimpanzee named Viki was reared by another scientist couple (Catherine and Keith Hayes) in their own home, exactly as if she was a human child. These foster parents spent five years attempting to get Viki to "say" English words by trying to shape her mouth as she produced sounds. Viki eventually managed to produce some words, rather poorly articulated versions of *mama*, *papa* and *cup*. In retrospect, this was a remarkable achievement since it has become clear that non-human primates do not actually have a physically structured vocal tract which is suitable for articulating the sounds used in speech. Apes and gorillas can, like chimpanzees, communicate with a wide range of vocal calls, but they just can't make human speech sounds.

Washoe

Recognizing that a chimpanzee was a poor candidate for spoken language learning, another scientist couple (Beatrix and Allen Gardner) set out to teach a female chimpanzee called Washoe to use a version of American Sign Language. As described later in Chapter 15, this sign language has all the essential properties of human language and is learned by many congenitally deaf children as their natural first language.

From the beginning, the Gardners and their research assistants raised Washoe like a human child in a comfortable domestic environment. Sign language was always used when Washoe was around and she was encouraged to use signs, even her own incomplete "baby-versions" of the signs used by adults. In a period of three and a half years, Washoe came to use signs for more than a hundred words, ranging from *airplane*, *baby* and *banana* through to *window*, *woman* and *you*. Even more impressive was Washoe's ability to take these forms and combine them to produce "sentences" of the type *gimme tickle*, *more fruit* and *open food drink* (to get someone to open the refrigerator). Some of the forms appear to have been inventions by Washoe, as in her novel sign for *bib* and in the combination *water bird* (referring to a swan), which would seem to indicate that her communication system had the potential for productivity. Washoe also demonstrated understanding of a much larger number of signs than she produced and was capable of holding rudimentary conversations, mainly in the form of question–answer sequences. A similar ability with sign language was reported by Francine Patterson working with a gorilla named Koko not long after.

Sarah and Lana

At the same time as Washoe was learning sign language, another chimpanzee was being taught (by Ann and David Premack) to use a set of plastic shapes for the purpose of communicating with humans. These plastic shapes represented "words" that could be arranged in sequence to build "sentences" (Sarah preferred a vertical order). The basic approach was quite different from that of the Gardners. Sarah was systematically trained to associate these shapes with objects or actions. She remained an animal in a cage, being trained with food rewards to manipulate a set of symbols. Once she had learned to use a large number of these plastic shapes, Sarah was capable of getting an apple by selecting the correct plastic shape (a blue triangle) from a large array. Notice that this symbol is arbitrary since it would be hard to argue for any natural connection between an apple and a blue plastic triangle. Sarah was also capable of producing

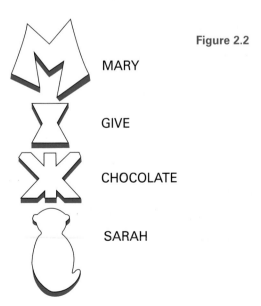

Figure 2.2

MARY

GIVE

CHOCOLATE

SARAH

"sentences" such as *Mary give chocolate Sarah* and had the impressive capacity to understand complex structures such as *If Sarah put red on green, Mary give Sarah chocolate*. Sarah got the chocolate.

A similar training technique with another artificial language was used (by Duane Rumbaugh) to train a chimpanzee called Lana. The language she learned was called Yerkish and consisted of a set of symbols on a large keyboard linked to a computer. When Lana wanted some water, she had to press four symbols, in the correct sequence, to produce the message *please machine give water*.

Figure 2.3

Both Sarah and Lana demonstrated an ability to use what look like word symbols and basic structures in ways that superficially resemble the use of language. There is, however, a lot of skepticism regarding these apparent linguistic skills. It has been pointed out that when Lana used the symbol for "please" she did not have to understand the meaning of the English word *please*. The symbol for "please" on the computer keyboard might simply be the equivalent of a button on a vending machine and, so the argument goes, we could learn to operate vending machines without necessarily knowing language. This is only one of the many arguments that have been presented against the idea that the use of signs and symbols by these chimpanzees is similar to the use of language.

The controversy

On the basis of his work with another chimpanzee called Nim, the psychologist Herbert Terrace argued that chimpanzees simply produce signs in response to the demands of people and tend to repeat signs those people use, yet they are treated (by naive researchers) as if they are taking part in a "conversation." As in many critical studies of animal learning, the chimpanzees' behavior is viewed as a type of conditioned response to cues provided (often unwittingly) by human trainers. Herbert's conclusion was that chimpanzees are clever creatures who learn to produce a certain type of behavior (signing or symbol selection) in order to get rewards and are essentially performing sophisticated "tricks."

In response, the Gardners argued that they were not animal trainers, nor were they inculcating and then eliciting conditioned responses from Washoe. In complex experiments, designed to eliminate any possible provision of cues by humans, they showed that in the absence of any human, Washoe could produce correct signs to identify objects in pictures. They also emphasize a major difference between the experiences of Washoe and Nim. While Nim was kept in a windowless cell as a research animal and had to deal with a lot of different research assistants who were often not fluent in American Sign Language, Washoe lived in a domestic environment with a lot of opportunity for imaginative play and interaction with fluent signers who were also using sign language with each other. They also report that another group of younger chimpanzees not only learned sign language, but also occasionally used signs with each other and with Washoe, even when there were no humans present.

Kanzi

In a more recent set of studies, an interesting development relevant to this controversy came about almost by accident. While Sue Savage-Rumbaugh was attempting to train a bonobo (a pygmy chimpanzee) called Matata how to use the symbols of Yerkish, Matata's adopted baby, Kanzi, was always with her. Although Matata did not do very well, her son Kanzi spontaneously started using the symbol system with great ease. He had learned not by being taught, but by being exposed to, and observing, a kind of language in use at a very early age. Kanzi eventually developed a large symbol vocabulary (over 250 forms). By the age of eight, he was reported to be able, through the association of symbols with spoken words, to demonstrate understanding of spoken English at a level comparable to a two-and-a-half-year-old human child. There was also evidence that he was using a consistently distinct set of "gentle noises" as words to refer to things such as bananas, grapes and juice. He had also become capable of using his symbol system to ask to watch his favorite movies, *Quest for Fire* (about primitive humans) and *Greystoke* (about the Tarzan legend).

Using language

Important lessons have been learned from attempts to teach chimpanzees how to use forms of language. We have answered some questions. Were Washoe and Kanzi capable of taking part in interaction with humans by using a symbol system chosen by humans and not chimpanzees? The answer is clearly "Yes." Did Washoe and Kanzi go on to perform linguistically on a level comparable to a human child about to begin pre-school? The answer is just as clearly "No." In arriving at these answers, we have also had to face the fact that, even with our list of key properties, we still don't seem to have a non-controversial definition of what counts as "using language."

One solution might be to stop thinking of language, at least in the phrase "using language," as a single thing that one can either have or not have. We could then say that there are (at least) two ways of thinking about what "using language" means. In a very broad sense, language does serve as a type of communication system that can be observed in a variety of different situations. In one situation, we look at the behavior of a two-year-old human child interacting with a caregiver as an example of "using language" in the broad sense. In another situation, we observe very similar behavior from chimpanzees and bonobos when they are interacting with humans they know. It has to be fair to say that, in both cases, we observe the participants "using language."

However, there is a difference. Underlying the two-year-old's communicative activity is the capacity to develop a highly complex system of sounds and structures, plus a set of computational procedures, that will allow the child to produce extended discourse containing a potentially infinite number of novel utterances. No other creature has been observed "using language" in this sense. It is in this more fundamental or abstract sense that we say that language is uniquely human. In the following chapters, we will begin to look in detail at the many elements that make up this uniquely human phenomenon.

Study questions

1 Why is reflexivity considered to be a special property of human language?
2 What kind of evidence is used to support the idea that language is culturally transmitted?
3 What is the difference between a communication system with productivity and one with fixed reference?
4 How did the Gardners try to show that Washoe was not simply repeating signs made by interacting humans?
5 If Sarah could use a gray plastic shape to convey the meaning of the word *red*, which property does her "language" seem to have?
6 What was considered to be the key element in Kanzi's language learning?

Tasks

A In studies of communication involving animals and humans, there is sometimes a reference to "the Clever Hans phenomenon." Who or what was Clever Hans, why was he/she/it famous and what exactly is the "phenomenon"?
B We recognized a distinction early in the chapter between communicative and informative signals. How would "body language" be characterized? Also, what kind of signaling is involved in "distance zones"? What about "eye contact" and "eyebrow flashes"?
C What is meant by "sound symbolism" and how does it relate to the property of arbitrariness?
D What was the significance of the name given to the chimpanzee in the research conducted by the psychologist Herbert Terrace?
E We reviewed studies involving chimpanzees and bonobos learning to communicate with humans. Can only African apes accomplish this task? Are there any studies involving the Asian great ape, the orangutan, learning how to use a human communication system?
F Consider these statements about the symbol-using abilities of chimpanzees in animal language studies and decide if they are correct or not. What evidence can be used to argue for or against the accuracy of these statements?
   1 They can create combinations of signs that look like the telegraphic speech produced by young children.
   2 They can invent new sign combinations.
   3 They can understand structures with complex word order, such as conditionals (i.e. *if X, then Y*).

4   They overgeneralize the references of signs, using one sign for many different things, just as human children do in the early stages.

5   They don't use signs spontaneously and only produce them in response to humans.

6   They have complex concepts such as time because they produce sign combinations such as "time eat."

7   They use signs to interact with each other, just as three-year-old children do with speech.

8   They steadily increase the length of their utterances, so that their average utterance length of 3.0 is equivalent to that of a three-and-a-half-year-old child.

Discussion topics/projects

I   Listed below are six other properties (or "design features") that are often discussed when human language is compared to other communication systems.

vocal-auditory channel use (language signals are sent using the vocal organs and received by the ears)

specialization (language signals do not serve any other type of purpose such as breathing or feeding)

non-directionality (language signals have no inherent direction and can be picked up by anyone within hearing, even unseen)

rapid fade (language signals are produced and disappear quickly)

reciprocity (any sender of a language signal can also be a receiver)

prevarication (language signals can be false or used to lie or deceive)

(i)   Are these properties found in all forms of human communication via language?

(ii) Are these special properties of human language or can they be found in the communication systems of other creatures?

(For background reading, see chapter 17 of O'Grady *et al.*, 2005.)

II The most persistent criticism of the chimpanzee language-learning projects is that the chimpanzees are simply making responses like trained animals for rewards and are consequently not using language to express anything. Read over the following reports and try to decide how the different behaviors of these chimpanzees (Dar, Washoe and Moja) should be characterized. Signs are represented by words in capital letters.

After her nap, Washoe signed OUT. I was hoping for Washoe to potty herself and did not comply. Then Washoe took my hands and put them together to make OUT and then signed OUT with her own hands to show me how.

Greg was hooting and making other sounds, to prevent Dar from falling asleep. Dar put his fist to Greg's lips and made kissing sounds. Greg asked WHAT WANT? and Dar replied QUIET, placing the sign on Greg's lips.

Moja signed DOG on Ron and me and looked at our faces, waiting for us to "woof." After several rounds I made a "meeow" instead. Moja signed DOG again, I repeated "meeow" again, and Moja slapped my leg harder. This went on. Finally I woofed and Moja leapt on me and hugged me.

Moja stares longingly at Dairy Queen as we drive by. Then for a minute or more signs NO ICE CREAM many times, by shaking her head while holding fist to mouth, index edge up.

(For background reading, see Rimpau *et al.*, 1989, which is the source of these examples.)

Further reading

Basic treatments
Aitchison, J. (2008) *The Articulate Mammal* (chapter 2) (5th edition) Routledge
Friend, T. (2004) *Animal Talk* Simon and Schuster
More detailed treatments
Anderson, S. (2004) *Doctor Dolittle's Delusion* Yale University Press
Rogers, L. and G. Kaplan (2000) *Songs, Roars and Rituals* Harvard University Press
General properties of language
Hockett, C. (1960) "The origin of speech" *Scientific American* 203: 89–96
Animal communication and consciousness
Griffin, D. (2001) *Animal Minds* University of Chicago Press
Hauser, M. (1996) *The Evolution of Communication* MIT Press
Bee communication
von Frisch, K. (1993) *The Dance Language and Orientation of Bees* Harvard University Press
Vervet monkey communication
Cheney, D. and R. Seyfarth (1990) *How Monkeys See the World* University of Chicago Press
Individual chimpanzees, gorillas and bonobos
(Gua) Kellogg, W. and L. Kellogg (1933) *The Ape and the Child* McGraw-Hill
(Viki) Hayes, C. (1951) *The Ape in Our House* Harper
(Washoe) Gardner, R., B. Gardner and T. van Cantfort (eds.) (1989) *Teaching Sign Language to Chimpanzees* State University of New York Press

(Koko) Patterson, F. and E. Linden (1981) *The Education of Koko* Holt

(Sarah) Premack, A. and D. Premack (1991) "Teaching language to an ape" In W. Wang (ed.) *The Emergence of Language* (16–27) W. H. Freeman

(Lana) Rumbaugh, D. (ed.) (1977) *Language Learning by a Chimpanzee: The LANA Project* Academic Press

(Nim) Terrace, H. (1979) *Nim: A Chimpanzee Who Learned Sign Language* Knopf

Hess, E. (2008) *Nim Chimpsky: The Chimp Who Would Be Human* Bantam Books

(Kanzi) Savage-Rumbaugh, S. and R. Lewin (1994) *Kanzi: The Ape at the Brink of the Human Mind* John Wiley

Other references

O'Grady, W., J. Archibald, M. Aronoff and J. Rees-Miller (2005) *Contemporary Linguistics* (chapter 17) (5th edition) Bedford/St. Martin's Press

Rimpau, J., R. Gardner and B. Gardner (1989) "Expression of person, place and instrument in ASL utterances of children and chimpanzees" In R. Gardner, B. Gardner and T. van Cantfort (eds.) *Teaching Sign Language to Chimpanzees* (240–268) State University of New York Press

3 The sounds of language

I take it you already know
Of tough and bough and cough and dough?
Others may stumble but not you
On hiccough, thorough, lough and through.
Well done! And now you wish, perhaps,
To learn of less familiar traps?

Beware of heard, a dreadful word,
That looks like beard and sounds like bird.
And dead: it's said like bed, not bead –
For goodness sake don't call it "deed"!
Watch out for meat and great and threat
(They rhyme with suite and straight and debt).

T. S. W. quoted in Mackay (1970)

Imagine the manager of a small restaurant, a man who has always had trouble with
the spelling of unusual words, writing out a sign which he puts in the front window,
advertising that they have a new SEAGH. You see the sign and you decide to ask what kind
of new thing this is. When you hear the pronunciation, you recognize the word usually
written as *chef*. How did he arrive at that other spelling? Well, it's very simple, he says.
Take the first sound of the word *sure*, the middle sound of the word *dead*, and the final
sound of the word *laugh*. Isn't that a *seagh*?

This tale, however unlikely, may serve as a reminder that the sounds of spoken English do not match up, a lot of the time, with letters of written English. If we cannot use the letters of the alphabet in a consistent way to represent the sounds we make, how do we go about describing the sounds of a language like English? One solution is to produce a separate alphabet with symbols that represent sounds. Such a set of symbols does exist and is called the **phonetic alphabet**. In this chapter, we will look at how these symbols are used to represent both the consonant and vowel sounds of English words and what physical aspects of the human vocal tract are involved in the production of those sounds.

Phonetics

The general study of the characteristics of speech sounds is called **phonetics**. Our main interest will be in **articulatory phonetics**, which is the study of how speech sounds are made, or articulated. Other areas of study are **acoustic phonetics**, which deals with the physical properties of speech as sound waves in the air, and **auditory phonetics** (or perceptual phonetics) which deals with the perception, via the ear, of speech sounds.

Voiced and voiceless sounds

In articulatory phonetics, we investigate how speech sounds are produced using the fairly complex oral equipment we have. We start with the air pushed out by the lungs up through the trachea (or windpipe) to the larynx. Inside the larynx are your **vocal folds** (or vocal cords), which take two basic positions.

1   When the vocal folds are spread apart, the air from the lungs passes between them unimpeded. Sounds produced in this way are described as **voiceless**.
2   When the vocal folds are drawn together, the air from the lungs repeatedly pushes them apart as it passes through, creating a vibration effect. Sounds produced in this way are described as **voiced**.

The distinction can be felt physically if you place a fingertip gently on the top of your Adam's apple (i.e. that part of your larynx you can feel in your neck below your chin), then produce sounds such as Z-Z-Z-Z or V-V-V-V. Because these are voiced sounds, you should be able to feel some vibration. Keeping your fingertip in the same position, now make the sounds S-S-S-S or F-F-F-F. Because these are voiceless sounds, there should be no vibration. Another trick is to put a finger in each ear, not too far, and produce the voiced sounds (e.g. Z-Z-Z-Z) to hear and feel some vibration, whereas no vibration will be heard or felt if you make voiceless sounds (e.g. S-S-S-S) in the same way.

Place of articulation

Once the air has passed through the larynx, it comes up and out through the mouth and/or the nose. Most consonant sounds are produced by using the tongue and other parts of the mouth to constrict, in some way, the shape of the oral cavity through which the air is passing. The terms used to describe many sounds are those which denote the place of articulation of the sound: that is, the location inside the mouth at which the constriction takes place.

What we need is a slice of head. If you crack a head right down the middle, you will be able to see which parts of the oral cavity are crucially involved in speech production. To describe the place of articulation of most consonant sounds, we can start at the front of the mouth and work back. We can also keep the voiced–voiceless distinction in mind and begin using the symbols of the phonetic alphabet for specific sounds. These symbols will be enclosed within square brackets [ ].

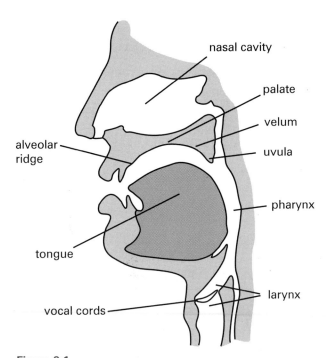

Figure 3.1

Bilabials

These are sounds formed using both (= bi) upper and lower lips (= labia). The initial sounds in the words *pat*, *bat* and *mat* are all **bilabials**. They are represented by the symbols [p], which is voiceless, and [b] and [m], which are voiced. We can also describe the [w] sound found at the beginning of *way*, *walk* and *world* as a bilabial.

Labiodentals

These are sounds formed with the upper teeth and the lower lip. The initial sounds of the words *fat* and *vat* and the final sounds in the words *safe* and *save* are **labiodentals**. They are represented by the symbols [f], which is voiceless, and [v], which is voiced. Notice that the final sound in the word *cough*, and the initial sound in *photo*, despite the spelling differences, are both pronounced as [f].

Dentals

These sounds are formed with the tongue tip behind the upper front teeth. The initial sound of *thin* and the final sound of *bath* are both voiceless **dentals**. The symbol used for this sound is [θ], usually referred to as "theta." It is the symbol you would use for the first and last sounds in the phrase *three teeth*.

The voiced dental is represented by the symbol [ð], usually called "eth." This sound is found in the pronunciation of the initial sound of common words like *the*, *there*, *then* and *thus*. It is also the middle consonant sound in *feather* and the final sound of *bathe*.

The term "interdentals" is sometimes used for these consonants when they are pronounced with the tongue tip between (= inter) the upper and lower teeth.

Alveolars

These are sounds formed with the front part of the tongue on the alveolar ridge, which is the rough, bony ridge immediately behind and above the upper teeth. The initial sounds in *top*, *dip*, *sit*, *zoo* and *nut* are all **alveolars**. The symbols for these sounds are easy to remember – [t], [d], [s], [z], [n]. Of these, [t] and [s] are voiceless whereas [d], [z] and [n] are voiced.

It may be clear that the final sounds of the words *bus* and *buzz* have to be [s] and [z] respectively, but what about the final sound of the word *raise*? The spelling is misleading because the final sound in this word is voiced and so must be represented by [z]. Notice also that despite the different spelling of *knot* and *not*, both of these words are pronounced with [n] as the initial sound.

Other alveolars are the [l] sound found at the beginning of words such as *lap* and *lit*, and the [r] sound at the beginning of *right* and *write*.

Palatals

If you feel back behind the alveolar ridge, you should find a hard part in the roof of your mouth. This is called the hard palate or just the palate. Sounds produced with the tongue and the palate are called **palatals** (or alveo-palatals). Examples of palatals are the initial sounds in the words *shout* and *child*, which are both voiceless. The "sh" sound is represented as [ʃ] and the "ch" sound is represented as [tʃ]. So, the word *shoe-brush* begins and ends with the voiceless palatal sound [ʃ] and the word *church* begins and ends with the other voiceless palatal sound [tʃ].

One of the voiced palatals, represented by the symbol [ʒ], is not very common in English, but can be found as the middle consonant sound in words like *treasure* and *pleasure*, or the final sound in *rouge*. The other voiced palatal is [dʒ], which is the initial sound in words like *joke* and *gem*. The word *judge* and the name *George* both begin and end with the sound [dʒ] despite the obvious differences in spelling.

One other voiced palatal is the [j] sound used at the beginning of words like *you* and *yet*.

Velars

Even further back in the roof of the mouth, beyond the hard palate, you will find a soft area, which is called the soft palate, or the velum. Sounds produced with the back of the tongue against the velum are called **velars**. There is a voiceless velar sound, represented by the symbol [k], which occurs not only in *kid* and *kill*, but is also the initial sound in *car* and *cold*. Despite the variety in spelling, this [k] sound is both the initial and final sound in the words *cook*, *kick* and *coke*.

The voiced velar sound heard at the beginning of words like *go*, *gun* and *give* is represented by [g]. This is also the final sound in words like *bag*, *mug* and, despite the spelling, *plague*.

The velum can be lowered to allow air to flow through the nasal cavity and thereby produce another voiced velar, represented by the symbol [ŋ], typically referred to as "angma." In written English, this sound is normally spelled as the two letters "ng." So, the [ŋ] sound is at the end of *sing*, *sang* and, despite the spelling, *tongue*. It occurs twice in the form *ringing*. Be careful not to be misled by the spelling of a word like *bang* – it ends with the [ŋ] sound only. There is no [g] sound in this word.

Glottals

There is one sound that is produced without the active use of the tongue and other parts of the mouth. It is the sound [h] which occurs at the beginning of *have* and *house* and, for most speakers, as the first sound in *who* and *whose*. This sound is usually described as a voiceless **glottal**. The "glottis" is the space between the vocal folds in the larynx. When the glottis is open, as in the production of other voiceless sounds, and there is no manipulation of the air passing out of the mouth, the sound produced is that represented by [h].

Charting consonant sounds

Having described in some detail the place of articulation of English consonant sounds, we can summarize the basic information in the accompanying chart. Along the top of the chart are the different labels for places of articulation and, under each, the labels −V (= voiceless) and +V (= voiced). Also included in this chart, on the left-hand side, is a set of terms used to describe manner of articulation which we will discuss in the following section.

	Bilabial		Labiodental		Dental		Alveolar		Palatal		Velar		Glottal	
	−V	+V	−V	+V	−V	+V	−V	+V	−V	+V	−V	+V	−V	+V
Stops	p	b					t	d			k	g		
Fricatives			f	v	θ	ð	s	z	ʃ	ʒ				h
Affricates									ʧ	ʤ				
Nasals		m						n				ŋ		
Liquids								l r						
Glides		w								j				

Figure 3.2

Limitations of the chart

This chart is far from complete. It contains the majority of consonant sounds used in the basic description of English pronunciation. There are, however, several differences between this basic set of symbols and the much more comprehensive chart produced by the International Phonetic Association (IPA). The most obvious difference is in the range of sounds covered.

We would go to an IPA chart for a description of the sounds of all languages. It includes, for example, symbols for the velar fricative sound you may have heard in the German pronunciation of the "ch" part of *Bach* or *Achtung*. It also includes sounds made with the back of the tongue and the uvula (the "little grape" hanging at the end of the velum) which represents the "r" parts of the French pronunciation of *rouge* and *lettre*. Uvular sounds also occur in many native languages of North and South America. Other non-English sounds such as pharyngeals (produced in the pharynx) occur in languages such as Arabic. There are many other consonant sounds in the languages of the world.

Another way in which the chart is incomplete is the single entry covering "r" sounds in English. There can be a lot of variation among speakers in the pronunciation of the initial sound in *raw* and *red*, the medial sound in *very*, and the final sound in *hour* and *air*. Different symbols (e.g. [ɹ], [ʀ]) may be encountered in transcriptions where the different "r" sounds are distinguished.

Finally, in some phonetic descriptions, there are different symbols for a few of the sounds represented here. These alternatives are [š] for [ʃ], [ž] for [ʒ], [č] for [ʧ], [ǰ] for [ʤ] and [y] for [j]. For a fuller discussion of the use of these symbols, see Ladefoged (2006).

Manner of articulation

So far, we have concentrated on describing consonant sounds in terms of where they are articulated. We can also describe the same sounds in terms of how they are articulated. Such a description is necessary if we want to be able to differentiate between some sounds which, in the preceding discussion, we have placed in the same category. For example, we can say that [t] and [s] are both voiceless alveolar sounds. How do they differ? They differ in their manner of articulation, that is, in the way they are pronounced. The [t] sound is one of a set of sounds called stops and the [s] sound is one of a set called fricatives.

Stops

Of the sounds we have already mentioned, the set [p], [b], [t], [d], [k], [g] are all produced by some form of "stopping" of the air stream (very briefly) then letting it go abruptly. This type of consonant sound, resulting from a blocking or stopping effect on the air stream, is called a **stop** (or a "plosive"). A full description of the [t] sound at the beginning of a word like *ten* is as a voiceless alveolar stop. In some discussions, only the manner of articulation is mentioned, as when it is said that the word *bed*, for example, begins and ends with voiced stops.

Fricatives

The manner of articulation used in producing the set of sounds [f], [v], [θ], [ð], [s], [z], [ʃ], [ʒ] involves almost blocking the air stream and having the air push through the very narrow opening. As the air is pushed through, a type of friction is produced and the resulting sounds are called **fricatives**. If you put your open hand in front of your mouth when making these sounds, [f] and [s] in particular, you should be able to feel the stream of air being pushed out. The usual pronunciation of the word *fish* begins and ends with the voiceless fricatives [f] and [ʃ]. The word *those* begins and ends with the voiced fricatives [ð] and [z].

The sound [h], as in *Hi* or *Hello*, is voiceless and also usually included in the set of fricatives.

Affricates

If you combine a brief stopping of the air stream with an obstructed release which causes some friction, you will be able to produce the sounds [ʧ] and [ʤ]. These are called **affricates** and occur at the beginning of the words *cheap* and *jeep*. In the first of these, there is a voiceless affricate [ʧ], and in the second, a voiced affricate [ʤ].

Nasals

Most sounds are produced orally, with the velum raised, preventing airflow from entering the nasal cavity. However, when the velum is lowered and the air stream is allowed to flow out through the nose to produce [m], [n] and [ŋ], the sounds are described as **nasals**. These three sounds are all voiced. The words *morning, knitting* and *name* begin and end with nasals.

Liquids

The initial sounds in *led* and *red* are described as **liquids**. They are both voiced. The [l] sound is called a lateral liquid and is formed by letting the air stream flow around the sides of the tongue as the tip of the tongue makes contact with the middle of the alveolar ridge. The [r] sound at the beginning of *red* is formed with the tongue tip raised and curled back near the alveolar ridge.

Glides

The sounds [w] and [j] are described as **glides**. They are both voiced and occur at the beginning of *we, wet, you* and *yes*. These sounds are typically produced with the tongue in motion (or "gliding") to or from the position of a vowel and are sometimes called semi-vowels.

In some approaches, the liquids [l], [r] and glides [w], [j] are combined in one category called "approximants."

Glottal stops and flaps

There are two common terms used to describe ways of pronouncing consonants which are not included in the chart presented earlier.

The **glottal stop**, represented by the symbol [ʔ], occurs when the space between the vocal folds (the glottis) is closed completely (very briefly), then released. Try saying the expression *Oh oh!*. Between the first *Oh* and the second *oh*, we typically produce a glottal stop. Some people do it in the middle of *Uh-uh* (meaning "no"), and others put one in place of "t" when they pronounce *Batman* quickly. You can also produce a glottal stop if you try to say the words *butter* or *bottle* without pronouncing the "-tt-" part in the middle. This sound is considered to be characteristic of Cockney (London) speech. (Try saying the name *Harry Potter* as if it didn't have the "H" or the "tt.") You will also hear glottal stops in the pronunciation of some Scottish speakers and also New Yorkers.

If, however, you are someone who pronounces the word *butter* in a way that is close to "budder," then you are making a **flap**. It is represented by [D] or sometimes [ɾ]. This sound is produced by the tongue tip tapping the alveolar ridge briefly. Many American English speakers have a tendency to "flap" the [t] and [d] consonants between vowels so that, in casual speech, the pairs *latter* and *ladder* do not have distinct middle consonants. Nor do *writer* and *rider*, *metal* and *medal*. They all have flaps. The student who was told about the importance of *Plato* in class and wrote it in his notes as *play-dough* was clearly a victim of a misinterpreted flap.

This rather lengthy list of the phonetic features of English consonant sounds is not presented as a challenge to your ability to memorize a lot of terminology and symbols. It is presented as an illustration of how a thorough description of the physical aspects of speech production will allow us to characterize the sounds of spoken English, independently of the vagaries of spelling found in written English. There are, however, some sounds that we have not yet investigated. These are the types of sounds known as vowels and diphthongs.

Vowels

While the consonant sounds are mostly articulated via closure or obstruction in the vocal tract, **vowel** sounds are produced with a relatively free flow of air. They are all typically voiced. To describe vowel sounds, we consider the way in which the tongue influences the shape through which the airflow must pass. To talk about a place of articulation, we think of the space inside the mouth as having a front versus a back and a high versus a low area. Thus, in the pronunciation of *heat* and *hit*, we talk about "high, front" vowels because the sound is made with the front part of the tongue in a raised position.

In contrast, the vowel sound in *hat* is produced with the tongue in a lower position and the sound in *hot* can be described as a "low, back" vowel. The next time you're facing the bathroom mirror, try saying the words *heat, hit, hat, hot*. For the first two, your mouth will stay fairly closed, but for the last two, your tongue will move lower and cause your mouth to open wider. (The sounds of relaxation and pleasure typically contain lower vowels.)

The terminology for describing vowel sounds in English (e.g. "high front") is usually based on their position in a chart, like the one shown here (based on Ladefoged, 2006), which provides a means of classifying the most common vowel sounds. Following the chart is a list of the major vowels with examples of familiar words illustrating some of the variation in spelling that is possible for each sound.

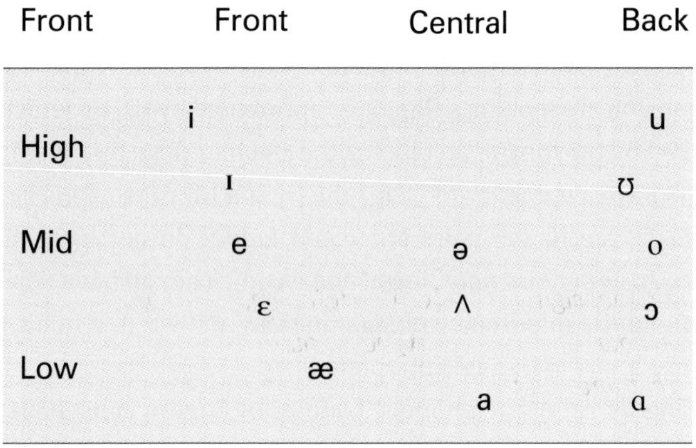

	Front	Front	Central	Back
High		i		u
		ɪ		ʊ
Mid		e	ə	o
		ɛ	ʌ	ɔ
Low		æ		
			a	ɑ

Figure 3.3

Front vowels
[i] *bead, beef, key, me*
[ɪ] *bid, myth, women*
[ɛ] *bed, dead, said*
[æ] *bad, laugh, wrap*

Central vowels
[ə] *above, oven, support*
[ʌ] *butt, blood, dove, tough*

Back vowels
[u] *boo, move, two, you*
[ʊ] *book, could, put*
[ɔ] *born, caught, fall, raw*
[ɑ] *Bob, cot, swan*

Diphthongs

In addition to single vowel sounds, we regularly create sounds that consist of a combination of two vowel sounds, known as **diphthongs**. When we produce diphthongs, our vocal organs move from one vocalic position [a] to another [ɪ] as we produce the sound [aɪ], as in *Hi* or *Bye*. The movement in this diphthong is from low towards high front. Alternatively, we can use movement from low towards high back, combining [a] and [ʊ] to produce the sound [aʊ], which is the diphthong repeated in the traditional speech training exercise [haʊ naʊ braʊn kaʊ]. In some descriptions, the movement is interpreted as involving a glide such as [j] or [w], so that the diphthongs we are representing as [aɪ] and [aʊ] may sometimes be seen as [aj] or [aw].

While the vowels [e], [a] and [o] are used as single sounds in other languages, and in some other varieties of English, they are only typically used as the first sounds of diphthongs in American English. The accompanying diagram provides a rough idea of how diphthongs are produced and is followed by a list of the sounds, with examples to illustrate some of the variation in the spelling of these sounds.

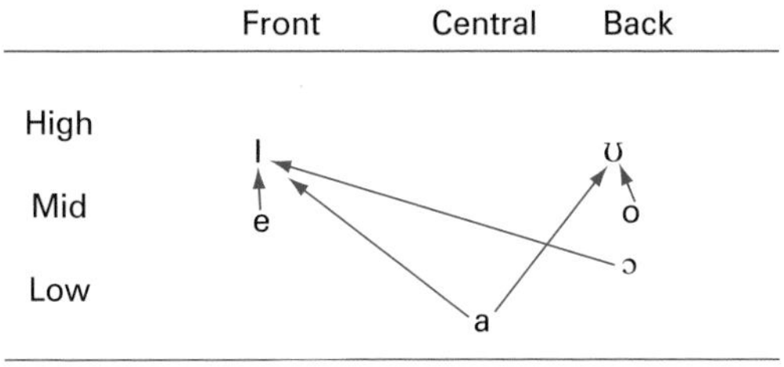

Figure 3.4

Diphthongs

[aɪ] *buy, eye, I, my, pie, sigh*   [oʊ] *boat, home, throw, toe*
[aʊ] *bough, doubt, cow*   [ɔɪ] *boy, noise*
[eɪ] *bait, eight, great, late, say*

Subtle individual variation

Vowel sounds are notorious for varying between one variety of English and the next, often being a key element in what we recognize as different accents. So, you may feel that some of the words offered in the earlier lists as examples don't seem to be pronounced with the vowel sounds exactly as listed. Also, some of the sound distinctions shown here may not even be used regularly in your own speech. It may be, for example, that you make no distinction between the vowels in the words *caught* and *cot* and use [ɑ] in both. You may also be used to seeing the vowel sound of *pet* represented as [e] in dictionaries rather than with [ɛ] as used here.

You may not make a significant distinction between the central vowels [ə], called "**schwa**," and [ʌ], called "wedge." If you're trying to transcribe, just use schwa [ə]. In fact, in casual speech, we all use schwa more than any other single sound. It is the unstressed vowel (underlined) in the everyday use of words such as *afford*, *collapse*, *photograph*, *wanted*, and in those very common words *a* and *the*.

There are many other variations in the actual physical articulation of the sounds we have considered here. The more we focus on the subtle differences in the actual articulation of each sound, the more likely we are to find ourselves describing the pronunciation of small groups or even individual speakers. Such subtle differences enable us to identify individual voices and recognize people we know as soon as they speak. But those differences don't help us understand how we are able to work out what total strangers with unfamiliar voices are saying. We are clearly able to disregard all the subtle individual variation in the phonetic detail of voices and recognize each underlying sound type as part of a word with a particular meaning. To make sense of how we do that, we need to look at the more general sound patterns, or the phonology, of a language.

Study questions

1   What is the difference between acoustic phonetics and articulatory phonetics?

2   Which of the following words normally end with voiceless (−V) sounds and which end with voiced sounds (+V) sounds?

(a) bang ____   (d) fizz____   (g) splat ____
(b) crash ____   (e) rap____   (h) thud ____
(c) ding ____   (f) smack ____   (i) wham ____

3   Try to pronounce the initial sounds of the following words and identify the place of articulation of each one (e.g. bilabial, alveolar, etc.).

(a) calf _____   (e) hand _____   (i) shoulder _____
(b) chin _____   (f) knee _____   (j) stomach _____
(c) foot _____   (g) mouth _____   (k) thigh _____
(d) groin _____   (h) pelvis _____   (l) toe _____

4   Identify the manner of articulation of the initial sounds in the following words (stop, fricative, etc.).

(a) cheery _____   (d) funny _____   (g) merry _____
(b) crazy _____   (e) jolly _____   (h) silly _____
(c) dizzy _____   (f) loony _____   (i) wimpy _____

5   Which written English words are usually pronounced as they are transcribed here?

(a) baɪk _____   (e) haʊl_____   (i) maɪn _____
(b) bɔt _____   (f) hoʊpɪŋ _____   (j) kju _____
(c) əndʒɔɪ _____   (g) hu _____   (k) tʃip _____
(d) feɪs _____   (h) kloʊk _____   (l) ðə _____

6   Using symbols introduced in this chapter, write a basic phonetic transcription of the most common pronunciation of the following words.

(a) catch _____   (e) noise _____   (i) thought _____
(b) doubt _____   (f) phone _____   (j) tough _____
(c) gem _____   (g) shy _____   (k) would _____
(d) measure_____   (h) these _____   (l) wring _____

Tasks

A The relationship between the spelling and pronunciation of English words is not always simple. Keeping this in mind, try to provide a basic phonetic representation of the following words.

although, beauty, bomb, ceiling, charisma, choice, cough, exercise, hour, light, phase, quiche, quake, sixteen, thigh, tongue, whose, writhe

B Using a dictionary if necessary, try to decide how each of the following words is usually pronounced. Then, put the words in five lists as illustrations of each of the sounds [eɪ], [i], [f], [k] and [ʃ]. Some words will be in more than one list.

air, belief, critique, crockery, Danish, gauge, giraffe, headache, keys, meat, mission, nation, ocean, pear, people, philosopher, queen, receipt, scene, Sikh, sugar, tough, weight

C We can create a definition for each consonant (e.g. [k]) by using the distinction between voiced and voiceless plus the terms for place (i.e. velar) and manner of articulation (i.e. fricative). So we say that [k] is a voiceless velar fricative. Write similar definitions for the initial sounds in the normal pronunciation of the following words.

fan, lunch, goal, jail, mist, shop, sun, tall, yellow, zoo

Are there any definitions in which the voiced/voiceless distinction is actually unnecessary and could be omitted?

D The terms "obstruent" and "sonorant" are sometimes used in descriptions of how consonants are pronounced. Among the types of consonants already described (affricates, fricatives, glides, liquids, nasals, stops), which are obstruents, which are sonorants, and why?

E (i) How would you make a retroflex sound?
  (ii) How are retroflex sounds identified in phonetic transcription?
  (iii) With which varieties of English are retroflex sounds generally associated?

F What is forensic phonetics?

Discussion topics/projects

I When we concentrate on the articulation of sounds, it's easy to forget that people listening to those sounds often have other clues to help them recognize what we're saying. In front of a mirror (or enlist a cooperative friend to be the speaker), say the following pairs of words. As you are doing this, can you decide which are rounded or unrounded vowels and which are tense or lax vowels? What clues are you using to help you make your decision?

bet/bought   coat/caught   feed/food   late/let   mail/mole   neat/knit

(For background reading, see chapter 5 of Ashby and Maidment, 2005.)

II English has a number of expressions such as *chit-chat* and *flip-flop* which never seem to occur in the reverse order (i.e. not *chat-chit* or *flop-flip*). Perhaps you can add examples to the following list of similar expressions.

criss-cross	*hip-hop*	*riff-raff*
dilly-dally	*knick-knacks*	*see-saw*
ding-dong	*mish-mash*	*sing-song*
fiddle-faddle	*ping-pong*	*tick-tock*
flim-flam	*pitter-patter*	*zig-zag*

(i)   Can you think of a phonetic description of the regular pattern of sounds in these expressions?

(ii) What kind of phonetic description might account for these other common pairings?

fuddy-duddy	*hocus-pocus*	*namby-pamby*
fuzzy-wuzzy	*hurly-burly*	*razzle-dazzle*
hanky-panky	*lovey-dovey*	*roly-poly*
helter-skelter	*mumbo-jumbo*	*super-duper*

(For background reading, see chapter 6 of Pinker, 1994.)

Further reading

Basic treatments
Ladefoged, P. (2006) *A Course in Phonetics* (5th edition) Thomson
Roach, P. (2001) *Phonetics* Oxford University Press
More detailed treatments
Ashby, M. and J. Maidment (2005) *Introducing Phonetic Science* Cambridge University Press
Catford, J. (2002) *A Practical Introduction to Phonetics* Oxford University Press
On acoustic and auditory phonetics
Johnson, K. (2003) *Acoustic and Auditory Phonetics* (2nd edition) Blackwell
On phonetic symbols
Pullum, G. and W. Ladusaw (1996) *Phonetic Symbol Guide* (2nd edition) University of Chicago Press

Phonetic descriptions of other languages

Handbook of the International Phonetic Association (1999) Cambridge University Press

A phonetics dictionary

Crystal, D. (2008) *A Dictionary of Linguistics and Phonetics* (6th edition) Blackwell

On pronunciation

Cruttenden, A. (2008) *Gimson's Pronunciation of English* (7th edition) Arnold Education

Jones, D., P. Roach, J. Hartman and J. Setter (2006) *Cambridge English Pronouncing Dictionary* (17th edition) Cambridge University Press

Kreidler, C. (2004) *The Pronunciation of English* (2nd edition) Blackwell

Other references

Pinker, S. (1994) *The Language Instinct* William Morrow

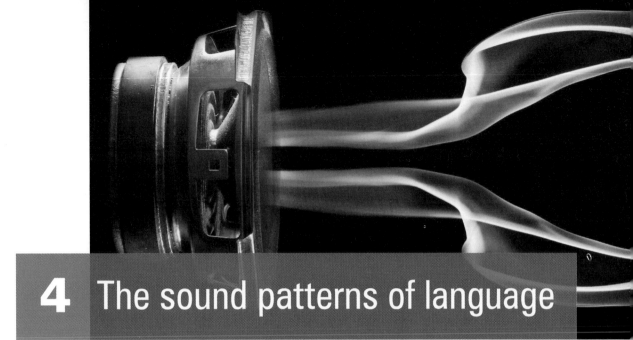

4 The sound patterns of language

Uans appona taim uas tri berres; mamma berre, pappa berre, e beibi berre. Live inne contri nire foresta. NAISE AUS. No mugheggia. Uanna dei pappa, mamma, e beibi go bice, orie e furghetta locche di dorra.

Bai ene bai commese Goldilocchese. Sci garra natingha tu du batte meiche troble. Sci puscia olle fudde daon di maute; no live cromma. Den sci gos appesterrese enne slipse in olle beddse.   Bob Belviso, quoted in Espy (1975)

In the preceding chapter, we investigated the physical production of speech sounds in terms of the articulatory mechanisms of the human vocal tract. That investigation was possible because of some rather amazing facts about the nature of language. When we considered the human vocal tract, we didn't have to specify whether we were talking about a fairly large person, over six feet tall, weighing over 200 pounds, or about a rather small person, about five feet tall, weighing less than 100 pounds. Yet those two physically different individuals would inevitably have physically different vocal tracts, in terms of size and shape. In a sense, every individual has a physically different vocal tract. Consequently, in purely physical terms, every individual will pronounce sounds differently. There are, then, potentially millions of physically different ways of saying the simple word *me*.

In addition, each individual will not pronounce the word *me* in a physically identical manner on every occasion. Obvious differences occur when that individual is shouting, is suffering from a bad cold or is asking for a sixth martini. Given this vast range of potential differences in the actual physical production of a speech sound, how do we manage consistently to recognize all those versions of *me* as the form [mi], and not [ni] or [si] or [ma] or [mo] or something else entirely? The answer to that question is provided to a large extent by the study of phonology.

Phonology

Phonology is essentially the description of the systems and patterns of speech sounds in a language. It is, in effect, based on a theory of what every speaker of a language unconsciously knows about the sound patterns of that language. Because of this theoretical status, phonology is concerned with the abstract or mental aspect of the sounds in language rather than with the actual physical articulation of speech sounds. If we can manage to make sense of Bob Belviso's comic introduction to the story of Goldilocks and the Three Bears quoted earlier, we must be using our phonological knowledge of likely combinations of sounds in English words to overcome some very unusual spellings of those words. (See the end of the chapter for a translation.)

Phonology is about the underlying design, the blueprint of each sound type, which serves as the constant basis of all the variations in different physical articulations of that sound type in different contexts. When we think of the [t] sound in the words *tar*, *star*, *writer* and *eighth* as being "the same," we actually mean that, in the phonology of English, they would be represented in the same way. In actual speech, these [t] sounds are all very different.

However, all these articulation differences in [t] sounds are less important to us than the distinction between the [t] sounds in general and the [k] sounds, or the [f] sounds, or the [b] sounds, because there are meaningful consequences related to the use of one rather than the others. These sounds must be distinct meaningful sounds, regardless of which individual vocal tract is being used to pronounce them, because they are what make the words *tar*, *car*, *far* and *bar* meaningfully distinct. Considered from this point of view, we can see that phonology is concerned with the abstract set of sounds in a language that allows us to distinguish meaning in the actual physical sounds we say and hear.

Phonemes

Each one of these meaning-distinguishing sounds in a language is described as a **phoneme**. When we learn to use alphabetic writing, we are actually using the concept of the phoneme as the single stable sound type which is represented by a single written symbol. It is in this sense that the phoneme /t/ is described as a sound type, of which all the different spoken versions of [t] are tokens. Note that slash marks are conventionally used to indicate a phoneme, /t/, an abstract segment, as opposed to the square brackets, as in [t], used for each phonetic or physically produced segment.

An essential property of a phoneme is that it functions contrastively. We know there are two phonemes /f/ and /v/ in English because they are the only basis of the contrast in meaning between the words *fat* and *vat*, or *fine* and *vine*. This contrastive property is the basic operational test for determining the phonemes that exist in a language. If we substitute one sound for another in a word and there is a change of meaning, then the two sounds represent different phonemes. The basic phonemes of English are listed with the consonant, vowel and diphthong diagrams in Chapter 3.

The technical terms used in creating those charts can be considered "features" that distinguish each phoneme from the next. If the feature is present, we mark it with a plus sign (+) and if it's not present, we use a minus sign (−). Thus /p/ can be characterized as [−voice, +bilabial, +stop] and /k/ as [−voice, +velar, +stop]. Because these two sounds share some features (i.e. both are voiceless stops), they are sometimes described as members of a natural class of sounds. The prediction would be that sounds which have features in common would behave phonologically in some similar ways. A sound which does not share those features would be expected to behave differently.

For example, /v/ has the features [+voice, +labiodental, +fricative] and so cannot be in the same "natural" class of sounds as /p/ and /k/. Although other factors will be involved, this feature-analysis could lead us to suspect that there may be a good phonological reason why words beginning with /pl-/ and /kl-/ are common in English, but words beginning with /vl-/ are not. Could it be that there are some definite sets of features required in a sound in order for it to occur word-initially before /l/? If so, then we will be on our way to producing a phonological account of permissible sound sequences in the language.

Phones and allophones

While the phoneme is the abstract unit or sound-type ("in the mind"), there are many different versions of that sound-type regularly produced in actual speech ("in the mouth"). We can describe those different versions as **phones**. Phones are phonetic units and appear in square brackets. When we have a set of phones, all of which are versions of one phoneme, we add the prefix "allo-" (= one of a closely related set) and refer to them as **allophones** of that phoneme.

For example, the [t] sound in the word *tar* is normally pronounced with a stronger puff of air than is present in the [t] sound in the word *star*. If you put the back of your hand in front of your mouth as you say *tar*, then *star*, you should be able to feel some physical evidence of **aspiration** (the puff of air) accompanying the [t] sound at the beginning of *tar* (but not in *star*). This aspirated version is represented more precisely as [tʰ]. That's one phone. In the last chapter, we noted that the [t] sound between vowels in a word like *writer* often becomes a flap, which we can represent as [D]. That's another phone. In the pronunciation of a word like *eighth* (/etθ/), the influence of the final dental [θ] sound causes a dental articulation of the [t] sound. This can be represented more precisely as [t̪]. That's yet another phone. There are even more variations of this sound which, like [tʰ], [D] and [t̪], can be represented in a more precise way in a detailed, or narrow, phonetic transcription. Because these variations are all part of one set of phones, they are referred to as allophones of the phoneme /t/.

The crucial distinction between phonemes and allophones is that substituting one phoneme for another will result in a word with a different meaning (as well as a different pronunciation), but substituting allophones only results in a different (and perhaps unusual) pronunciation of the same word.

Let's look at another quick example, using a vowel sound. In English, there is a subtle difference in the pronunciation of /i/ in the words *seed* and *seen*. In the second word, the effect of the nasal consonant [n] makes the [i] sound nasalized. We can represent this **nasalization** with a small mark (˜), called "tilde," over the symbol [ĩ] in a narrow phonetic transcription. So, there are at least two phones, [i] and [ĩ], used to realize the single phoneme. They are both allophones of /i/ in English.

It is possible, of course, for two languages to have the same pair of phonetic segments, but to treat them differently. In English, the effect of nasalization on a vowel is treated as allophonic variation because the nasalized version is not meaningfully contrastive. Whether we try to say [sin] or [sĩn], people will only recognize one word *seen*. In French, however, the pronunciation [so] for the word *seau* ("pail") contrasts with [sõ] for the word *son* ("sound") and *beau* [bo] ("good-looking") contrasts with *bon* [bõ] ("good"). Clearly, in these cases, the distinction is phonemic.

Minimal pairs and sets

Phonemic distinctions in a language can be tested via pairs and sets of words. When two words such as *pat* and *bat* are identical in form except for a contrast in one phoneme, occurring in the same position, the two words are described as a **minimal pair**. More accurately, they would be classified as a minimal pair in the phonology of English. (Arabic, for example, does not have this contrast between /p/ and /b/.) Other examples of English minimal pairs are *fan–van*, *bet–bat*, *site–side*. Such pairs have traditionally been used in the teaching and testing of English as a second or foreign language to help students develop the ability to understand the contrast in meaning based on the minimal sound contrast.

When a group of words can be differentiated, each one from the others, by changing one phoneme (always in the same position in the word), then we have a **minimal set**.

For example, one minimal set based on the vowel phonemes of English could include *feat, fit, fat, fate, fought, foot,* and another minimal set based on consonant phonemes could have *big, pig, rig, fig, dig, wig.*

Phonotactics

This type of exercise involving minimal sets also allows us to see that there are definite patterns in the types of sound combinations permitted in a language. In English, the minimal set we have just listed does not include forms such as *lig* or *vig.* According to the dictionary, these are not English words, but they could be viewed as possible English words. That is, our phonological knowledge of the pattern of sounds in English words would allow us to treat these forms as acceptable if, at some future time, they came into use. They might, for example, begin as invented abbreviations (*I think Bubba is one very ignorant guy.* ~ *Yeah, he's a big vig!*). Until then, they represent "accidental" gaps in the vocabulary of English.

It is, however, no accident that forms such as [fsɪɡ] or [rnɪɡ] do not exist or are unlikely ever to exist. They have been formed without obeying some constraints on the sequence or position of English phonemes. Such constraints are called the **phono-tactics** (i.e. permitted arrangements of sounds) in a language and are obviously part of every speaker's phonological knowledge. Because these constraints operate on a unit that is larger than the single segment or phoneme, we have to move on to a consideration of the basic structure of that larger phonological unit called the syllable.

Syllables

A **syllable** must contain a vowel or vowel-like sound, including diphthongs. The most common type of syllable in language also has a consonant (C) before the vowel (V) and is typically represented as CV. Technically, the basic elements of the syllable are the **onset** (one or more consonants) followed by the **rhyme**. The rhyme (sometimes

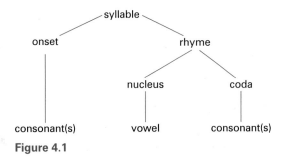

Figure 4.1

written as "rime") consists of a vowel, which is treated as the **nucleus**, plus any following consonant(s), described as the **coda**.

Syllables like *me*, *to* or *no* have an onset and a nucleus, but no coda. They are known as **open syllables**. When a coda is present, as in the syllables *up*, *cup*, *at* or *hat*, they are called **closed syllables**. The basic structure of the kind of syllable found in English words like *green* (CCVC), *eggs* (VCC), *and* (VCC), *ham* (CVC), *I* (V), *do* (CV), *not* (CVC), *like* (CVC), *them* (CVC), *Sam* (CVC), *I* (V), *am* (VC) is shown in the accompanying diagram.

Consonant clusters

Both the onset and the coda can consist of more than one consonant, also known as a **consonant cluster**. The combination /st/ is a consonant cluster (CC) used as onset in the word *stop*, and as coda in the word *post*. There are many CC onset combinations permitted in English phonotactics, as in *black*, *bread*, *trick*, *twin*, *flat* and *throw*. Note that liquids (/l/, /r/) and a glide (/w/) are being used in second position.

English can actually have larger onset clusters, as in the words *stress* and *splat*, consisting of three initial consonants (CCC). The phonotactics of these larger onset consonant clusters is not too difficult to describe. The first consonant must always be /s/, followed by one of the voiceless stops (/p/, /t/, /k/) and a liquid or glide (/l/, /r/, /w/). You can check if this description is adequate for the combinations in *splash*, *spring*, *strong*, *scream* and *square*. Does the description also cover the second syllable in the pronunciation of *exclaim*? How about /ɛk-skleɪm/? Remember that it is the onset of the syllable that is being described, not the beginning of the word.

It is quite unusual for languages to have consonant clusters of this type. Indeed, the syllable structure of many languages (e.g. Japanese) is predominantly CV. It is also noticeable in English that large consonant clusters may be reduced in casual conversational speech, particularly if they occur in the middle of a word. This is just one example of a process that is usually discussed in terms of coarticulation effects.

Coarticulation effects

In much of the preceding discussion, we have been describing speech sounds in syllables and words as if they are always pronounced carefully and deliberately, almost in slow motion. Speech isn't normally like that. Mostly our talk is fast and spontaneous, and it requires our articulators to move from one sound to the next without stopping. The process of making one sound almost at the same time as the next sound is called **coarticulation**. There are two well-known coarticulation effects, described as assimilation and elision.

Assimilation

When two sound segments occur in sequence and some aspect of one segment is taken or "copied" by the other, the process is known as **assimilation**. If we think of the physical production of speech, we realize that this regular process happens simply because it's quicker, easier and more efficient for our articulators as they do their job. Think of the word *have* /hæv/ by itself, then think of how it is pronounced in the phrase *I have to go* in everyday speech. In this phrase, as we start to say the /t/ sound in *to*, which is voiceless, we tend to produce a voiceless version of the preceding sound, resulting in what sounds more like /f/ than /v/. So, we typically say [hæftə] in this phrase and you may even see it written informally as "hafta," showing how the assimilation from a voiced to a voiceless sound is perceived.

Vowels are also subject to assimilation. In isolation, we would typically pronounce [ɪ] and [æ] without any nasal quality at all. However, when we say words like *pin* and *pan* in everyday speech, the anticipation of forming the final nasal consonant will make it easier to go into the nasalized articulation in advance and consequently the vowel sounds in these words will be, in more precise transcription, [ĩ] and [æ̃] This is a very regular feature of English speakers' pronunciation. It is so regular, in fact, that a phonological rule can be stated in the following way: "Any vowel becomes nasal whenever it immediately precedes a nasal."

This type of assimilation process occurs in a variety of different contexts. By itself, the word *can* may be pronounced as [kæn], but, when we say *I can go*, the influence of the following velar [g] will almost certainly make the preceding nasal sound come out as [ŋ] (the velar nasal) rather than [n] (the alveolar nasal). The most commonly observed conversational version of the phrase is [aɪkəŋgoʊ]. Notice that the vowel in *can* has also changed to schwa [ə] from the isolated-word version [æ]. In many words spoken carefully, the vowel receives stress, but in the course of ordinary everyday talk, that vowel may no longer receive any stress and naturally reduce to schwa. We may, for example, pronounce *and* as [ænd] by itself, but in the normal use of the phrase *you and me*, we usually say [ən], as in [juənmi].

Elision

In the last example, illustrating the normal pronunciation of *you and me*, the [d] sound of the word *and* was not included in the transcription. That's because it isn't usually pronounced in this phrase. In the environment of a preceding nasal [n] and a following nasal [m], we simply don't devote speech energy to including the stop sound [d]. This isn't laziness, it's efficiency. There is also typically no [d] sound included in the everyday pronunciation of a word like *friendship* [frɛnʃɪp]. This process of not pronouncing a sound segment that might be present in the deliberately careful pronunciation of a word in isolation is described as **elision**. In consonant clusters, especially in coda position, /t/ is a common casualty in this process, as in the typical pronunciation [æspɛks] for *aspects*, or in [himəsbi] for the phrase *he must be*. We can, of course, slowly and deliberately pronounce each part of the phrase *we asked him*, but the process of elision (of /k/) in casual conversation is likely to produce [wiæstəm]. Vowels also disappear, as in [ɛvri] for *every*, [ɪntrɪst] for *interest*, [kæbnət] for *cabinet*, [kæmrə] for *camera*, [prɪznər] for *prisoner* and [spoʊz] for *suppose*.

Normal speech

These two processes of assimilation and elision occur in everyone's normal speech and should not be regarded as some type of sloppiness or laziness in speaking. In fact, consistently avoiding the regular patterns of assimilation and elision used in a language would result in extremely artificial-sounding talk. The point of investigating these phonological processes is not to arrive at a set of rules about how a language should be pronounced, but to try to come to an understanding of the regularities and patterns which underlie the actual use of sounds in language.

Study questions

1   What is the difference between a phoneme and an allophone?
2   What is an aspirated sound and which of the following words would normally be pronounced with one: *kill, pool, skill, spool, stop, top*?
3   Which of the following words would be treated as minimal pairs?

   ban, fat, pit, bell, tape, heat, meal, more, pat, tap, pen, chain, vote, bet, far, bun, goat, heel, sane, tale, vet

4   What is meant by the phonotactics of a language?
5   What is the difference between an open and a closed syllable?
6   Which segments in the pronunciation of the following words are most likely to be affected by elision?
   (i) *government*   (ii) *postman*   (iii) *pumpkin*   (iv) *sandwich*   (v) *victory*

Tasks

A   What are diacritics and which ones were used in this chapter to identify sounds?
B   In the phonology of Hawaiian there are only open syllables. Using this information, can you work out how English "Merry Christmas" became "Mele Kalikimaka" for people in Hawai'i? Also, based on this slender evidence, which two English consonants are probably not phonemes in Hawaiian?
C   The word *central* has a consonant cluster (-*ntr*-) in the middle and two syllables. What do you think is the best way to divide the word into two syllables (*ce + ntral, centr + al, cen + tral, cent + ral*) and why?
D   Individual sounds are described as segments. What are suprasegmentals?
E   The English words *lesson* and *little* are typically pronounced with syllabic consonants.
   (i)   What exactly is a syllabic consonant and how would it appear in a phonetic transcription?
   (ii) Which of these words would most likely be pronounced with a syllabic consonant: *bottle, bottom, button, castle, copper, cotton, paddle, schism, wooden*?
F   A general distinction can be made among languages depending on their basic rhythm, whether they have syllable-timing or stress-timing. How are these two types of rhythm distinguished and which type characterizes the pronunciation of English, French and Spanish?

Discussion topics/projects

I We can form negative versions of words such as *audible* and *edible* in English by adding *in-* to produce *inaudible* and *inedible*. How would you describe the special phonological processes involved in the pronunciation of the negative versions of the following words?

balance, compatible, complete, decent, glorious, gratitude, legal, literate, mature, perfect, possible, rational, responsible, sane, tolerant, variable

(For background reading, see chapter 3 (pages 75–78) of Payne, 2006.)

II The use of plural *-s* in English has three different, but very regular, phonological alternatives. We add /s/ to words like *bat*, *book*, *cough* and *ship*. We add /z/ to words like *cab*, *cave*, *lad*, *rag* and *thing*. We add /əz/ to words like *bus*, *bush*, *church*, *judge* and *maze*.

(a) Can you identify the sets of sounds that regularly precede each of these alternative pronunciations of the plural ending?

(b) What features do each of these sets have in common?

(For background reading, see chapter 2 (pages 55–56) of Jeffries, 2006.)

Bob Belviso translated

One attempt to interpret those very unusual spellings might be as follows:

Once upon a time was three bears; mama bear, papa bear, and baby bear. Live in the country near the forest. NICE HOUSE. No mortgage. One day papa, mama, and baby go beach, only they forget to lock the door.

By and by comes Goldilocks. She got nothing to do but make trouble. She push all the food down the mouth; no leave a crumb. Then she goes upstairs and sleeps in all the beds.

Further reading

Basic treatments
Davenport, M. and S. Hannahs (2005) *Introducing Phonetics and Phonology* (2nd edition) Hodder Arnold
McMahon, A. (2002) *An Introduction to English Phonology* Edinburgh University Press
More detailed treatments
Odden, D. (2005) *Introducing Phonology* Cambridge University Press
Roach, P. (2000) *English Phonetics and Phonology* (3rd edition) Cambridge University Press
Syllables
Duanmu, S. (2008) *Syllable Structure* Oxford University Press

Coarticulation

Hardcastle, W. and N. Hewlett (1999) *Coarticulation: Theory, Data and Techniques* Cambridge
University Press

Assimilation and elision

Brown, G. (1990) *Listening to Spoken English* Longman

Other references

Jeffries, L. (2006) *Discovering Language* Palgrave Macmillan

Payne, T. (2006) *Exploring Language Structure* Cambridge University Press

5 Word formation

Though the Dutch were only a passing political presence in America, their linguistic legacy is immense. From their earliest days of contact, Americans freely appropriated Dutch terms – *blunderbuss* (literally "thunder gun") as early as 1654, *scow* in 1660, *sleigh* in 1703. By the mid-eighteenth century Dutch words flooded into American English: *stoop, span, coleslaw, boss, pit* in the sense of the stone of a fruit, *bedpan, bedspread* (previously known as a *counterpane*), *cookie, waffle, nitwit* (from the colloquial Dutch *Ik niet weet*, meaning "I don't know"), the distinctive American interrogative *how come?* (a literal translation of the Dutch *hoekom*), *poppycock* (from *pappekak*, "soft dung"), *dunderhead*, and probably the *caboodle* in *kit and caboodle*.

Two particularly durable Americanisms that emanate from Dutch are *Santa Claus* (out of *Sinter Klaas*, a familiar form of *St Nicholas*), first recorded in American English in 1773, and *Yankee* (probably from either *Janke*, a diminutive equivalent to the English *Johnny*, or *Jan Kaas*, "John Cheese," intended originally as a mild insult). Bryson (1994)

Around 1900, in New Berlin, Ohio, a department-store worker named J. Murray Spangler invented a device which he called an *electric suction sweeper*. This device eventually became very popular and could have been known as a *spangler*. People could have been *spanglering* their floors or they might even have *spanglered* their rugs and curtains. The use could have extended to a type of person who droned on and on (and really sucked), described as *spanglerish*, or to a whole style of behavior called *spanglerism*. However, none of that happened.

Instead, Mr. Spangler sold his new invention to a local businessman called William H. Hoover, whose Hoover Suction Sweeper Company produced the first machine called a "Hoover." Not only did the word *hoover* (without a capital letter) become as familiar as *vacuum cleaner* all over the world, but in Britain, people still talk about *hoovering* (and not *spanglering*) their carpets.

The point of this small tale is that, although we had never heard of Mr. Spangler before, we really had no difficulty coping with the new words: *spangler*, *spanglerish*, *spanglerism*, *spanglering* or *spanglered*. That is, we can very quickly understand a new word in our language (a **neologism**) and accept the use of different forms of that new word. This ability must derive in part from the fact that there is a lot of regularity in the word-formation processes in a language. In this chapter, we will explore some of the basic processes by which new words are created.

Etymology

The study of the origin and history of a word is known as its **etymology**, a term which, like many of our technical words, comes to us through Latin, but has its origins in Greek (*étymon* "original form" + *logia* "study of"), and is not to be confused with *entomology*, also from Greek (*éntomon* "insect"). When we look closely at the etymologies of less technical words, we soon discover that there are many different ways in which new words can enter the language. We should keep in mind that these processes have been at work in the language for some time and a lot of words in daily use today were, at one time, considered barbaric misuses of the language. It is difficult now to understand the views expressed in the early nineteenth century over the "tasteless innovation" of a word like *handbook*, or the horror expressed by a London newspaper in 1909 over the use of the newly coined word *aviation*. Yet many new words can cause similar outcries as they come into use today. Rather than act as if the language is being debased, we might prefer to view the constant evolution of new words and new uses of old words as a reassuring sign of vitality and creativeness in the way a language is shaped by the needs of its users.

Coinage

One of the least common processes of word formation in English is **coinage**, that is, the invention of totally new terms. The most typical sources are invented trade names for commercial products that become general terms (usually without capital letters) for any version of that product. Older examples are *aspirin*, *nylon*, *vaseline* and *zipper*;

more recent examples are *granola, kleenex, teflon* and *xerox*. It may be that there is an obscure technical origin (e.g. te(tra)-fl(uor)-on) for some of these invented terms, but after their first coinage, they tend to become everyday words in the language.

The most salient contemporary example of coinage is the word *google*. Originally a misspelling for the word *googol* (= the number 1 followed by 100 zeros), in the creation of the word *Googleplex*, which later became the name of a company (*Google*), the term *google* (without a capital letter) has become a widely used expression meaning "to use the internet to find information." New products and concepts (*ebay*) and new activities ("Have you tried *ebaying* it?") are the usual sources of coinage.

New words based on the name of a person or a place are called **eponyms**. When we talked about a *hoover* (or even a *spangler*), we were using an eponym. Other common eponyms are *sandwich* (from the eighteenth-century Earl of Sandwich who first insisted on having his bread and meat together while gambling) and *jeans* (from the Italian city of Genoa where the type of cloth was first made). Some eponyms are technical terms, based on the names of those who first discovered or invented things, such as *fahrenheit* (from the German, Gabriel Fahrenheit), *volt* (from the Italian, Alessandro Volta) and *watt* (from the Scottish inventor, James Watt).

Borrowing

As Bill Bryson observed in the quotation presented earlier, one of the most common sources of new words in English is the process simply labeled **borrowing**, that is, the taking over of words from other languages. (Technically, it's more than just borrowing because English doesn't give them back.) Throughout its history, the English language has adopted a vast number of words from other languages, including *croissant* (French), *dope* (Dutch), *lilac* (Persian), *piano* (Italian), *pretzel* (German), *sofa* (Arabic), *tattoo* (Tahitian), *tycoon* (Japanese), *yogurt* (Turkish) and *zebra* (Bantu).

Other languages, of course, borrow terms from English, as in the Japanese use of *suupaa* or *suupaamaaketto* ("supermarket") and *taipuraitaa* ("typewriter"), Hungarians talking about *sport, klub* and *futbal*, or the French discussing problems of *le stress*, over a glass of *le whisky*, during *le weekend*. In some cases, the borrowed words may be used with quite different meanings, as in the contemporary German use of the English words *partner* and *look* in the phrase *im Partnerlook* to describe two people who are together and are wearing similar clothing. There is no equivalent use of this expression in English.

A special type of borrowing is described as **loan-translation** or **calque** (/kælk/). In this process, there is a direct translation of the elements of a word into the borrowing language. Interesting examples are the French term *gratte-ciel*, which literally translates as "scrape-sky," the Dutch *wolkenkrabber* ("cloud scratcher") or the German *Wolkenkratzer* ("cloud scraper"), all of which were calques for the English *skyscraper*. The English word *superman* is thought to be a loan-translation of the German *Übermensch*, and the term *loan-word* itself is believed to have come from the German *Lehnwort*. The English expression *moment of truth* is believed to be a calque from the Spanish phrase *el momento de la verdad*, though not restricted to the original use as the final thrust of the sword to end a bullfight. Nowadays, some Spanish speakers eat *perros calientes* (literally "dogs hot") or *hot dogs*. The American concept of "boyfriend" was a borrowing, with sound modification, into Japanese as *boyifurendo*, but as a calque into Chinese as "male friend" or *nan pengyu*.

Compounding

In some of the examples we have just considered, there is a joining of two separate words to produce a single form. Thus, *Lehn* and *Wort* are combined to produce *Lehnwort* in German. This combining process, technically known as **compounding**, is very common in languages such as German and English, but much less common in languages such as French and Spanish. Common English compounds are *bookcase*, *doorknob*, *fingerprint*, *sunburn*, *textbook*, *wallpaper*, *wastebasket* and *waterbed*. All these examples are nouns, but we can also create compound adjectives (*good-looking*, *low-paid*) and compounds of adjective (*fast*) plus noun (*food*) as in *a fast-food restaurant* or *a full-time job*.

This very productive source of new terms has been well documented in English and German, but can also be found in totally unrelated languages, such as Hmong (spoken in South East Asia), which combines *hwj* ("pot") and *kais* ("spout") to produce *hwjkais* ("kettle"). Recent creations are *paj* ("flower") plus *kws* ("corn") for *pajkws* ("popcorn") and *hnab* ("bag") + *rau* ("put") + *ntawv* ("paper" or "book") for *hnabrauntawv* ("schoolbag").

Blending

The combination of two separate forms to produce a single new term is also present in the process called **blending**. However, blending is typically accomplished by taking only the beginning of one word and joining it to the end of the other word. In some parts of the USA, there's a product that is used like *gasoline*, but is made from *alcohol*, so the "blended" word for referring to this product is *gasohol*. To talk about the combined effects of *smoke* and *fog*, we can use the word *smog*. In places where they have a lot of this stuff, they can jokingly make a distinction between *smog*, *smaze* (smoke + haze) and *smurk* (smoke + murk). In Hawai'i, near the active volcano, they have problems with *vog*. Some other commonly used examples of blending are *bit* (binary/digit), *brunch* (breakfast/lunch), *motel* (motor/hotel) and *telecast* (television/broadcast).

The activity of fund-raising on television that feels like a marathon is typically called a *telethon*, while *infotainment* (information/entertainment) and *simulcast* (simultaneous/broadcast) are other new blends from life with television. To describe the mixing of languages, some people talk about *Franglais* (French/Anglais) and *Spanglish* (Spanish/English). In a few blends, we combine the beginnings of both words, as in terms from information technology, such as *telex* (teleprinter/exchange) or *modem* (modulator/demodulator). There is also the word *fax*, but that is not a blend. It's an example of our next category.

Clipping

The element of reduction that is noticeable in blending is even more apparent in the process described as **clipping**. This occurs when a word of more than one syllable (*facsimile*) is reduced to a shorter form (*fax*), usually beginning in casual speech. The term *gasoline* is still used, but most people talk about *gas*, using the clipped form. Other common examples are *ad* (advertisement), *bra* (brassiere), *cab* (cabriolet), *condo* (condominium), *fan* (fanatic), *flu* (influenza), *perm* (permanent wave), *phone*, *plane* and *pub* (public house). English speakers also like to clip each other's names, as in *Al*, *Ed*, *Liz*, *Mike*, *Ron*, *Sam*, *Sue* and *Tom*.

There must be something about educational environments that encourages clipping because so many words get reduced, as in *chem*, *exam*, *gym*, *lab*, *math*, *phys-ed*, *poly-sci*, *prof* and *typo*.

A particular type of reduction, favored in Australian and British English, produces forms technically known as **hypocorisms**. In this process, a longer word is reduced to a single syllable, then *-y* or *-ie* is added to the end. This is the process that results in *movie* ("moving pictures") and *telly* ("television"). It has also produced *Aussie* ("Australian"), *barbie* ("barbecue"), *bookie* ("bookmaker"), *brekky* ("breakfast") and *hankie* ("handkerchief"). You can probably guess what *Chrissy pressies* are.

Backformation

A very specialized type of reduction process is known as **backformation**. Typically, a word of one type (usually a noun) is reduced to form a word of another type (usually a verb). A good example of backformation is the process whereby the noun *television* first came into use and then the verb *televise* was created from it. Other examples of words created by this process are: *donate* (from "donation"), *emote* (from "emotion"), *enthuse* (from "enthusiasm"), *liaise* (from "liaison") and *babysit* (from "babysitter"). Indeed, when we use the verb *backform* (*Did you know that "opt" was backformed from "option"?*), we are using a backformation.

One very regular source of backformed verbs in English is based on the common pattern *worker – work*. The assumption seems to have been that if there is a noun ending in *-er* (or something close in sound), then we can create a verb for what that noun *-er* does. Hence, an *editor* will *edit*, a *sculptor* will *sculpt* and *burglars*, *peddlers* and *swindlers* will *burgle*, *peddle* and *swindle*.

Conversion

A change in the function of a word, as for example when a noun comes to be used as a verb (without any reduction), is generally known as **conversion**. Other labels for this very common process are "category change" and "functional shift." A number of nouns such as *bottle*, *butter*, *chair* and *vacation* have come to be used, through conversion, as verbs: *We bottled the home-brew last night*; *Have you buttered the toast?*; *Someone has to chair the meeting*; *They're vacationing in Florida*. These conversions are readily accepted, but some examples, such as the noun *impact* being used as a verb, seem to *impact* some people's sensibilities rather negatively.

The conversion process is particularly productive in Modern English, with new uses occurring frequently. The conversion can involve verbs becoming nouns, with *guess*, *must* and *spy* as the sources of *a guess*, *a must* and *a spy*. Phrasal verbs (*to print out*, *to take over*) also become nouns (*a printout*, *a takeover*). One complex verb combination (*want to be*) has become a new noun, as in *He isn't in the group, he's just a wannabe*.

Verbs (*see through*, *stand up*) also become adjectives, as in *see-through material* or *a stand-up comedian*. Or adjectives, as in *a dirty floor, an empty room, some crazy ideas* and *those nasty people*, can become the verbs *to dirty* and *to empty*, or the nouns *a crazy* and *the nasty*.

Some compound nouns have assumed adjectival or verbal functions, exemplified by *the ball park* appearing in *a ball-park figure* or asking someone *to ball-park an estimate of the cost*. Other nouns of this type are *carpool*, *mastermind*, *microwave* and *quarterback*, which are all regularly used as verbs. Other forms, such as *up* and *down*, can also become verbs, as in *They're going to up the price of oil* or *We downed a few beers at the Chimes*.

It is worth noting that some words can shift substantially in meaning when they change category through conversion. The verb *to doctor* often has a negative sense, not normally associated with the source noun *a doctor*. A similar kind of reanalysis of meaning is taking place with respect to the noun *total* and the verb *run around*, which do not have negative meanings. However, after conversion, if you *total* (= verb) your car, and your insurance company gives you the *runaround* (= noun), then you will have a double sense of the negative.

Acronyms

Acronyms are new words formed from the initial letters of a set of other words. These can be forms such as *CD* ("compact disk") or *VCR* ("video cassette recorder") where the pronunciation consists of saying each separate letter. More typically, acronyms are pronounced as new single words, as in *NATO*, *NASA* or *UNESCO*. These examples have kept their capital letters, but many acronyms simply become everyday terms such as *laser* ("light amplification by stimulated emission of radiation"), *radar* ("radio detecting and ranging"), *scuba* ("self-contained underwater breathing apparatus") and *zip* ("zone improvement plan") code. You might even hear talk of a *snafu*, which is reputed to have its origins in "situation normal, all fouled up," though there is some dispute about the appropriate f-word in there.

Names for organizations are often designed to have their acronym represent an appropriate term, as in "mothers against drunk driving" (*MADD*) and "women against rape" (*WAR*). Some new acronyms come into general use so quickly that many speakers do not think of their component meanings. Innovations such as the *ATM* ("automatic teller machine") and the required *PIN* ("personal identification number") are regularly used with one of their elements repeated, as in *I sometimes forget my PIN number when I go to the ATM machine.*

Derivation

In our list so far, we have not dealt with what is by far the most common word-formation process to be found in the production of new English words. This process is called **derivation** and it is accomplished by means of a large number of small "bits" of the English language which are not usually given separate listings in dictionaries. These small "bits" are generally described as **affixes**. Some familiar examples are the elements *un-*, *mis-*, *pre-*, *-ful*, *-less*, *-ish*, *-ism* and *-ness* which appear in words like *unhappy*, *misrepresent*, *prejudge*, *joyful*, *careless*, *boyish*, *terrorism* and *sadness*.

Prefixes and suffixes

Looking more closely at the preceding group of words, we can see that some affixes have to be added to the beginning of the word (e.g. *un-*, *mis-*). These are called **prefixes**. Other affixes have to be added to the end of the word (e.g. *-less*, *-ish*) and are called **suffixes**. All English words formed by this derivational process have either prefixes or suffixes, or both. Thus, *mislead* has a prefix, *disrespectful* has both a prefix and a suffix, and *foolishness* has two suffixes.

Infixes

There is a third type of affix, not normally used in English, but found in some other languages. This is called an **infix** and, as the term suggests, it is an affix that is incorporated inside another word. It is possible to see the general principle at work in certain expressions, occasionally used in fortuitous or aggravating circumstances by emotionally aroused English speakers: *Halle**bloody**lujah!*, *Abso**goddam**lutely!* and *Un**fuckin**believable!*. In the film *Wish You Were Here*, the main character expresses her aggravation (at another character who keeps trying to contact her) by screaming *Tell him I've gone to Singa**bloody**pore!*. The expletive may even have an infixed element, as in *god**triple**dammit!*.

Kamhmu

We could view these "inserted" forms as a special version of infixing in English. However, a much better set of examples can be provided from Kamhmu, a language spoken in South East Asia.

	Verb	Noun	
("to drill")	*see*	*srnee*	("a drill")
("to chisel")	*toh*	*trnoh*	("a chisel")
("to eat with a spoon")	*hiip*	*hrniip*	("a spoon")
("to tie")	*hoom*	*hrnoom*	("a thing with which to tie")

From these examples, we can see that there is a regular pattern whereby the infix *-rn-* is added to verbs to form corresponding nouns. If this pattern is generally found in the language and we know that the form *krnap* is the Kamhmu noun for "tongs," then we can work out the corresponding verb "to grasp with tongs." According to Merrifield *et al.* (2003), the source of these examples, it is *kap*.

Multiple processes

Although we have concentrated on each of these word-formation processes in isolation, it is possible to trace the operation of more than one process at work in the creation of a particular word. For example, the term *deli* seems to have become a common American English expression via a process of first borrowing *delicatessen* (from German) and then clipping that borrowed form. If someone says that *problems with the project have snowballed*, the final word can be analyzed as an example of compounding in which *snow* and *ball* were combined to form the noun *snowball*, which was then turned into a verb through conversion. Forms that begin as acronyms can also go through other processes, as in the use of *lase* as a verb, the result of backformation from *laser*. In the expression *waspish attitudes*, the acronym *WASP* ("white Anglo-Saxon Protestant") has lost its capital letters and gained a suffix (*-ish*) in the derivation process.

An acronym that never seems to have had capital letters comes from "young urban professional", plus the *-ie* suffix, as in hypocorism, to produce the word *yuppie* (first recorded in 1984). The formation of this new word, however, was helped by a quite different process, known simply as **analogy**, whereby new words are formed to be similar in some way to existing words. *Yuppie* was made possible as a new word by analogy with the earlier word *hippie* and another short-lived analogy *yippie*. The word *yippie* also had an acronym basis ("youth international party") and was used for some students in the USA who were protesting against the war in Vietnam. One joke has it that *yippies* just grew up to be *yuppies*. And the process continues. Another analogy, with the word *yap* ("to make shrill noises"), helped label some of the noisy young professionals as *yappies*.

Many of these new words can, of course, have a very brief life-span. Perhaps the generally accepted test of the "arrival" of recently formed words in a language is their published appearance in a dictionary. However, even this may not occur without protests from some conservative voices, as Noah Webster found when his first dictionary, published in 1806, was criticized for citing words like *advocate* and *test* as verbs, and for including such "vulgar" words as *advisory* and *presidential*. It would seem that Noah had a keener sense than his critics of which new word-forms in the language were going to last.

Study questions

1   What is the difference between etymology and entomology?

2   Which of the following pairs contains an example of calque? How would you describe the other(s)?

(a)   *footobooru* (Japanese) – *football* (English)

(b)   *tréning* (Hungarian) – *training* (English)

(c)   *luna de miel* (Spanish "moon of honey") – *honeymoon* (English)

(d)   *jardin d'enfants* (French "garden of children") – *Kindergarten* (German "children garden")

3   Can you identify the different word-formation processes involved in producing each of the underlined words in these sentences?

(a)   *Don't you ever worry that you might get AIDS?*

(b)   *Do you have a xerox machine?*

(c)   *That's really fandamntastic!*

(d)   *Shiel still parties every Saturday night.*

(e)   *These new skateboards from Zee Designs are kickass.*

(f)   *When I'm ill, I want to see a doc, not a vet.*

(g)   *The house next door was burgled when I was babysitting the Smiths' children.*

(h)   *I like this old sofa – it's nice and comfy.*

4   Identify the prefixes and suffixes used in these words: *misfortune, terrorism, carelessness, disagreement, ineffective, unfaithful, prepackaged, biodegradable, reincarnation, decentralization*

5   In Kamhmu, the word *sal* means "to put an ornament in the ear." What would be the word for "an ear ornament"?

6   More than one process was involved in the creation of the forms underlined in these sentences. Can you identify the processes involved in each case?

(a)   *Are you still using that old car-phone?*

(b)   *Can you FedEx the books to me today?*

(c)   *Police have reported an increase in carjackings in recent months.*

(d)   *Welcome, everyone, to karaokenight at Cathy's Bar and Grill!*

(e)   *Jeeves, could you tell the maid to be sure to hoover the bedroom carpet?*

(f)   *Would you prefer a decaf?*

Tasks

A   What are "initialisms"? Were there any examples in this chapter?

B   Who invented the term "portmanteau words"? How many examples were included in this chapter?

C   Using a dictionary with etymological information, identify which of the following words are borrowings and from which languages they were borrowed. Are any of them eponyms?

assassin, clone, cockroach, denim, diesel, horde, kayak, kiosk, nickname, penguin, robot, shampoo, sherry, slogan, snoop, taboo, tea, tomato, umbrella, voodoo

D   There are a lot of new words in English from IT (an acronym for "information technology") and the widespread use of the internet (a blend from "international" and "network"). Using a dictionary if necessary, try to describe the word-formation processes involved in the creation of the underlined words in these sentences.

(1)   *There are some teenage netizens who rarely leave their rooms.*
(2)   *How much RAM do you have?*
(3)   *I can't get some of the students to keyboard more carefully.*
(4)   *Your friend Jason is such a techie!*
(5)   *Doesn't every new computer have a webcam now?*
(6)   *You should bookmark that site.*
(7)   *We're paying too much attention to bloggers.*
(8)   *Subscribers have unlimited downloads.*
(9)   *You should check the faq because the information is usually helpful.*
(10)   *Hey, just heard about the accident, ruok?*

E   Another type of affix is called a circumfix. Here are some examples from Indonesian.

("big")	*besar*	*kebesaran*	("bigness")
("beautiful")	*indah*	*keindahan*	("beauty")
("healthy")	....	*kesehatan*	("health")
("free")	....	*kebebasan*	("freedom")
("kind")	*baik*	....	("kindness")
("honest")	*jujur*	....	("honesty")

1   Can you provide the missing forms in these examples?
2   What is the circumfix illustrated here?
3   For what type of word-formation process is the circumfix being used here?
4   Given the words *tersedia* ("available"), *sulit* ("difficult"), *sesuai* ("suitable") and *seimbang* ("balanced"), how would you translate "availability," "difficulty," "suitability" and "balance"?
5   Consider the following examples:
   ketidakjujuran ("dishonesty")

ketidaksenangan ("unhappiness")

ketidakadilan ("injustice")

ketidakpuasan ("dissatisfaction")

What do you think the corresponding Indonesian words would be for "happy," "just/fair" and "satisfied"?

F When Hmong speakers (from Laos and Vietnam) settled in the USA, they had to create some new words for the different objects and experiences they encountered. Using the following translations (provided by Bruce Downing and Judy Fuller), can you work out the English equivalents of the Hmong expressions listed below?

chaw ("place")	*kho* ("fix")	*hlau* ("iron")	*cai* ("right")
dav ("bird")	*muas* ("buy")	*hniav* ("teeth")	*daim* ("flat")
hnab ("bag")	*nres* ("stand")	*looj* ("cover")	*mob* ("sickness")
kev ("way")	*ntaus* ("hit")	*ntoo* ("wood")	*nqaj* ("rail")
kws ("expert")	*tos* ("wait")	*ntawv* ("paper")	*tshuaj* ("medicine")
tsheb ("vehicle")	*zaum* ("sit")	*tes* ("hand")	

chawkhomob   *kwshlau*

chawnrestsheb   *kwskhohniav*

chawzaumtos   *kwsntausntawv*

davhlau   *kwsntoo*

hnabloojtes   *kwskhotsheb*

kevcai   *kwstshuaj*

kevkhomob   *tshebnqajhlau*

kevnqajhlau   *daimntawvmuastshuaj*

Discussion topics/projects

I When we form compounds in English, how do we know whether to join the words (*hairspray*), join them with a hyphen (*hair-spray*) or leave a space between them (*hair spray*)? Using the examples below, and any others that you want to include in the discussion, try to decide if there are any typical patterns in the way we form compounds.

backpack, back-pedal, back seat, blackboard, black hole, black-tie affair, bulletin board, double bed, double-cross, house husband, house-warming, housewife, life-saving, lifestyle, life insurance, mother-in-law, mother tongue, postcard, Post-its, post office, workbook, work experience, work-to-rule

(For background reading, see chapter 3 of Denning, Kessler and Leben, 2007.)

II When we derive new words with a suffix such as *-able*, there seems to be some type of constraint on what is permitted. The words in the left column below are "acceptable" (that's one!), but the forms in the other two columns don't seem to be current English words. They are marked with an asterisk * to show that we think they are "unacceptable" (there's another one!). From these examples, and any others that you think might be relevant to the discussion, can you work out what the rule(s) might be for making new adjectives with the suffix *-able*?

breakable	*carable	*dieable
doable	*chairable	*disappearable
downloadable	*diskable	*downable
inflatable	*hairable	*pinkable
movable	*housable	*runable
understandable	*pencilable	*sleepable
wearable	*quickable	*smilable

(For background reading, see File 4.4 of *Language Files*, 2007.)

Further reading

Basic treatments

Denning, K., B. Kessler and W. Leben (2007) *English Vocabulary Elements* (2nd edition) Oxford University Press

Minkova, D. and R. Stockwell (2009) *English Words: History and Structure* (2nd edition) Cambridge University Press

More detailed treatments

Adams, V. (2001) *Complex Words in English* Longman

Plag, I. (2003) *Word-formation in English* Cambridge University Press

Etymology

Crystal, D. (2003) *The Cambridge Encyclopedia of the English Language* (chapters 10–12) (2nd edition) Cambridge University Press

Googling

Vise, D. and M. Malseed (2005) *The Google Story* Delacorte Press

Borrowing

Stubbs, M. (2001) *Words and Phrases* (chapter 8) Blackwell

Compounding

Fabb, N. (1998) "Compounding" In A. Spencer and A. Zwicky (eds.) *The Handbook of Morphology* (66–83) Blackwell

Hypocorisms

Allan, K. (1986) *Linguistic Meaning* Routledge

Conversion

Aitchison, J. (2003) *Words in the Mind* (part 3) (3rd edition) Blackwell

Derivation

Lieber, R. (2004) *Morphology and Lexical Semantics* Cambridge University Press

Infixes

Yu, A. (2007) *A Natural History of Infixation* Oxford University Press

Other references

Language Files (2007) (10th edition) Ohio State University Press

Merrifield, W., C. Naish, C. Rensch and G. Story (2003) *Laboratory Manual for Morphology and Syntax* (7th edition) Summer Institute of Linguistics

6 Morphology

BAMBIFICATION: The mental conversion of flesh and blood living creatures into cartoon characters possessing bourgeois Judeo-Christian attitudes and morals.   Coupland (1991)

Throughout the preceding chapter, we approached the description of processes involved in word formation as if the unit called the "word" was always a regular and easily identifiable form, even when it is a form such as *bambification* that we may never have seen before. This doesn't seem unreasonable when we look at a text of written English, since the "words" in the text are, quite obviously, those sets of things marked in black with the bigger spaces separating them. Unfortunately, there are a number of problems with using this observation as the basis of an attempt to describe language in general, and individual linguistic forms in particular.

Morphology

In many languages, what appear to be single forms actually turn out to contain a large number of "word-like" elements. For example, in Swahili (spoken throughout East Africa), the form *nitakupenda* conveys what, in English, would have to be represented as something like *I will love you*. Now, is the Swahili form a single word? If it is a "word," then it seems to consist of a number of elements which, in English, turn up as separate "words." A rough correspondence can be presented in the following way:

ni-	ta-	ku-	penda
"I	will	you	love"

It would seem that this Swahili "word" is rather different from what we think of as an English "word." Yet, there clearly is some similarity between the languages, in that similar elements of the whole message can be found in both. Perhaps a better way of looking at linguistic forms in different languages would be to use this notion of "elements" in the message, rather than depend on identifying only "words."

The type of exercise we have just performed is an example of investigating basic forms in language, generally known as **morphology**. This term, which literally means "the study of forms," was originally used in biology, but, since the middle of the nineteenth century, has also been used to describe the type of investigation that analyzes all those basic "elements" used in a language. What we have been describing as "elements" in the form of a linguistic message are technically known as "morphemes."

Morphemes

We do not actually have to go to other languages such as Swahili to discover that "word forms" may consist of a number of elements. We can recognize that English word forms such as *talks*, *talker*, *talked* and *talking* must consist of one element *talk*, and a number of other elements such as *-s*, *-er*, *-ed* and *-ing*. All these elements are described as **morphemes**. The definition of a morpheme is "a minimal unit of meaning or grammatical function." Units of grammatical function include forms used to indicate past tense or plural, for example.

In the sentence *The police reopened the investigation*, the word *reopened* consists of three morphemes. One minimal unit of meaning is *open*, another minimal unit of meaning is *re-* (meaning "again") and a minimal unit of grammatical function is *-ed* (indicating past tense). The word *tourists* also contains three morphemes. There is one minimal unit of meaning *tour*, another minimal unit of meaning *-ist* (marking "person who does something"), and a minimal unit of grammatical function *-s* (indicating plural).

Free and bound morphemes

From these examples, we can make a broad distinction between two types of morphemes. There are **free morphemes**, that is, morphemes that can stand by themselves as single words, for example, *open* and *tour*. There are also **bound morphemes**, which are those forms that cannot normally stand alone and are typically attached to another form, exemplified as *re-, -ist, -ed, -s*. These forms were described in Chapter 5 as affixes. So, we can say that all affixes (prefixes and suffixes) in English are bound morphemes. The free morphemes can generally be identified as the set of separate English word forms such as basic nouns, adjectives, verbs, etc. When they are used with bound morphemes attached, the basic word forms are technically known as **stems**. For example:

	undressed			*carelessness*	
un-	dress	-ed	care	-less	-ness
prefix	stem	suffix	stem	suffix	suffix
(bound)	(free)	(bound)	(free)	(bound)	(bound)

We should note that this type of description is a partial simplification of the morphological facts of English. There are a number of English words in which the element treated as the stem is not, in fact, a free morpheme. In words such as *receive, reduce* and *repeat*, we can identify the bound morpheme *re-* at the beginning, but the elements *-ceive, -duce* and *-peat* are not separate word forms and hence cannot be free morphemes. These types of forms are sometimes described as "bound stems" to keep them distinct from "free stems" such as *dress* and *care*.

Lexical and functional morphemes

What we have described as free morphemes fall into two categories. The first category is that set of ordinary nouns, adjectives and verbs that we think of as the words that carry the "content" of the messages we convey. These free morphemes are called **lexical morphemes** and some examples are: *girl, man, house, tiger, sad, long, yellow, sincere, open, look, follow, break*. We can add new lexical morphemes to the language rather easily, so they are treated as an "open" class of words.

Other types of free morphemes are called **functional morphemes**. Examples are *and, but, when, because, on, near, above, in, the, that, it, them*. This set consists largely of the functional words in the language such as conjunctions, prepositions, articles and pronouns. Because we almost never add new functional morphemes to the language, they are described as a "closed" class of words.

Derivational and inflectional morphemes

The set of affixes that make up the category of bound morphemes can also be divided into two types. One type is described in Chapter 5 in terms of the derivation of words. These are the **derivational morphemes**. We use these bound morphemes to make new words or to make words of a different grammatical category from the stem. For example, the addition of the derivational morpheme *-ness* changes the adjective *good* to the noun *goodness*. The noun *care* can become the adjectives *careful* or *careless* by the addition of the derivational morphemes *-ful* or *-less*. A list of derivational morphemes will include suffixes such as the *-ish* in *foolish*, *-ly* in *quickly*, and the *-ment* in *payment*. The list will also include prefixes such as *re-, pre-, ex-, mis-, co-, un-* and many more.

The second set of bound morphemes contains what are called **inflectional morphemes**. These are not used to produce new words in the language, but rather to indicate aspects of the grammatical function of a word. Inflectional morphemes are used to show if a word is plural or singular, if it is past tense or not, and if it is a comparative or possessive form.

English has only eight inflectional morphemes (or "inflections"), illustrated in the following sentences.

Jim's two sisters are really different.
One likes to have fun and is always laughing.
The other liked to read as a child and has always taken things seriously.
One is the loudest person in the house and the other is quieter than a mouse.

In the first sentence, both inflections (-'s, -s) are attached to nouns, one marking possessive and the other marking plural. Note that -'s here is a possessive inflection and different from the -'s used as an abbreviation for *is* or *has* (e.g. *she's singing, it's happened again*). There are four inflections attached to verbs: *-s* (3rd person singular), *-ing* (present participle), *-ed* (past tense) and *-en* (past participle). There are two inflections attached to adjectives: *-er* (comparative) and *-est* (superlative). In English, all the inflectional morphemes are suffixes.

Noun +   -'s, -s
Verb +   -s, -ing, -ed, -en
Adjective +   -er, -est

There is some variation in the form of these inflectional morphemes. For example, the possessive sometimes appears as -s' (*those boys' bags*) and the past participle as -ed (*they have finish**ed***).

Morphological description

The difference between derivational and inflectional morphemes is worth emphasizing. An inflectional morpheme never changes the grammatical category of a word. For example, both *old* and *older* are adjectives. The *-er* inflection here (from Old English *-ra*) simply creates a different version of the adjective. However, a derivational morpheme can change the grammatical category of a word. The verb *teach* becomes the noun *teacher* if we add the derivational morpheme *-er* (from Old English *-ere*). So, the suffix *-er* in Modern English can be an inflectional morpheme as part of an adjective and also a distinct derivational morpheme as part of a noun. Just because they look the same (*-er*) doesn't mean they do the same kind of work.

Whenever there is a derivational suffix and an inflectional suffix attached to the same word, they always appear in that order. First the derivational (*-er*) is attached to *teach*, then the inflectional (*-s*) is added to produce *teachers*.

Armed with all these terms for different types of morphemes, we can now take most sentences of English apart and list all the "elements." For example, in the sentence *The child's wildness shocked the teachers*, we can identify eleven morphemes.

The	*child*	*-'s*	*wild*	*-ness*	*shock*
functional	lexical	inflectional	lexical	derivational	lexical
-ed	*the*	*teach*	*-er*	*-s*	
inflectional	functional	lexical	derivational	inflectional	

A useful way to remember all these different types of morphemes is in the following chart.

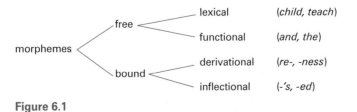

Figure 6.1

Problems in morphological description

The rather neat chart presented here conceals a number of outstanding problems in the analysis of English morphology. So far, we have only considered examples of English words in which the different morphemes are easily identifiable as separate elements. The inflectional morpheme -s is added to *cat* and we get the plural *cats*. What is the inflectional morpheme that makes *sheep* the plural of *sheep*, or *men* the plural of *man*? And if -al is the derivational suffix added to the stem *institution* to give us *institutional*, then can we take -al off the word *legal* to get the stem *leg*? Unfortunately, the answer is "No."

There are other problematic cases, especially in the analysis of different languages, but the solutions to some of these problems are clearer in some instances than in others. For example, the relationship between *law* and *legal* is a reflection of the historical influence of different languages on English word forms. The modern form *law* is a result of a borrowing into Old English (*lagu*) from a Scandinavian source over 1,000 years ago. The modern word *legal* was borrowed about 500 years later from the Latin form *legalis* ("of the law"). Consequently, there is no derivational relationship between the noun *law* and the adjective *legal* in English, nor between the noun *mouth* (from Old English) and the adjective *oral* (a Latin borrowing). An extremely large number of English words owe their morphological patterning to languages like Latin and Greek. Consequently, a full description of English morphology will have to take account of both historical influences and the effect of borrowed elements.

Morphs and allomorphs

One way to treat differences in inflectional morphemes is by proposing variation in morphological realization rules. In order to do this, we draw an analogy with some processes already noted in phonology (Chapter 4). Just as we treated phones as the actual phonetic realization of phonemes, so we can propose **morphs** as the actual forms used to realize morphemes. For example, the form *cats* consists of two morphs, *cat* + -s, realizing a lexical morpheme and an inflectional morpheme ("plural"). The form *buses* also consists of two morphs (*bus* + -es), realizing a lexical morpheme and an inflectional morpheme ("plural"). So there are at least two different morphs (-s and -es, actually /s/ and /əz/) used to realize the inflectional morpheme "plural." Just as we noted that there were "allophones" of a particular phoneme, so we can recognize the existence of **allomorphs** of a particular morpheme. That is, when we find a group of different morphs, all versions of one morpheme, we can use the prefix *allo-* (= one of a closely related set) and describe them as allomorphs of that morpheme.

Take the morpheme "plural." Note that it can be attached to a number of lexical morphemes to produce structures like "*cat* + plural," "*bus* + plural," "*sheep* + plural," and "*man* + plural." In each of these examples, the actual forms of the morphs that result from the morpheme "plural" are different. Yet they are all allomorphs of the one morpheme. So, in addition to /s/ and /əz/, another allomorph of "plural" in English seems to be a zero-morph because the plural form of *sheep* is actually "*sheep* + ø." When we look at "*man* + plural," we have a vowel change in the word (æ → ε) as the morph that produces the "irregular" plural form *men*.

There are a number of other morphological processes at work in a language like English, such as those involved in the range of allomorphs for the morpheme "past tense." These include the common pattern in "*walk* + past tense" that produces *walked* and also the special pattern that takes "*go* + past tense" and produces the "irregular" past form *went*.

Other languages

When we look at the morphology of other languages, we can find other forms and patterns realizing the basic types of morphemes we have identified. The first example below is from English and the second from a language called Aztec (from Central America). In both cases, we attach a derivational morpheme to a stem, then add an inflectional morpheme.

Stem	Derivational	Inflectional	
dark	+ *en* ("make")	+ *ed* ("past")	= *darkened*
mic ("die")	+ *tia* ("cause to")	+ *s* ("future")	= *mictias* ("will kill")

Different patterns occur in other languages. In the following examples, from a range of languages originally described in Gleason (1955), we can try to work out how different forms in the languages are used to realize morphological processes and features.

Kanuri

This first set of examples is from Kanuri, a language spoken in Nigeria.

	Adjective	Noun	
("excellent")	*karite*	*nəmkarite*	("excellence")
("big")	*kura*	*nəmkura*	("bigness")
("small")	*gana*	*nəmgana*	("smallness")
("bad")	*dibi*	*nəmdibi*	("badness")

From this set, we can propose that the prefix *nəm-* is a derivational morpheme that can be used to derive nouns from adjectives. Discovering a regular morphological feature of this type will enable us to make certain predictions when we encounter other forms in the language. For example, if the Kanuri word for "length" is *nəmkurugu*, then we can be reasonably sure that "long" is *kurugu*.

Ganda

Different languages also employ different means to produce inflectional marking on forms. Here are some examples from Ganda, a language spoken in Uganda.

	Singular	Plural	
("doctor")	*omusawo*	*abasawo*	("doctors")
("woman")	*omukazi*	*abakazi*	("women")
("girl")	*omuwala*	*abawala*	("girls")
("heir")	*omusika*	*abasika*	("heirs")

From this small sample, we can observe that there is an inflectional prefix *omu-* used with singular nouns, and a different inflectional prefix *aba-* used with the plural of those nouns. If you are told that *abalenzi* is a Ganda plural, meaning "boys," you should be able to work out the singular form meaning "boy." It is, of course, *omulenzi*.

Ilocano

When we look at Ilocano, a language of the Philippines, we find a quite different way of marking plurals.

	Singular	Plural	
("head")	*úlo*	*ulúlo*	("heads")
("road")	*dálan*	*daldálan*	("roads")
("life")	*bíag*	*bibíag*	("lives")
("plant")	*múla*	*mulmúla*	("plants")

In these examples, there seems to be repetition of the first part of the singular form. When the first part is *bi-* in the singular, the plural begins with this form repeated *bibi-*. The process involved here is technically known as **reduplication** (= "repeating all or part of a form"). There are many languages that use this repetition device as a means of inflectional marking. Having seen how plurals differ from singular forms in Ilocano, you should be able to take this plural form *taltálon* ("fields") and work out what the singular ("field") would be. If you follow the observed pattern, you should get *tálon*.

Tagalog

Here are some other intriguing examples from Tagalog, another language spoken in the Philippines.

basa ("read")	*tawag* ("call")	*sulat* ("write")
bumasa ("Read!")	*tumawag* ("Call!")	*sumulat* ("Write!")
babasa ("will read")	*tatawag* ("will call")	*susulat* ("will write")

If we assume that the first form in each column can be treated as a stem, then it appears that, in the second item in each column, an element *-um-* has been inserted after the first consonant, or more precisely, after the syllable onset. It is an example of an infix (described in Chapter 5). In the third example in each column, note that the change in form involves, in each case, a repetition of the first syllable. So, the marking of future reference in Tagalog appears to be accomplished via reduplication. Using this information, you should be able to complete these examples:

lakad ("walk")	_____ ("Walk!")	_____ ("will walk")
lapit ("come here")	_____ ("Come here!")	_____ ("will come here")

In the second column, with an infix, you'll have *lumakad* and *lumapit*, while in the third column, with reduplication, you'll have *lalakad* and *lalapit*.

As we have been exploring all these different morphological processes, we have moved from the basic structure of words to a consideration of some topics traditionally associated with grammar. We will focus more fully on issues relating to grammar in the next chapter.

Study questions

1   What are the functional morphemes in the following sentence?

   *When he arrived in the morning, the old man had an umbrella and a large plastic
   bag full of books.*

2   (a)   List the bound morphemes in these words: *fearlessly, misleads, previewer,
         shortened, unhappier*
   (b)   Which of these words has a bound stem: *construct, deceive, introduce,
         repeat*?
   (c)   Which of these words contains an allomorph of the morpheme "past tense":
         are, have, must, sitting, waits?

3   What are the inflectional morphemes in these expressions?
   (a)   *Have you eaten yet?*
   (b)   *Do you know how long I've been waiting?*
   (c)   *She's younger than me and always dresses in the latest style.*
   (d)   *We looked through my grandmother's old photo albums.*

4   What are the allomorphs of the morpheme "plural" in this set of English words:
   criteria, dogs, oxen, deer, judges, stimuli?

5   What is reduplication?

6   Provide equivalent forms, in the languages listed, for the English translations
   shown on the right below.

Ganda	*omuloŋgo*	("twin")	–	("twins")	_____
Ilocano	*tawtáwa*	("windows")	–	("window")	_____
Kanuri	*nəmkəǰi*	("sweetness")	–	("sweet")	_____
Tagalog	*bili*	("buy")	–	("will buy")	_____
Tagalog	*kain*	("eat")	–	("Eat!")	_____

Tasks

A   What is "suppletion"? Was there an example of an English suppletive form
   described in this chapter?

B   The selection of appropriate allomorphs is based on three different effects:
   lexical conditioning, morphological conditioning or phonological conditioning.
   What type of conditioning do you think is involved in the relationship between
   the words in each of the following pairs?

   1   *stitch – stitches*
   2   *exclaim – exclamation*
   3   *child – children*

4   *conclude – conclusion*

5   *cliff – cliffs*

6   *tooth – teeth*

C   What are enclitics and proclitics? Does English have both? What are some typical English examples? Why aren't they just called affixes?

D   Using what you learned about Swahili and information provided in the set of examples below, create appropriate forms as translations of the English expressions (1–6) that follow.

nitakupenda ("I will love you")   *alipita* ("She passed by")

watanilipa ("They will pay me")   *uliwapika* ("You cooked them")

tutaondoka ("We will leave")   *walimpiga* ("They beat him")

1 ("She loved you")   4 ("We paid him")

2 ("I will cook them")   5 ("She will beat me")

3 ("You will pass by")   6 ("They left")

E   These examples are from Samoan, as reported in Yu (2007: 24), and based on Mosel and Hovdhaugen (1992). (The consonant represented by ʔ is a glottal stop, as described in Chapter 3.)

	Singular	Plural
("love")	*alófa*	*alolófa*
("clever")	*atamái*	*atamamái*
("work")	*galúe*	*galulúe*
("brave")	*tóa*	*totóa*

(i)   What is the morphological process involved here and where exactly does it take place in the word form?

(ii) What would be the plural of *avága* ("elope"), *má* ("ashamed"), *maʔalíli* ("cold") and *toʔúlu* ("fall")?

F   Using what you learned about Tagalog, plus information from the set of examples here, create appropriate forms of these verbs for (1–10) below.

basag ("break"), *bili* ("buy"), *hanap* ("look for"), *kain* ("eat")

("Write!")	*sumulat*	("Call!")	*tumawag*
("was written")	*sinulat*	("was called")	*tinawag*
("is writing")	*sumusulat*	("is calling")	*tumatawag*
("is being written")	*sinusulat*	("is being called")	*tinatawag*

1 ("Buy!")   6 ("is eating")

2 ("was bought")   7 ("is breaking")

3 ("was broken")   8 ("is being broken")
4 ("was looked for")   9 ("is being looked for")
5 ("is looking for")   10 ("is being eaten")

Discussion topics/projects

I   In English, plural forms such as *mice* appear to be treated in a different way from plurals such as *rats*. If you tell people that a place is infested with mice or rats, they will accept the compounds *mice-infested* and *rat-infested*, but not *rats-infested*. This would suggest that the forms which have the regular plural affix (-*s*) follow a different rule in compounding than irregular plural forms such as *mice*. Can you think of a way to state a rule (or sequence of rules) that would accommodate all the examples given here? (The asterisk * designates an unacceptable form.)

teethmarks	*the feet-cruncher*	*lice-infested*	*a people-mover*
clawmarks	*the finger-cruncher*	*roach-infested*	*a dog-mover*
clawsmarks	*the fingers-cruncher*	*roaches-infested*	*a dogs-mover*

(For background reading, see chapter 6 of Pinker, 1999.)

II   In Turkish, there is some variation in the plural inflection.

	Singular	Plural	
("man")	*adam*	*adamlar*	("men")
("gun")	_____	*toplar*	("guns")
("lesson")	*ders*	_____	("lessons")
("place")	*yer*	*yerler*	("places")
("road")	_____	*yollar*	("roads")
("lock")	_____	*kilitler*	("locks")
("arrow")	*ok*	_____	("arrows")
("hand")	*el*	_____	("hands")
("arm")	*kol*	_____	("arms")
("bell")	_____	*ziller*	("bells")
("friend")	_____	*dostlar*	("friends")
("apple")	*elma*	_____	("apples")

(i)   Can you provide the missing forms?

(ii)   What are the two plural morphs exemplified here?

(iii) Treat the written forms of *a* and *o* as representing back vowels and *e* and *i* as representing front vowels. Using this information, can you state the conditions under which each of the plural morphs is used?

(iv) On the basis of the following phrases, how would you describe the Turkish translation equivalents of *your* and the conditions for their use?

dishin ("your tooth")   *topun* ("your gun")
okun ("your arrow")   *dersin* ("your lesson")
kushun ("your bird")   *kibritlerin* ("your matches")

(v) While English usually marks location with prepositions (**in** *a house* or **at** *a place*), Turkish has postpositions (*house-**in*** or *place-**at***). After looking at the following examples, try to identify the three versions of the "location" suffix and the conditions for their use.

("book")	*kitap*	*kitapta*	("in a book")
("chair")	*koltuk*	*koltukta*	("in a chair")
("room")	*oda*	*odada*	("in a room")
("restaurant")	*lokanta*	*lokantada*	("in a restaurant")
("house")	*ev*	*evde*	("in a house")
("place")	*yer*	*yerlerde*	("in places")
("hand")	*el*	*ellerimde*	("in my hands")
("road")	*yol*	*yollarda*	("in roads")

(vi) When Turkish borrowed (from French) the word *randevu*, meaning "an appointment," how do you think they expressed "in an appointment"? (For more examples, see Gleason, 1955. For more on Turkish, see Lewis, 2000.)

Further reading

Basic treatments
Coates, R. (1999) *Word Structure* Routledge
Payne, T. (2006) *Exploring Language Structure* (chapters 1–3) Cambridge University Press
More detailed treatments
Bauer, L. (2003) *Introducing Linguistic Morphology* (2nd edition) Edinburgh University Press
Booij, G. (2007) *The Grammar of Words: An Introduction to Morphology* (2nd edition) Oxford University Press
Specifically on English morphology
Carstairs-McCarthy, A. (2002) *An Introduction to English Morphology* Edinburgh University Press
Morphology exercises
Language Files (2007) (10th edition) Ohio State University Press
Other references
Gleason, H. (1955) *Workbook in Descriptive Linguistics* Holt

Lewis, G. (2000) *Turkish Grammar* (2nd edition) Oxford University Press

Mosel, U. and E. Hovdhaugen (1992) *Samoan Reference Grammar* Scandinavian University Press

Pinker, S. (1999) *Words and Rules* HarperCollins

Yu, A. (2007) *A Natural History of Infixation* Oxford University Press

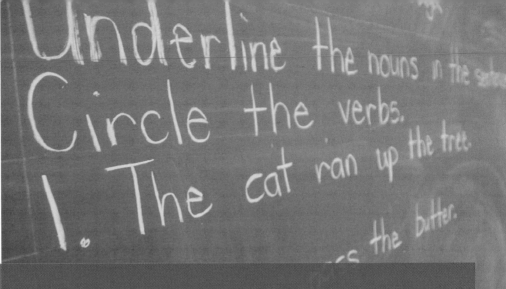

7 Grammar

Dear Ann Landers,

My husband recently ran for public office. He went to the local radio station to record an ad to be read on the air. The copy was written by someone at the station.

One of the sentences was, "Me and my family will be moving to this town." When I heard it on the air, I was shocked. My husband said, "that's the way they wrote it. It didn't sound right to me, either."

I immediately went to the station and challenged them. They said, "You are wrong." We then telephoned a graduate of Northwestern University who was an English major. He said it could be either "I" or "me."

Am I an ignoramus? I was taught to diagram sentences when in doubt. It comes out, "*Me will be moving.*" Does this sound like correct English to you? Please settle it.

Feeling Like a Fool.

Quoted in Lakoff (1990)

We have already considered two levels of description used in the study of language. We have described linguistic expressions as sequences of sounds that can be represented in the phonetic alphabet and described in terms of their features.

ðəlʌkibɔɪz

Voiced fricative   voiceless stop   diphthong

Figure 7.1

We can take the same expression and describe it as a sequence of morphemes.

the	*luck*	*-y*	*boy*	*-s*
functional	lexical	derivational	lexical	inflectional

With these descriptions, we could characterize all the words and phrases of a language in terms of their phonology and morphology.

Grammar

However, we have not accounted for the fact that these words can only be combined in a limited number of patterns. We recognize that the phrase *the lucky boys* is a well-formed phrase in English, but that the following two "phrases" are not at all well-formed.

   *boys the lucky   *lucky boys the

(We use an asterisk * to indicate that a form is unacceptable or ungrammatical.)

From these examples, we can see that English has strict rules for combining words into phrases. The article (*the*) must go before the adjective (*lucky*), which must go before the noun (*boys*). So, in order to be grammatical, this type of phrase must have the sequence article + adjective + noun (and not *noun + article + adjective, for example).

The process of describing the structure of phrases and sentences in such a way that we account for all the grammatical sequences in a language and rule out all the ungrammatical sequences is one way of defining **grammar**. It is the kind of definition assumed when we talk about the grammar of English as opposed to the grammar of Swahili, Tagalog or Turkish. As illustrated in Chapter 6, each of these languages has different ways of forming grammatical phrases and sentences. Studying grammar in this way has a very long tradition.

Traditional grammar

The terms "article," "adjective" and "noun" that we used to label the grammatical categories of the words in the phrase *the lucky boys* come from traditional grammar, which has its origins in the description of languages such as Latin and Greek. Since there were well-established grammatical descriptions of these languages, it seemed appropriate to adopt the existing categories from these descriptions and apply them in the analysis of "newer" languages such as English. After all, Latin and Greek were the languages of scholarship, religion, philosophy and "knowledge," so the grammar of these languages was taken to be the model for other grammars. The best-known terms from that tradition are those used in describing the parts of speech.

The parts of speech

Terms such as "adjective" and "noun" are used to label forms in the language as the parts of speech or word classes. The technical terms used to describe each part of speech are illustrated in the following sentence and simple definitions of each term are listed below.

The	*lucky*	*boys*	*found*	*a*	*backpack*	*in*
article	adjective	noun	verb	article	noun	preposition

the	*park*	*and*	*they*	*opened*	*it*	*carefully*
article	noun	conjunction	pronoun	verb	pronoun	adverb

Nouns are words used to refer to people (*boy*), objects (*backpack*), creatures (*dog*), places (*school*), qualities (*roughness*), phenomena (*earthquake*) and abstract ideas (*love*) as if they were all "things."

Articles are words (*a, an, the*) used with nouns to form noun phrases classifying those "things" (*You can have **a** banana or **an** apple*) or identifying them as already known (*I'll take **the** apple*).

Adjectives are words used, typically with nouns, to provide more information about the things referred to (**happy** *people,* **large** *objects, a* **strange** *experience*).

Verbs are words used to refer to various kinds of actions (*go, talk*) and states (*be, have*) involving people and things in events (*Jessica **is** ill and **has** a sore throat so she can't **talk** or **go** anywhere*).

Adverbs are words used, typically with verbs, to provide more information about actions, states and events (*slowly, yesterday*). Some adverbs (*really, very*) are also used with adjectives to modify information about things (**Really** *large objects move* **slowly**. *I had a* **very** *strange experience* **yesterday**).

Prepositions are words (*at, in, on, near, with, without*) used with nouns in phrases providing information about time (**at** *five o'clock,* **in** *the morning*),

Pronouns   place (**on** *the table*, **near** *the window*) and other connections (**with** *a knife*, **without** *a thought*) involving actions and things.
are words (*she, herself, they, it, you*) used in place of noun phrases, typically referring to people and things already known (**She** *talks to* **herself. They** *said* **it** *belonged to* **you**).

Conjunctions   are words (*and, but, because, when*) used to make connections and indicate relationships between events (*Chantel's husband was so sweet* **and** *he helped her a lot* **because** *she couldn't do much* **when** *she was pregnant*).

Basic definitions of this type are useful for identifying most forms in a language such as English, but they are not completely reliable. A different approach might focus on some other properties of the parts of speech. For example, a noun can be defined as a form that comes after an article (*a, the*) and can take inflections for possessive (*-'s*) and plural (*-s*). Of course, not all nouns (e.g. *information, mud*) have all these characteristics. Moreover, these characteristics are unlikely to be true of nouns in other languages that we might want to describe. As we shall see, an alternative way of looking at nouns and other parts of speech had to be found in order to carry out structural analysis.

Agreement

In addition to the terms used for the parts of speech, traditional grammatical analysis has also given us a number of other categories, including "number," "person," "tense," "voice" and "gender." These categories can be discussed in isolation, but their role in describing language structure becomes clearer when we consider them in terms of **agreement**. For example, we say that the verb *loves* "agrees with" the noun *Cathy* in the sentence *Cathy loves her dog*.

This agreement is partially based on the category of **number**, that is, whether the noun is singular or plural. It is also based on the category of **person**, which covers the distinctions of first person (involving the speaker), second person (involving the hearer) and third person (involving any others). The different forms of English pronouns can be described in terms of person and number. We use *I* for first person singular, *you* for second person singular, and *he, she, it* (or *Cathy*) for third person singular. So, in the sentence *Cathy loves her dog*, we have a noun *Cathy*, which is third person singular, and we use the verb *loves* (not *love*) to "agree with" the noun.

In addition, the form of the verb must be described in terms of another category called **tense**. In this case, the verb *loves* is in the present tense, which is different from the past tense (*loved*). The sentence is also in the **active voice**, describing what Cathy does (i.e. she performs the action of the verb). An alternative would be the **passive voice**, which can be used to describe what happens to Cathy (i.e. she doesn't perform the action), as in *Cathy is loved by her dog* or just *Cathy is loved*.

Our final category is **gender**, which helps us describe the agreement between *Cathy* and *her* in our example sentence. In English, we have to describe this relationship in terms of **natural gender**, mainly derived from a biological distinction between male and female. The agreement between *Cathy* and *her* is based on a distinction made in English between reference to female entities (*she, her*), male entities (*he, his*) and things or creatures, when the sex is unknown or irrelevant (*it, its*).

Grammatical gender

The type of biological distinction used in English is quite different from the more common distinction found in languages that use **grammatical gender**. Whereas natural gender is based on sex (male and female), grammatical gender is based on the type of noun (masculine and feminine) and is not tied to sex. In this latter sense, nouns are classified according to their gender class and, typically, articles and adjectives have different forms to "agree with" the gender of the noun.

Spanish, for example, has two grammatical genders, masculine and feminine, illustrated by the expressions *el sol* ("the sun") and *la luna* ("the moon"). German uses three genders, masculine *der Mond* ("the moon"), feminine *die Sonne* ("the sun") and neuter *das Feuer* ("the fire"). The different forms of the articles in both the Spanish (*el* or *la*) and German (*der, die* or *das*) examples correspond to differences in the gender class of the nouns.

We should emphasize that this gender distinction is not based on a distinction in sex. A young girl is biologically "female," but the German noun *das Mädchen* used to talk about her is grammatically neuter. The French noun in *le livre* ("the book") is grammatically masculine, but neither we nor the French people consider a book to be biologically male. So, the grammatical category of gender is very usefully applied in describing a number of languages (including Latin), but may not be appropriate for describing forms in other languages such as English. (For more on gender, see Chapter 20.)

Traditional analysis

The notion of "appropriateness" of analytic categories for a particular language has not always been a consideration. In traditional grammar books, tables such as the following were often presented for English verbs, constructed by analogy with similar tables of forms in Latin grammars. The forms for the Latin verb *amare* ("to love") are listed on the right.

	First person singular	(*I*)	*love*	*amo*
Present tense, active voice	Second person singular	(*you*)	*love*	*amas*
	Third person singular	(*she*)	*loves*	*amat*
	First person plural	(*we*)	*love*	*amamus*
	Second person plural	(*you*)	*love*	*amatis*
	Third person plural	(*they*)	*love*	*amant*

Each of the Latin verb forms is different, according to the categories of person and number, yet the English verb forms are (with one exception) mostly the same. Thus it makes sense, in describing a language such as Latin, to have all those descriptive categories to characterize verb forms, but they don't really describe verb forms in English. In English, it makes more sense to say the categories describe different pronouns. The influence of Latin, however, goes beyond the types of descriptive labels.

The prescriptive approach

It is one thing to adopt the grammatical labels (e.g. "noun," "verb") to categorize words in English sentences; it is quite another thing to go on to claim that the structure of English sentences should be like the structure of sentences in Latin. That was an approach taken by a number of influential grammarians, mainly in eighteenth-century England, who set out rules for the "proper" use of English. This view of grammar as a set of rules for the "proper" use of a language is still to be found today and may be best characterized as the **prescriptive approach**. Some familiar examples of prescriptive rules for English sentences are:

You must not split an infinitive.
You must not end a sentence with a preposition.

Following these types of rules, traditional teachers would correct sentences like *Who did you go with?* to *With whom did you go?* (making sure that the preposition *with* was not at the end of the sentence). And *Mary runs faster than me* would be corrected to *Mary runs faster than I*. And *Me and my family* would certainly have to be corrected to *My family and I*, as Ann Landers would recommend. And, in proper English writing, one should never begin a sentence with *and*!

It may, in fact, be a valuable part of one's education to be made aware of this "linguistic etiquette" for the proper use of the language. If it is a social expectation that someone who writes well should obey these prescriptive rules, then social judgments such as "poorly educated" may be made about someone who does not follow these rules. However, it is worth considering the origins of some of these rules and asking whether they are appropriately applied to the English language. Let's take one example: "You must not split an infinitive."

Captain Kirk's infinitive

The infinitive in English has the form *to* + the base form of the verb, as in *to go*, and can be used with an adverb such as *boldly*. At the beginning of each televised *Star Trek* episode, one of the main characters, Captain Kirk, always used the expression *To boldly go* … This is an example of a split infinitive. Captain Kirk's teacher might have expected him to say *To go boldly* or *Boldly to go*, so that the adverb didn't split the infinitive. If Captain Kirk had been a Roman space traveler, speaking Latin, he would have used the expressions *ire* ("to go") and *audacter* ("boldly"). Now, in saying *Ire audacter* … in Latin, Capitaneus Kirkus would not even have the opportunity to split his infinitive (*ire*), because Latin infinitives are single words and just do not split.

It would be very appropriate in Latin grammar to say you cannot split an infinitive. But is it appropriate to carry this idea over into English where the infinitive form does not consist of a single word, but of two words, *to* and *go*? If it is a typical feature of the use of English that speakers and writers regularly produce forms such as *to boldly go*, *to solemnly swear* or *to never ever say goodbye*, then we may simply wish to note that there are structures in English that differ from those found in Latin, rather than think of the English forms as "bad" because they are breaking a rule of Latin grammar.

The descriptive approach

It may be that using a well-established grammatical description of Latin is a useful guide for some European languages (e.g. Italian or Spanish), is less useful for others (e.g. English), and may be absolutely misleading if you are trying to describe some non-European languages. This last point became clear to those linguists who were trying to describe the structure of the native languages of North America toward the end of the nineteenth century. The categories and rules that were appropriate for Latin grammar just did not seem to fit these languages. As a consequence, for most of the twentieth century, a rather different approach was adopted. Analysts collected samples of the language they were interested in and attempted to describe the regular structures of the language as it was used, not according to some view of how it should be used. This is called the **descriptive approach**.

Structural analysis

One type of descriptive approach is called **structural analysis** and its main concern is to investigate the distribution of forms in a language. The method involves the use of "test-frames" that can be sentences with empty slots in them. For example:

> The _____ makes a lot of noise.
> I heard a _____ yesterday.

There are a lot of forms that can fit into these slots to produce good grammatical sentences of English (e.g. *car, child, donkey, dog, radio*). As a result, we can propose that because all these forms fit in the same test-frame, they are likely to be examples of the same grammatical category. The label we give to this grammatical category is, of course, "noun."

However, there are many forms that do not fit those test-frames. Examples would be *Cathy, someone, the dog, a car*, and many others. (That is, we wouldn't say *The Cathy ... or *The the dog ... here.) For these forms, we require different test-frames, which could look like this:

> _____ makes a lot of noise.
> I heard _____ yesterday.

Among the other forms that comfortably fit these test-frames are *it, the big dog, an old car, Ani Difranco, the professor with the Scottish accent*, and many more. Once again, we can suggest that these forms are likely to be examples of the same grammatical category. The common label for this category is "noun phrase."

Observing that *it* fits in this second set of test-frames, and not in the first set (**The it makes a lot of noise*), allows us to improve on the older, Latin-influenced, analysis of pronouns in English. In the older analysis, pronouns were described as "words used in place of nouns." We can now see that it is more accurate to say that pronouns are used in place of noun phrases (not just nouns). By developing a set of test-frames of this type and discovering which forms fit the slots in the test-frames, we can produce a description of (at least some) aspects of the sentence structures of a language.

Constituent analysis

An approach with the same descriptive aims is called **constituent analysis**. The technique employed in this approach is designed to show how small constituents (or components) in sentences go together to form larger constituents. One basic step is determining how words go together to form phrases. In the following sentence, we can identify nine constituents at the word level: *An old man brought a shotgun to the wedding.* How do those nine constituents go together to form constituents at the phrase level? Does it seem appropriate to put the words together as follows?

An old   man brought   brought a   shotgun to   to the

We don't normally think of these combinations as phrases in English. We are more likely to say that the phrase-like constituents here are combinations of the following types: *an old man, a shotgun, the wedding,* which are noun phrases; *to the wedding,* which is a prepositional phrase; and *brought a shotgun,* which is a verb phrase.

This analysis of the constituent structure of the sentence can be represented in different types of diagrams. One type of diagram simply shows the distribution of the constituents at different levels.

An	old	man	brought	a	shotgun	to	the	wedding

Figure 7.2

Using this kind of diagram we can determine the types of forms that can be substituted for each other at different levels of constituent structure. One advantage of this type of analysis is that it shows rather clearly that proper nouns or names (*Gwen, Kingston*) and pronouns (*I, him, her*), though they are single words, can be used as noun phrases and fill the same constituent space as longer phrases (e.g. *an old man*).

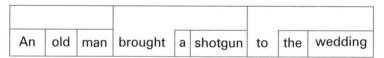

An	old	man	brought	a	shotgun	to	the	wedding
The	woman		kept	a	large	snake	in	a	cage
Gwen			took		Kingston		with		her
I			saw		him		recently		

Figure 7.3

Labeled and bracketed sentences

An alternative type of diagram is designed to show how the constituents in sentence structure can be marked off by using labeled brackets. The first step is to put brackets (one on each side) round each constituent, and then more brackets round each combination of constituents. For example:

Figure 7.4

With this procedure, the different constituents of the sentence are shown at the word level [*the*] or [*dog*], at the phrase level [*the dog*] or [*loved the girl*], and at the sentence level [*The dog loved the girl*].

We can then label each constituent using these abbreviated grammatical terms:

Art (= article)   V (= verb)
N (= noun)   VP (= verb phrase)
NP (= noun phrase)   S (= sentence)

In the next diagram, these labels are placed beside each bracket that marks the beginning of a constituent. The result is a labeled and bracketed analysis of the constituent structure of the sentence.

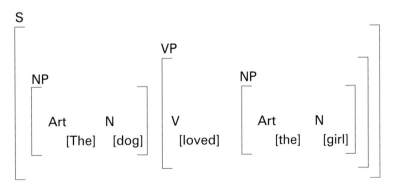

Figure 7.5

In performing this type of analysis, we have not only labeled all the constituents, we have revealed the **hierarchical organization** of those constituents. In this hierarchy, the sentence (S) is higher than and contains the noun phrase (NP). The noun phrase

(NP) is higher than and contains the noun (N). We can also see that the sentence (S) contains a verb phrase (VP) which contains a verb (V) and another noun phrase (NP). We will return to the important concept of hierarchical organization in grammatical structure in the next chapter.

Before moving on, however, we should note that constituent analysis is not only useful for describing the structure of English sentences. We can take a sample sentence from a language with a grammatical structure that is really quite different from English and apply the same type of analysis.

A Gaelic sentence

Here is a sentence from Scottish Gaelic which would be translated as "The boy saw the black dog."

Chunnaic	*an*	*gille*	*an*	*cu*	*dubh*
saw	the	boy	the	dog	black

One very obvious difference between the structure of this Gaelic sentence and its English counterpart is the fact that the verb comes first in the sentence. Another noticeable feature is that, when an adjective is used, it goes after the noun and not before it. We can represent these structural observations in a labeled and bracketed diagram.

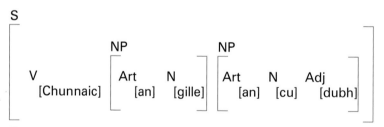

Figure 7.6

The diagram makes it clear that this Gaelic sentence is organized with a V NP NP structure, which is rather different from the NP V NP structure we found in the English sentence analyzed earlier.

It is not, of course, the aim of this type of analysis that we should be able to draw complicated-looking diagrams in order to impress our friends. The aim is to make explicit, via the diagram, what we believe to be the structure of grammatical sentences in the language. It also enables us to describe clearly how English sentences are put together as combinations of phrases which, in turn, are combinations of words. We can then look at similar descriptions of sentences in other languages such as Gaelic, Japanese or Spanish and see clearly what structural differences exist. At a very practical level, it may help us understand why a Spanish learner of English produces phrases like *the wine red* (instead of *the red wine*), using a structural organization of constituents that is possible in Spanish, but not in English.

Study questions

1   Identify all the parts of speech used in this sentence (e.g. *woman* = noun): *The woman kept a large snake in a cage, but it escaped recently.*

2   What is the difference between grammatical gender and natural gender?

3   What prescriptive rules for the "proper" use of English are not obeyed in the following sentences and how would they be "corrected"?

   (i)   *The old theory consistently failed to fully explain all the data.*

   (ii) *I can't remember the name of the person I gave the book to.*

4   What was wrong with the older Latin-influenced definition of English pronouns?

5   Given these other Gaelic words, translate the following sentences into English.

   mor ("big")   *beag* ("small")   *bhuail* ("hit")   *duine* ("man")

   (i)   Bhuail an gille beag an cu dubh.

   (ii) Chunnaic an cu an duine mor.

6   Create a labeled and bracketed analysis of this sentence: *The thief stole a wallet.*

Tasks

A   Another term used in the description of the parts of speech is "determiner." What are determiners? How many examples were included in this chapter?

B   In this chapter, we discussed "correction" in grammar. What is hypercorrection?

C   What is aspect? How is it used in the description of the underlined forms in these sentences?

   (1)   *I hope no one calls while I'm eating lunch.*

   (2)   *She's writing a story about her dog.*

   (3)   *I've eaten lunch already, thanks.*

   (4)   *She's written a story about her cat and the cat next door.*

   (5)   *I was eating lunch, so I didn't answer.*

   (6)   *She had written a story about her goldfish before that.*

   (7)   *As a child, she used to write stories about the insects in the garden.*

D   What is the basis of the categorization of English verbs as transitive, intransitive or ditransitive? Can you use this categorization to explain why these sentences are ungrammatical?

   (1)   **I thought I had lost my sunglasses, but Ali found in his car.*

   (2)   **Mark didn't win, but he didn't care that.*

   (3)   **They had a problem so we discussed.*

   (4)   **Suzy needed a jacket so I lent mine.*

(5) *We're always waiting you because you're late.

(6) *I didn't have a pen so Anne gave one.

(7) *When it's your birthday, people bring you.

(8) *She smiled me yesterday when I saw her, so I think she really likes.

E The structural analysis of a basic English sentence (NP + V + NP) is often described as "Subject Verb Object" or SVO. The basic sentence order in a Gaelic sentence (V + NP + NP) is described as "Verb Subject Object" or VSO.

  (i) After looking at the examples below (based on Inoue, 1979), would you describe the basic sentence order in these Japanese sentences as SVO or VSO or something else?

  (ii) Given the forms *tabemashita* ("ate"), *ringo* ("apple") and *-ni* ("in"), how would you translate these two sentences: *Jack ate an apple* and *John is in school*?

(1) *Jakku-ga gakkoo-e ikimasu*
Jack   school to go
("Jack goes to school")

(2) *Kazuko-ga gakkoo-de eigo-o naratte imasu*
Kazuko   school at English learn   be
("Kazuko is learning English at school")

(3) *Masuda-ga tegami-o kakimasu*
Masuda   letter   write
("Masuda writes a letter")

(4) *Jon-ga shinbun-o yomimasu*
John   newspaper read
("John reads a newspaper")

F The sample sentences below are from (i) Latin and (ii) Amuzgo, a language of Mexico (adapted from Merrifield *et al.*, 2003).

1 Using what you have learned about Latin, carefully translate this sentence: *The doves love the small girl.*

2 How would you write *A big woman is reading the red book* in Amuzgo?

3 In terms of basic sentence order, which of these languages is most similar to Amuzgo: English, Gaelic, Japanese or Latin ?

  (i) Latin

puellae aquilas portant	"The girls carry the eagles"
feminae columbas amant	"The women love the doves"
puella aquilam salvat	"The girl saves the eagle"
femina parvam aquilam liberat	"The woman frees the small eagle"
magna aquila parvam columbam pugnat	"The big eagle fights the small dove"

(ii)   Amuzgo

macei'na tyocho kwi com   "The boy is reading a book"
kwil'a yonom kwi w'aa   "The men are building a house"
nnceihnda yusku kwi com we   "The woman will buy a red book"
kwil'a yonom ndee meisa   "The men are making three tables"
macei'na kwi tyocho com t'ma   "A boy is reading the big book"

Discussion topics/projects

I   In this chapter, we briefly mentioned the grammatical category of tense and illustrated the difference between past tense (*loved*) and present tense (*loves*). Using the examples below, and any others that you think are relevant, try to describe the "future tense" in English.

   (1)   *We may forgive, but we shall never forget.*
   (2)   *We'll leave if you want.*
   (3)   *Jenny's arriving at eight o'clock tonight.*
   (4)   *Your plane leaves at noon tomorrow.*
   (5)   *They were about to leave when I got there.*
   (6)   *We're going to visit Paris next year.*
   (7)   *She said Jim was leaving next Wednesday.*
   (8)   *I wish I had a million dollars.*
   (9)   *The president is to visit Japan in May.*
   (10) *Water will freeze at zero degrees centigrade.*

(For background reading, see the section on "Future" in Hurford, 1994.)

II   In the descriptive approach, "ungrammatical" simply means "not well-formed" in purely structural terms. However, the word "ungrammatical" is also used with a more general meaning. Which of the following sentences should be considered "ungrammatical" in your opinion and why?

   (1)   *There's hundreds of students waiting outside.*
   (2)   *Who's there? It's me and Lisa.*
   (3)   *Ain't nobody gonna tell me what to do.*
   (4)   *You wasn't here when he come looking for you.*
   (5)   *I hate lobsters anymore.*
   (6)   *Are y'all coming to see us soon?*
   (7)   *That chair's broke, so you shouldn't ought to sit on it.*
   (8)   *I can't remember the name of the hotel that we stayed in it.*
   (9)   *I never seen anything.*
   (10) *If you'd have come with, we'd have had more fun.*

(For background reading, see chapter 7 of Napoli, 2003.)

Further reading

Basic treatments

Hudson, R. (1998) *English Grammar* Routledge

Swan, M. (2005) *Grammar* Oxford University Press

More detailed treatments

Hurford, J. (1994) *Grammar: A Student's Guide* Cambridge University Press

Kroeger, P. (2005) *Analyzing Grammar* Cambridge University Press

On the prescriptive approach

Cameron, D. (1995) *Verbal Hygiene* Routledge

Constituent analysis

Payne, T. (2006) *Exploring Language Structure* (chapter 6) Cambridge University Press

Gaelic sentence structure

Brown, K. and J. Miller (1991) *Syntax: A Linguistic Introduction to Sentence Structure* (2nd edition) Routledge

English grammar courses

Celce-Murcia, M. and D. Larsen-Freeman (1999) *The Grammar Book* Heinle and Heinle

Yule, G. (1998) *Explaining English Grammar* Oxford University Press

English reference grammars

Huddleston, R. and G. Pullum (2005) *A Student's Introduction to English Grammar* Cambridge University Press

Quirk, R., S. Greenbaum, G. Leech and J. Svartvik (1985) *A Comprehensive Grammar of the English Language* Longman

Other references

Inoue, K. (1979) "Japanese" In T. Shopen (ed.) *Languages and Their Speakers* (241–300) Winthrop Publishers

Merrifield, W., C. Naish, C. Rensch and G. Story (2003) *Laboratory Manual for Morphology and Syntax* (7th edition) Summer Institute of Linguistics

Napoli, D. (2003) *Language Matters* Oxford University Press

8 Syntax

After a lecture on cosmology and the structure of the solar system, William James was accosted by a little old lady who told him that his view of the earth rotating round the sun was wrong.

"I've got a better theory," said the little old lady.
"And what is that, madam?" inquired James politely.
"That we live on a crust of earth which is on the back of a giant turtle."
"If your theory is correct, madam," he asked, "what does this turtle stand on?"
"You're a very clever man, Mr. James, and that's a very good question," replied the little old lady, "but I have an answer to it. And it's this: the first turtle stands on the back of a second, far larger, turtle, who stands directly under him."
"But what does this second turtle stand on?" persisted James patiently.
To this, the little old lady crowed triumphantly, "It's no use, Mr. James, it's turtles all the way down."

Adapted from Ross (1967)

In the last chapter, we moved from the general categories and concepts of traditional grammar to more specific methods of describing the structure of phrases and sentences. When we concentrate on the structure and ordering of components within a sentence, we are studying the **syntax** of a language. The word "syntax" comes originally from Greek and literally means "a putting together" or "arrangement." In earlier approaches to the analysis of syntax, as we saw in Chapter 7, there was an attempt to produce an accurate description of the sequence or ordering "arrangement" of elements in the linear structure of the sentence. In more recent attempts to analyze syntactic structure, there has been a greater focus on the underlying rule system that we use to produce or "generate" sentences.

Syntax

When we set out to provide an analysis of the syntax of a language, we try to adhere to the "all and only" criterion. This means that our analysis must account for *all* the grammatically correct phrases and sentences and *only* those grammatically correct phrases and sentences in whatever language we are analyzing. In other words, if we write rules for the creation of well-formed structures, we have to check that those rules, when applied logically, won't also lead to ill-formed structures.

For example, we might say informally that, in English, we put a preposition (*near*) before a noun (*London*) to form a prepositional phrase (*near London*). However, if we use this as a rule of the grammar to create structures, we will end up producing phrases like **near tree* or **with dog*. These don't seem to be grammatically correct, so we mark them with an asterisk *. We clearly need to be more careful in forming this rule. We might have more success with a rule stating that we put a preposition before a noun phrase (not just a noun). In Chapter 7, we saw that a noun phrase can consist of a proper noun (*London*), a pronoun (*you*) or a combination of an article (*a, the*) and a noun (*tree, dog*), so that the revised rule can produce these well-formed structures: *near London, with you, near a tree, with the dog*.

When we have an effective rule such as "a prepositional phrase in English consists of a preposition followed by a noun phrase," we can imagine an extremely large number of English phrases that could be produced using this rule. In fact, the potential number is unlimited. This reflects another goal of syntactic analysis, which is to have a small and finite (i.e. limited) set of rules that will be capable of producing a large and potentially infinite (i.e. unlimited) number of well-formed structures. This small and finite set of rules is sometimes described as a **generative grammar** because it can be used to "generate" or produce sentence structures and not just describe them.

This type of grammar should also be capable of revealing the basis of two other phenomena: first, how some superficially different sentences are closely related and, second, how some superficially similar sentences are in fact different.

Deep and surface structure

Two superficially different sentences are shown in these examples:

> *Charlie broke the window.*
> *The window was broken by Charlie.*

In traditional grammar, the first is called an active sentence, focusing on what *Charlie* did, and the second is a passive sentence, focusing on *The window* and what happened to it. The distinction between them is a difference in their **surface structure**, that is, the different syntactic forms they have as individual English sentences. However, this superficial difference in form disguises the fact that the two sentences are very closely related, even identical, at some less superficial level.

This other "underlying" level, where the basic components (Noun Phrase + Verb + Noun Phrase) shared by the two sentences can be represented, is called their **deep structure**. The deep structure is an abstract level of structural organization in which all the elements determining structural interpretation are represented. That same deep structure can be the source of many other surface structures such as *It was Charlie who broke the window* and *Was the window broken by Charlie?*. In short, the grammar must be capable of showing how a single underlying abstract representation can become different surface structures.

Structural ambiguity

Let's say we have two distinct deep structures. One expresses the idea that "Annie had an umbrella and she bumped into a man with it." The other expresses the idea that "Annie bumped into a man and the man happened to be carrying an umbrella." Now, these two different versions of events can actually be expressed in the same surface structure form: *Annie bumped into a man with an umbrella*. This sentence provides an example of **structural ambiguity**. It has two distinct underlying interpretations that have to be represented differently in deep structure.

The comedian Groucho Marx knew how to have fun with structural ambiguity. In the film *Animal Crackers*, he first says *I once shot an elephant in my pajamas*, then follows it with *How he got into my pajamas I'll never know*. In the non-funny interpretation, part of the underlying structure of the first sentence could be something like: "I shot an elephant (while I was) in my pajamas." In the other (ho, ho) interpretation, part of the underlying structure would be something like: "I shot an elephant (which was) in my pajamas." There are two different underlying structures with the same surface structure.

Phrases can also be structurally ambiguous, as in expressions like *small boys and girls*. The underlying interpretation can be either "small boys and (small) girls" or "small boys and (all) girls." Our syntactic analysis will have to be capable of showing the structural distinction between these underlying representations.

Recursion

The rules of the grammar will also need the crucial property of **recursion**. Recursive ("repeatable any number of times") rules have the capacity to be applied more than once in generating a structure. For example, we can have one prepositional phrase describing location (*on the table*) in the sentence *The gun was on the table*. We can also repeat this type of phrase, using different words (*near the window*), for as long as the sentence still makes sense (*in the bedroom*). So, in order to generate a sentence such as *The gun was on the table near the window in the bedroom*, we must be able to repeat the rule that creates a prepositional phrase over and over again.

We must also be able to put sentences inside other sentences. For example, when we produce a sentence such as *Cathy knew that Mary helped George*, we do so with the sentence *Mary helped George* inside it. And those two sentences can be generated inside another sentence such as *John believed that Cathy knew that Mary helped George*. In principle, there is no end to the recursion that would produce ever longer versions of complex sentences with this structure.

Basically, the grammar will have to capture the fact that a sentence can have another sentence inside it or that a phrase can be repeated as often as required. We should note that recursion of this type is not only a feature of grammar, but can also be an essential part of a theory of cosmic structure, as in the role of turtles in one little old lady's view of the universe (in the introductory quotation).

Tree diagrams

One of the most common ways to create a visual representation of syntactic structure is through **tree diagrams**. We can use the symbols introduced in Chapter 7 (Art = article, N = noun, NP = noun phrase) to label parts of the tree as we try to capture the hierarchical organization of those parts in the underlying structure of phrases and sentences. So, we can take the information in a labeled and bracketed format, shown on the left, and present it in a tree diagram, shown on the right.

Although this kind of "tree," with its "branches," shown on the right, seems to grow down rather than up, it functions rather well as a diagram representing all the grammatical information found in the other analysis on the left. It also shows very explicitly that there are different levels in the analysis. That is, there is a level of analysis at which a constituent such as NP is represented and a different, lower, level at

Figure 8.1

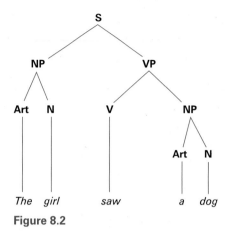

Figure 8.2

which a constituent such as N is represented. This type of hierarchical organization can be illustrated in a tree diagram for a whole sentence, beginning at the top with S.

If we start at the top of the tree diagram, we begin with a sentence (S) and divide it into two constituents (NP and VP). In turn, the NP constituent is divided into two other constituents (Art and N). Finally, one word is selected that fits the label Art (*the*) and another that fits N (*girl*). You can go through the same procedure with the VP branches.

Symbols used in syntactic analysis

We have already encountered some symbols that are used as abbreviations for syntactic categories. Examples are "S" (= sentence), "NP" (= noun phrase), "N" (= noun), "Art" (= article), "V" (= verb) and "VP" (= verb phrase). Others, such as "PP" (= prepositional phrase), seem fairly transparent. There are three more symbols that are commonly used in syntactic description.

The first is in the form of an arrow →. It can be interpreted as "consists of" or "rewrites as." It is typically used in the following type of rule:

NP → Art N

This is simply a shorthand way of saying that a noun phrase (NP) such as *the dog* consists of or rewrites as (→) an article (Art) *the* and a noun (N) *dog*.

The second symbol is a pair of round brackets ( ). Whatever occurs inside these round brackets will be treated as an optional constituent. For example, we can describe something as *the dog* or *the small dog*. We can say that both *the dog* and *the small dog* are examples of the category noun phrase (NP). When we want to use a noun phrase in

English, we can include an adjective (Adj) such as *small*, but we don't have to. It's an optional constituent in a grammatically well-formed noun phrase. We can represent this observation in the following type of rule:

NP → Art (Adj) N

This shorthand notation expresses the idea that a noun phrase rewrites as (→) an article (Art) and a noun (N), with the option of including an adjective (Adj) in a specific position between them. We use the round brackets to indicate that the adjective is optional. So, we can use this notation to generate *the dog, the small dog, a cat, a big cat, the book, a boring book* and an endless number of other similar noun phrases.

The third symbol is in the form of curly brackets { }.These indicate that only one of the elements enclosed within the curly brackets must be selected. We use these types of brackets when we want to indicate that there is a choice from two or more constituents. For example, we have seen already that a noun phrase can consist of an expression such as *the dog* (article plus noun), or *it* (pronoun), or *Cathy* (proper noun). Using the abbreviations "Pro" (for pronoun) and "PN" (for proper noun), we can try to capture this observation about English with three separate rules, as shown on the left. However, it is more succinct to write one rule, as shown in the middle or on the right, using curly brackets and including exactly the same information.

$$NP \rightarrow Art\ N$$
$$NP \rightarrow Pro \qquad NP \rightarrow \quad \begin{Bmatrix} Art\ N \\ Pro \\ PN \end{Bmatrix} \qquad NP \rightarrow \{Art\ N,\ Pro,\ PN\}$$
$$NP \rightarrow PN$$

It is important to remember that, although there are three constituents inside these curly brackets, only one of them can be selected on any occasion.

The list of common symbols and abbreviations is summarized here.

S sentence	**NP** noun phrase	**PN** proper noun
N noun	**VP** verb phrase	**Adv** adverb
V verb	**Adj** adjective	**Prep** preposition
Art article	**Pro** pronoun	**PP** prepositional phrase

*	ungrammatical sentence
→	consists of / rewrites as
( )	optional constituent
{ }	one and only one of these constituents must be selected

Phrase structure rules

When we use a tree diagram format, we can think of it in two different ways. In one way, we can simply treat it as a static representation of the structure of the sentence shown at the bottom of the diagram. We could then propose that, for every single sentence in English, a tree diagram of this type could be drawn. An alternative view is to treat the tree diagram as a dynamic format, in the sense that it represents a way of generating not only that one sentence, but a very large number of other sentences with similar structures.

This second approach is very appealing because it would enable us to generate a very large number of sentences with what look like a very small number of rules. These rules are called **phrase structure rules**. As the name suggests, these rules state that the structure of a phrase of a specific type will consist of one or more constituents in a particular order. We can use phrase structure rules to present the information of the tree diagram in another format. That is, the information shown in the tree diagram on the left can be expressed in the phrase structure rule on the right.

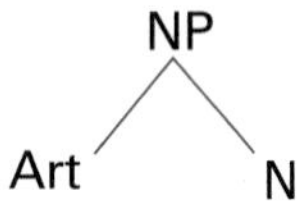

```
        NP
       /  \
    Art     N          NP → Art  N
```

Figure 8.3

According to this rule, "a noun phrase rewrites as an article followed by a noun."

The first rule in the following set of simple (and necessarily incomplete) phrase structure rules states that "a sentence rewrites as a noun phrase and a verb phrase." The second rule states that "a noun phrase rewrites as either an article plus an optional adjective plus a noun, or a pronoun, or a proper noun." The other rules follow a similar pattern.

$$S \rightarrow NP\ VP$$
$$NP \rightarrow \{Art\ (Adj)\ N,\ Pro,\ PN\}$$
$$VP \rightarrow V\ NP\ (PP)\ (Adv)$$
$$PP \rightarrow Prep\ NP$$

Lexical rules

Phrase structure rules generate structures. In order to turn those structures into recognizable English, we also need **lexical rules** that specify which words can be used when we rewrite constituents such as N. The first rule in the following set states that "a proper noun rewrites as *Mary* or *George*." (It's a very small world.)

PN → {*Mary, George*}
N → {*girl, dog, boy*}
Art → {*a, the*}
Pro → {*it, you*}
V → {*followed, helped, saw*}

We can rely on these rules to generate the grammatical sentences shown below as (1) to (6), but not the ungrammatical sentences shown as (7) to (12).

(1) *A dog followed the boy.*   (7) **Dog followed boy.*
(2) *Mary helped George.*   (8) **The helped you boy.*
(3) *George saw the dog.*   (9) **George Mary dog.*
(4) *The boy helped you.*   (10) **Helped George the dog.*
(5) *It followed Mary.*   (11) **You it saw.*
(6) *You saw it.*   (12) **Mary George helped.*

As a way of visualizing how the phrase structure rules form the basis of these sentences, we can draw the tree diagrams for sentences (1) and (6).

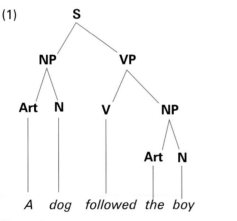
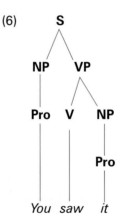

Figure 8.4

Movement rules

The very small set of phrase structure rules just described is a sample of what a more complex phrase structure grammar of English, with many more parts, would look like. These rules can be treated as a representation of the underlying or deep structures of sentences in English. One feature of these underlying structures is that they will generate sentences with a fixed word order. That is convenient for creating declarative forms (*You will help Mary*), but not for making interrogative forms, as used in questions (*Will you help Mary?*). In making the question, we move one part of the structure to a different position. This process is based on a **movement rule**.

In order to talk about this process, we need to expand our phrase structure rules to include an **auxiliary verb (Aux)** as part of the sentence. This is illustrated in the first rewrite rule below. Auxiliary verbs (sometimes described as "helping" verbs) take different forms in English, but one well-known set can be included in the rudimentary lexical rule for Aux below. We also need a lexical rule that specifies the basic forms of the verbs, shown as the third rewrite rule below.

> **S → NP Aux VP**
> **Aux → {*can, could, should, will, would*}**
> **V → {*follow, help, see*}**

With these components, we can specify a simple movement rule that is involved in the creation of one basic type of question in English.

> **NP Aux VP ⇒ Aux NP VP**

This type of rule has a special symbol ⇒ and can be illustrated in the process of one tree, on the right, being derived from the tree on the left.

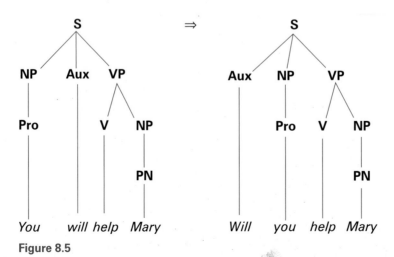

Figure 8.5

Using this simple rule, we can also generate these other questions:

Can you see the dog?   *Should George follow you?*
Could the boy see it?   *Would Mary help George?*

These are all surface structure variations of a single underlying structure. However, we still have not incorporated recursion.

Back to recursion

The simple phrase structure rules listed earlier have no recursive elements. Each time we start to create an S, we only create a single S (sentence structure). We actually need to be able to include sentence structures within other sentence structures. In traditional grammar, these "sentence structures" were described as "clauses." We know, for example, that *Mary helped George* is a sentence. We can put this sentence inside another sentence beginning *Cathy knew that [Mary helped George]*. And, being tediously recursive, we can put this sentence inside another sentence beginning *John believed that [Cathy knew that [Mary helped George]]*.

In these sentences, two new proper nouns and two new verbs have been used. We have to expand our earlier set of lexical rules to include PN → {*John, Cathy*} and V → {*believed, knew*}. After verbs such as *believe* and *know*, as in these examples, the word *that* introduces a complement phrase.

Mary helped George.
Cathy knew that Mary helped George.
John believed that Cathy knew that Mary helped George.

Complement phrases

The word *that*, as used in these examples, is called a **complementizer** (C). The role of *that* as a complementizer is to introduce a **complement phrase** (CP). For example, in the second sentence (*Cathy knew …*), we can identify one CP which contains *that* plus *Mary helped George*. We already know that *Mary helped George* is a sentence (S). So, we are now in a position to define a CP in the following way: "a complement phrase rewrites as a complementizer and a sentence," or CP → C S.

We can also see from the same sentence that the complement phrase (CP) comes after a verb (V) *knew*. This means that we are using the CP as part of a verb phrase (VP), as in *knew that Mary helped George*. So, there must be another rule that says: "a verb phrase rewrites as a verb and complement phrase," or VP → V CP.

If we now look at these two new rules in conjunction with an earlier rule, we can see how recursion is built into the grammar.

$$S \rightarrow NP \ VP$$
$$VP \rightarrow V \ CP$$
$$CP \rightarrow C \ S$$

We begin with S on the left and, as we rewrite symbols, we eventually have S on the right, allowing us to go back to the beginning and go through the set of rules again (and again). This means that we can, in principle, use these rules to create an endless sentence containing other sentence structures. In practice, it allows us to draw the following tree diagram and provide a clear representation of the syntactic structure of this one fairly complex sentence.

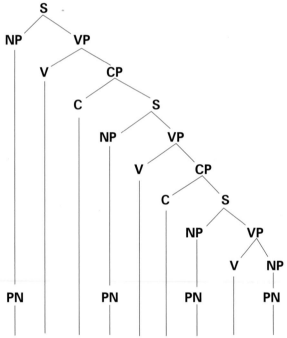

John believed that Cathy knew that Mary helped George

Figure 8.6

As we try to capture more aspects of the structure of complex English sentences, we inevitably need to identify more rules and concepts involved in the analysis of syntax. (We've barely scratched the surface structures.) However, having explored some of the basic issues and methods of syntactic analysis in order to talk about structure in language, we must move on to consider how we might incorporate the analysis of meaning in the study of language.

Study questions

1 What is the "all and only" criterion?

2 Do phrase structure rules represent deep structure or surface structure?

3 In what ways are these expressions structurally ambiguous?

(a) *The parents of the bride and groom were waiting outside.*

(b) *We met an English history teacher.*

(c) *Flying planes can be dangerous.*

(d) *The students complained to everyone that they couldn't understand.*

4 Which of the following expressions would be generated by this phrase structure rule: NP → {Art (Adj) N, Pro, PN}?

(a) *a lady*   (c) *her*   (e) *the widow*

(b) *the little girl*   (d) *Annie*   (f) *she's an old woman*

5 Which of these sentences would result from applying the rule: NP Aux VP ⇒ Aux NP VP?

(a) *John will follow Mary.*   (c) *Can George see the dog?*

(b) *You knew that Cathy helped the boy.* (d) *Should you believe that Mary saw it?*

6 Using information from the phrase structure rules presented in this chapter, complete the following tree diagrams.

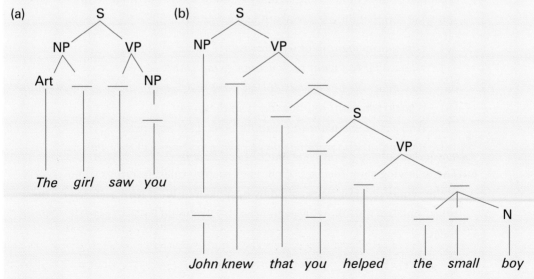

Figure 8.7

Tasks

A   What is the distinction made between "competence" and "performance" in the study of syntax?

B   What is meant by the expression "an embedded structure"? Were there any examples in this chapter?

C   Which of the following two tree diagrams could be used to represent the underlying structure of the sentence: *George saw the boy with a telescope*?

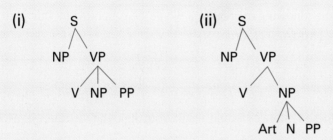

Figure 8.8

D   In spoken English, the sequence *want to* is sometimes contracted to *wanna*, as in *I don't wanna go* or *What do you wanna do tonight?*. However, as illustrated in the following set of sentences, there are some structures where *want to* cannot be contracted. English-speaking children know how to use *wanna* in the right places (and none of the wrong places) at a very early age. Can you work out what it is that they know about using *wanna*?

   (1) *Who do you **want to** or **wanna** visit?*
   (2) *Who would you **want to** or **wanna** go out with?*
   (3) *How many of your friends do you **want to** or **wanna** invite to the wedding?*
   (4) *Who do you **want to** (*wanna) win the game?*
   (5) *Who would you **want to** (*wanna) look after your pets?*
   (6) *How many of your friends do you **want to** (*wanna) stay with us?*

E   The following simplified set of phrase structure rules describes some aspects of the syntax of a language called Ewe, spoken in West Africa. Based on these rules, which of the following sentences (1–10) should have an asterisk * before them?

S   → NP VP   N   → {*oge, ika, amu*}
NP → N (Art)   Art → *ye*
VP → V NP   V   → {*xa, vo*}

(1) *Oge xa ika*	(6) *Vo oge ika*
(2) *Ye amu vo oge*	(7) *Amu ye vo ika*
(3) *Ika oge xa ye*	(8) *Ye ika xa ye oge*
(4) *Oge ye vo ika ye*	(9) *Xa amu ye*
(5) *Amu xa oge*	(10) *Oge ye xa amu*

F   Using these simple phrase structure rules for Scottish Gaelic, identify (with *) the ungrammatical sentences below and draw tree diagrams for the grammatical sentences.

S	→ V NP NP		NP	→ {Art N (Adj), PN}
Art	→ *an*			
N	→ {*cu, duine, gille*}		Adj	→ {*ban, beag, mor*}
PN	→ {*Calum, Mairi, Tearlach*}		V	→ {*bhuail, chunnaic, fhuair*}

(1)   *Calum chunnaic an gille.*

(2)   *Bhuail an beag cu Tearlach.*

(3)   *Bhuail an gille mor an cu.*

(4)   *Chunnaic Tearlach an gille.*

(5)   *Ban an cu an duine beag.*

(6)   *Fhuair Mairi an cu ban.*

Discussion topics/projects

I   There is a principle of syntax called "structure dependency" that is often used to show that the rules of language structure depend on hierarchical organization and not on linear position. For example, someone trying to learn English might be tempted to think that questions of the type in (2) are formed simply by moving the second word in a statement (1) to become the first word of a question (2).

(1) *Shaggy **is** tired.*   (2) ***Is** Shaggy tired?*

   *You **will** help him.*   ***Will** you help him?*

Using the sentences in (2)–(6), try to decide if this is the best way to describe how all of these English questions are formed and, if it is not, try to formulate a better rule.

(3)   *Are the exercises in this book too easy?*

(4)   *Is the cat that is missing called Blackie?*

> (5) Will the price of the new book you've ordered be really expensive?
> (6) Was the guy who scored the winning goal in the final playing for love or money?

(For background reading, see chapter 4 of Fromkin *et al.*, 2007.)

II We could propose that passive sentences (*George was helped by Mary*) are derived from active structures (*Mary helped George*) via a movement rule such as the following:

(active) NP_1 V NP_2 $\Rightarrow$ NP_2 *be* V-*ed by* NP_1 (passive)

Note that the tense, past or present, of the V (e.g. *helped*) in the active structure determines the tense of *be* in the passive structure (e.g. **was** *helped*).
Which of the following active sentences can be restructured into passive sentences
using this rule? What prevents the rule from working in the other cases?

> (1)   The dog chased the cat.
> (2)   Snow White kissed Grumpy.
> (3)   He loves them.
> (4)   Betsy borrowed some money from Christopher.
> (5)   The team played badly.
> (6)   The bank manager laughed.
> (7)   They have two children.
> (8)   The duckling became a swan.
> (9)   Someone mentioned that you played basketball.
> (10) The police will arrest violent demonstrators.

(For background reading, see chapter 5 of Morenberg, 2003).

Further reading

Basic treatments
Miller, J. (2008) *An Introduction to English Syntax* (2nd edition) Edinburgh University Press
Thomas, L. (1993) *Beginning Syntax* Blackwell
More detailed treatments
Morenberg, M. (2003) *Doing Grammar* (3rd edition) Oxford University Press
Tallerman, M. (2005) *Understanding Syntax* (2nd edition) Hodder Arnold
Specifically on English syntax
Radford, A. (2004) *English Syntax* Cambridge University Press

On generative grammar
Baker, M. (2001) *The Atoms of Language: The Mind's Hidden Rules of Grammar* Basic Books
On structural ambiguity
Pinker, S. (1994) *The Language Instinct* (chapter 4) William Morrow
Tree diagrams
Carnie, A. (2002) *Syntax* (chapter 12) Blackwell
On Gaelic syntax
Brown, K. and J. Miller (1991) *Syntax: A Linguistic Introduction to Sentence Structure* (2nd edition) Routledge
Other references
Fromkin, V., R. Rodman and N. Hyams (2007) *An Introduction to Language* (8th edition) Thomson

9 Semantics

The words *Fire Department* make it sound like they're the ones who are starting fires, doesn't it? It should be called the "Extinguishing Department." We don't call the police the "Crime Department." Also, the "Bomb Squad" sounds like a terrorist gang. The same is true of *wrinkle cream*. Doesn't it sound like it causes wrinkles? And why would a doctor prescribe pain pills? I already *have* pain! I need relief pills!

Carlin (1997)

Semantics is the study of the meaning of words, phrases and sentences. In semantic analysis, there is always an attempt to focus on what the words conventionally mean, rather than on what an individual speaker (like George Carlin) might want them to mean on a particular occasion. This approach is concerned with objective or general meaning and avoids trying to account for subjective or local meaning. Doing semantics is attempting to spell out what it is we all know when we behave as if we share knowledge of the meaning of a word, a phrase, or a sentence in a language.

Meaning

While semantics is the study of meaning in language, there is more interest in certain aspects of meaning than in others. We have already ruled out special meanings that one individual might attach to words. We can go further and make a broad distinction between **conceptual meaning** and **associative meaning**. Conceptual meaning covers those basic, essential components of meaning that are conveyed by the literal use of a word. It is the type of meaning that dictionaries are designed to describe. Some of the basic components of a word like *needle* in English might include "thin, sharp, steel instrument." These components would be part of the conceptual meaning of *needle*. However, different people might have different associations or connotations attached to a word like *needle*. They might associate it with "pain," or "illness," or "blood," or "drugs," or "thread," or "knitting," or "hard to find" (especially in a haystack), and these associations may differ from one person to the next. These types of associations are not treated as part of the word's conceptual meaning.

In a similar way, some people may associate the expression *low-calorie*, when used to describe a product, with "healthy," but this is not part of the basic conceptual meaning of the expression (i.e. "producing a small amount of heat or energy"). Poets, song-writers, novelists, literary critics, advertisers and lovers may all be interested in how words can evoke certain aspects of associative meaning, but in linguistic semantics we're more concerned with trying to analyze conceptual meaning.

Semantic features

One way in which the study of basic conceptual meaning might be helpful would be as a means of accounting for the "oddness" we experience when we read sentences such as the following:

The hamburger ate the boy.
The table listens to the radio.
The horse is reading the newspaper.

We should first note that the oddness of these sentences does not derive from their syntactic structure. According to the basic syntactic rules for forming English sentences (as presented in Chapter 8), we have well-formed structures.

	NP	V	NP
	The hamburger	*ate*	*the boy*

This sentence is syntactically good, but semantically odd. Since the sentence *The boy ate the hamburger* is perfectly acceptable, we may be able to identify the source of the problem. The components of the conceptual meaning of the noun *hamburger* must be significantly different from those of the noun *boy*, thereby preventing one, and not the other, from being used as the subject of the verb *ate*. The kind of noun that can be the subject of the verb *ate* must denote an entity that is capable of "eating." The noun *hamburger* does not have this property and the noun *boy* does.

We can make this observation more generally applicable by trying to determine the crucial element or feature of meaning that any noun must have in order to be used as the subject of the verb *ate*. Such an element may be as general as "animate being." We can then use this idea to describe part of the meaning of words as either having (+) or not having (−) that particular feature. So, the feature that the noun *boy* has is "+animate" (= denotes an animate being) and the feature that the noun *hamburger* has is "−animate" (= does not denote an animate being).

This simple example is an illustration of a procedure for analyzing meaning in terms of **semantic features**. Features such as "+animate, −animate," "+human, −human," "+female, −female," for example, can be treated as the basic elements involved in differentiating the meaning of each word in a language from every other word. If we had to provide the crucial distinguishing features of the meanings of a set of English words such as *table, horse, boy, man, girl, woman*, we could begin with the following diagram.

	table	horse	boy	man	girl	woman
animate	−	+	+	+	+	+
human	−	−	+	+	+	+
female	−	−	−	−	+	+
adult	−	+	−	+	−	+

From a feature analysis like this, we can say that at least part of the meaning of the word *girl* in English involves the elements [+human, +female, −adult]. We can also characterize the feature that is crucially required in a noun in order for it to appear as the subject of a particular verb, supplementing the syntactic analysis with semantic features.

The _____ is reading the newspaper.

      N [+human]

This approach would give us the ability to predict which nouns make this sentence semantically odd. Some examples would be *table, horse* and *hamburger*, because none of them have the required feature [+human].

The approach just outlined is a start on analyzing the conceptual components of word meaning, but it is not without problems. For many words in a language it may not be as easy to come up with neat components of meaning. If we try to think of the components or features we would use to differentiate the nouns *advice*, *threat* and *warning*, for example, we may not be very successful. Part of the problem seems to be that the approach involves a view of words in a language as some sort of "containers" that carry meaning components. There is clearly more to the meaning of words than these basic types of features.

Semantic roles

Instead of thinking of words as "containers" of meaning, we can look at the "roles" they fulfill within the situation described by a sentence. If the situation is a simple event, as in *The boy kicked the ball*, then the verb describes an action (*kick*). The noun phrases in the sentence describe the roles of entities, such as people and things, involved in the action. We can identify a small number of **semantic roles** (also called "thematic roles") for these noun phrases.

Agent and theme

In our example sentence, one role is taken by the noun phrase *The boy* as "the entity that performs the action," technically known as the **agent**. Another role is taken by *the ball* as "the entity that is involved in or affected by the action," which is called the **theme** (or sometimes the "patient"). The theme can also be an entity (*The ball*) that is simply being described (i.e. not performing an action), as in *The ball was red*.

Agents and themes are the most common semantic roles. Although agents are typically human (*The boy*), they can also be non-human entities that cause actions, as in noun phrases denoting a natural force (*The wind*), a machine (*A car*), or a creature (*The dog*), all of which affect *the ball* as theme.

The boy kicked the ball.
The wind blew the ball away.
A car ran over the ball.
The dog caught the ball.

The theme is typically non-human, but can be human (*the boy*), as in *The dog chased the boy*. In fact, the same physical entity can appear in two different semantic roles in a sentence, as in *The boy cut himself*. Here *The boy* is agent and *himself* is theme.

Instrument and experiencer

If an agent uses another entity in order to perform an action, that other entity fills the role of **instrument**. In the sentences *The boy cut the rope with an old razor* and *He drew the picture with a crayon*, the noun phrases *an old razor* and *a crayon* are being used in the semantic role of instrument.

When a noun phrase is used to designate an entity as the person who has a feeling, perception or state, it fills the semantic role of **experiencer**. If we *see*, *know* or *enjoy* something, we're not really performing an action (hence we are not agents). We are in the role of experiencer. In the sentence *The boy feels sad*, the experiencer (*The boy*) is the only semantic role. In the question, *Did you hear that noise?*, the experiencer is *you* and the theme is *that noise*.

Location, source and goal

A number of other semantic roles designate where an entity is in the description of an event. Where an entity is (*on the table*, *in the room*) fills the role of **location**. Where the entity moves from is the **source** (*from Chicago*) and where it moves to is the **goal** (*to New Orleans*), as in *We drove from Chicago to New Orleans*. When we talk about transferring money *from savings to checking*, the source is *savings* and the goal is *checking*.

All these semantic roles are illustrated in the following scenario. Note that a single entity (e.g. *George*) can appear in several different semantic roles.

| *Mary* | *saw* | *a fly* | *on the wall.* |
| EXPERIENCER | | THEME | LOCATION |

| *She* | *borrowed* | *a magazine* | *from George.* |
| AGENT | | THEME | SOURCE |

| *She* | *squashed* | *the bug* | *with the magazine.* |
| AGENT | | THEME | INSTRUMENT |

| *She* | *handed* | *the magazine* | *back to George.* |
| AGENT | | THEME | GOAL |

| *"Gee thanks,"* | *said* | *George.* |
| | | AGENT |

Lexical relations

Not only can words be treated as "containers" of meaning, or as fulfilling "roles" in events, they can also have "relationships" with each other. In everyday talk, we often explain the meanings of words in terms of their relationships. If we're asked the meaning of the word *conceal*, for example, we might simply say, "It's the same as *hide*," or give the meaning of *shallow* as "the opposite of *deep*," or the meaning of *daffodil* as "a kind of *flower*." In doing so, we are characterizing the meaning of each word, not in terms of its component features, but in terms of its relationship to other words. This approach is used in the semantic description of language and treated as the analysis of **lexical relations**. The lexical relations we have just exemplified are synonymy (*conceal/hide*), antonymy (*shallow/deep*) and hyponymy (*daffodil/flower*).

Synonymy

Two or more words with very closely related meanings are called **synonyms**. They can often, though not always, be substituted for each other in sentences. In the appropriate circumstances, we can say, *What was his answer?* or *What was his reply?* with much the same meaning. Other common examples of synonyms are the pairs: *almost/nearly, big/large, broad/wide, buy/purchase, cab/taxi, car/automobile, couch/sofa, freedom/ liberty*.

We should keep in mind that the idea of "sameness" of meaning used in discussing synonymy is not necessarily "total sameness." There are many occasions when one word is appropriate in a sentence, but its synonym would be odd. For example, whereas the word *answer* fits in the sentence *Sandy had only one answer correct on the test*, the word *reply* would sound odd. Synonymous forms may also differ in terms of formal versus informal uses. The sentence *My father purchased a large automobile* has virtually the same meaning as *My dad bought a big car*, with four synonymous replacements, but the second version sounds much more casual or informal than the first.

Antonymy

Two forms with opposite meanings are called **antonyms**. Some common examples are the pairs: *alive/dead, big/small, fast/slow, happy/sad, hot/cold, long/short, male/ female, married/single, old/new, rich/poor, true/false*.

Antonyms are usually divided into two main types, "gradable" (opposites along a scale) and "non-gradable" (direct opposites). **Gradable antonyms**, such as the pair *big/ small*, can be used in comparative constructions like *I'm bigger than you* and *A pony is smaller than a horse*. Also, the negative of one member of a gradable pair does not necessarily imply the other. For example, the sentence *My car isn't old*, doesn't necessarily mean *My car is new*.

With **non-gradable antonyms** (also called "complementary pairs"), comparative constructions are not normally used. We don't typically describe someone as *deader* or *more dead* than another. Also, the negative of one member of a non-gradable pair does imply the other member. That is, *My grandparents aren't alive* does indeed mean *My grandparents are dead*. Other non-gradable antonyms in the earlier list are the pairs: *male/female, married/single* and *true/false*.

Although we can use the "negative test" to identify non-gradable antonyms in a language, we usually avoid describing one member of an antonymous pair as the negative of the other. For example, while *undress* can be treated as the opposite of *dress*, it doesn't mean "not dress." It actually means "do the reverse of dress." Antonyms of this type are called **reversives**. Other common examples are *enter/exit, pack/unpack, lengthen/shorten, raise/lower, tie/untie*.

Hyponymy

When the meaning of one form is included in the meaning of another, the relationship is described as **hyponymy**. Examples are the pairs: *animal/dog, dog/poodle, vegetable/carrot, flower/rose, tree/banyan*. The concept of "inclusion" involved in this relationship is the idea that if an object is a *rose*, then it is necessarily a *flower*, so the meaning of *flower* is included in the meaning of *rose*. Or, *rose* is a hyponym of *flower*.

When we consider hyponymous connections, we are essentially looking at the meaning of words in some type of hierarchical relationship. We can represent the relationships between a set of words such as *animal, ant, asp, banyan, carrot,*

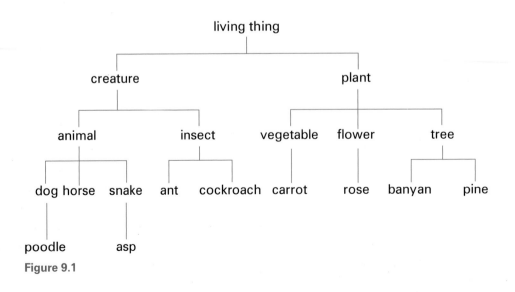

Figure 9.1

cockroach, creature, dog, flower, horse, insect, living thing, pine, plant, poodle, rose, snake, tree and *vegetable* as a hierarchical diagram.

Looking at the diagram, we can say that "*horse* is a hyponym of *animal*" or "*cockroach* is a hyponym of *insect*." In these two examples, *animal* and *insect* are called the **superordinate** (= higher-level) terms. We can also say that two or more words that share the same superordinate term are **co-hyponyms**. So, *dog* and *horse* are co-hyponyms and the superordinate term is *animal*.

The relation of hyponymy captures the concept of "is a kind of," as when we give the meaning of a word by saying, "an *asp* is a kind of *snake*." Sometimes the only thing we know about the meaning of a word is that it is a hyponym of another term. That is, we may know nothing more about the meaning of the word *asp* other than that it is a kind of *snake* or that *banyan* is a kind of *tree*.

It is worth emphasizing that it is not only words for "things" that are hyponyms. Words such as *punch*, *shoot* and *stab*, describing "actions," can all be treated as co-hyponyms of the superordinate term *injure*.

Prototypes

While the words *canary, cormorant, dove, duck, flamingo, parrot, pelican* and *robin* are all equally co-hyponyms of the superordinate *bird*, they are not all considered to be equally good examples of the category "bird." According to some researchers, the most characteristic instance of the category "bird" is *robin*. The idea of "the characteristic instance" of a category is known as the **prototype**. The concept of a prototype helps explain the meaning of certain words, like *bird*, not in terms of component features (e.g. "has feathers," "has wings"), but in terms of resemblance to the clearest example. Thus, even native speakers of English might wonder if *ostrich* or *penguin* should be hyponyms of *bird* (technically they are), but have no trouble deciding about *sparrow* or *pigeon*. These last two are much closer to the prototype.

Given the category label *furniture*, we are quick to recognize *chair* as a better example than *bench* or *stool*. Given *clothing*, people recognize *shirts* quicker than *shoes*, and given *vegetable*, they accept *carrot* before *potato* or *tomato*. It is clear that there is some general pattern to the categorization process involved in prototypes and that it determines our interpretation of word meaning. However, this is one area where individual experience can lead to substantial variation in interpretation and people may disagree over the categorization of a word like *avocado* or *tomato* as fruit or vegetable. These words seem to be treated as co-hyponyms of both *fruit* and *vegetable* in different contexts.

Homophones and homonyms

When two or more different (written) forms have the same pronunciation, they are described as **homophones**. Common examples are *bare/bear*, *meat/meet*, *flour/flower*, *pail/pale*, *right/write*, *sew/so* and *to/too/two*.

We use the term **homonyms** when one form (written or spoken) has two or more unrelated meanings, as in these examples:

bank (of a river) – *bank* (financial institution)
bat (flying creature) – *bat* (used in sports)
mole (on skin) – *mole* (small animal)
pupil (at school) – *pupil* (in the eye)
race (contest of speed) – *race* (ethnic group)

The temptation is to think that the two types of *bank* must be related in meaning. They are not. Homonyms are words that have separate histories and meanings, but have accidentally come to have exactly the same form.

Polysemy

When we encounter two or more words with the same form and related meanings, we have what is technically known as **polysemy**. Polysemy can be defined as one form (written or spoken) having multiple meanings that are all related by extension. Examples are the word *head*, used to refer to the object on top of your body, froth on top of a glass of beer, person at the top of a company or department, and many other things. Other examples of polysemy are *foot* (of person, of bed, of mountain) or *run* (person does, water does, colors do).

If we aren't sure whether different uses of a single word are examples of homonymy or polysemy, we can check in a dictionary. If the word has multiple meanings (i.e. it's polysemous), then there will be a single entry, with a numbered list of the different meanings of that word. If two words are treated as homonyms, they will typically have two separate entries. In most dictionaries, *bank*, *mail*, *mole* and *sole* are clearly treated as homonyms whereas *face*, *foot*, *get*, *head* and *run* are treated as examples of polysemy.

Of course, it is possible for two forms to be distinguished via homonymy and for one of the forms also to have various uses via polysemy. The words *date* (= a thing we can eat) and *date* (= a point in time) are homonyms. However, the "point in time" kind of *date* is polysemous in terms of a particular day and month (= on a letter), an arranged meeting time (= an appointment), a social meeting (= with someone we like), and even a person (= that person we like). So the question *How was your date?* could have several different interpretations.

Word play

These last three lexical relations are the basis of a lot of word play, usually for humorous effect. In the nursery rhyme *Mary had a little lamb*, we think of a small animal, but in the comic version *Mary had a little lamb, some rice and vegetables*, we think of a small amount of meat. The polysemy of *lamb* allows the two interpretations. We make sense of the riddle *Why are trees often mistaken for dogs?* by recognizing the homonymy in the answer: *Because of their bark*. And if you are asked the following question: *Why is 6 afraid of 7?*, you can understand why the answer is funny (*Because 789*) by identifying the homophones.

Metonymy

The relatedness of meaning found in polysemy is essentially based on similarity. The *head* of a company is similar to the *head* of a person on top of and controlling the body. There is another type of relationship between words, based simply on a close connection in everyday experience. That close connection can be based on a container–contents relation (*bottle/water*, *can/juice*), a whole–part relation (*car/wheels*, *house/roof*) or a representative–symbol relationship (*king/crown*, *the President/the White House*). Using one of these words to refer to the other is an example of **metonymy**.

It is our familiarity with metonymy that makes it possible for us to understand *He drank the whole bottle*, although it sounds absurd literally (i.e. he drank the liquid, not the glass object). We also accept *The White House has announced …* or *Downing Street protested …* without being puzzled that buildings appear to be talking. We use metonymy when we talk about *filling up the car*, *answering the door*, *boiling a kettle*, *giving someone a hand*, or *needing some wheels*.

Many examples of metonymy are highly conventionalized and easy to interpret. However, other examples depend on an ability to infer what the speaker has in mind. The metonymy in *Get your butt over here* is easier to understand if you are used to male talk in the United States, *The strings are too quiet* if you're familiar with orchestral music, and *I prefer cable* if you have a choice in how you receive television programs (in the USA). Making sense of such expressions often depends on context, background knowledge and inference. These are all topics we'll explore in the next chapter.

Collocation

One final aspect of our knowledge of words has nothing to do with any of the factors considered so far. We know which words tend to occur with other words. If you ask a thousand people what they think of when you say *hammer*, more than half will say *nail*. If you say *table*, they'll mostly say *chair*, and *butter* elicits *bread*, *needle* elicits *thread* and *salt* elicits *pepper*. One way we seem to organize our knowledge of words is simply on the basis of **collocation**, or frequently occurring together.

In recent years, the study of which words occur together and their frequency of co-occurrence has received a lot more attention in **corpus linguistics**. A corpus is a large collection of texts, spoken or written, typically stored as a database in a computer. Those doing corpus linguistics can then use the database to find out how often specific words or phrases occur and what types of collocations are most common.

One investigation looked at 84 occurrences of the phrase *true feelings* in a corpus (only a small sample is shown here). After looking at the types of verbs (e.g. *deny, try to communicate*) used with this phrase, the investigator noted that "English speakers use the phrase with *true feelings* when they want to give the meaning of reluctance to express deeply felt emotions" (Sinclair, 2003: 148).

(1) more accustomed to denying our *true feelings*, avoiding reflection and self- …
(2) We try to communicate our *true feelings* to those around us, and we are …
(3) the ability to express our *true feelings* and creativity because we are …
(4) we appease others, deny our *true feelings*, and conform, I suspected the …
(5) more of us in there, of our *true feelings*, rather than just ranting on …

This type of research provides more evidence that our understanding of what words and phrases mean is tied to the contexts in which they are typically used. We will look at other aspects of the role of context in the next chapter.

Study questions

1 How is the term "prototype" used in semantics?

2 Using semantic features, how would you explain the oddness of these sentences?
   (a) *The television drank my water.*
   (b) *His dog writes poetry.*

3 Identify the semantic roles of the seven noun phrases in this sentence.

   With her new golf club, Anne Marshall whacked the ball from the woods to the grassy area near the hole and she suddenly felt invincible.

4 What is the basic lexical relation between each pair of words listed here?

   (a) *damp/moist*   (c) *furniture/table*   (e) *move/run*
   (b) *deep/shallow*   (d) *married/single*   (f) *peace/piece*

5 Which of the following opposites are gradable, non-gradable, or reversive?

   (a) *absent/present*   (c) *fail/pass*   (e) *fill it/empty it*
   (b) *appear/disappear*   (d) *fair/unfair*   (f) *high/low*

6 Are these underlined words best described as examples of polysemy or metonymy?
   (a) *The pen is mightier than the sword.*
   (b) *I had to park on the shoulder of the road.*
   (c) *Yes, I love those. I ate a whole box on Sunday!*
   (d) *The bookstore has some new titles in linguistics.*
   (e) *Computer chips created an important new technology.*
   (f) *I'm going to sue your ass!*

Tasks

A What is the connection between an English doctor called Peter Mark Roget and the study of lexical relations?

B In this chapter, we discussed metonymy, but not metaphor. What is the difference between these two ways of using words?

C The adjective pairs listed here are antonyms with a marked and unmarked member in each pair. Can you list the unmarked members and explain your choices?

   big/small, empty/full, expensive/inexpensive, fast/slow, happy/unhappy, heavy/light, old/young, possible/impossible, short/tall, strong/weak

D   Which of these pairs of words are converses (also known as reciprocal antonyms)?

above/below, asleep/awake, brother/sister, buy/sell, doctor/patient, dry/wet,
enter/exit, follow/precede, husband/wife, older/younger, true/false

E   Another less common relation between word meanings is known as
    transferred epithet or hypallage. Why do we need to talk about this special type
    of meaning relation in the analysis of the meaning of the phrases listed here?
    Can you think of any other similar examples?

a quiet cup of coffee, a sleepless night, a nude photo, one of my clever days

F   We can *pour water into a glass* and we can *fill a glass with water*, but we can't
    **fill water into a glass* or **pour a glass with water*. Why not?

(i)   By focusing on the meaning of the verbs and their themes ("the affected
      objects"), try to find a semantic reason why some of the following
      sentences are ungrammatical.
      (1)   (a)   *We loaded furniture into the van.*
            (b)   *We loaded the van with furniture.*
      (2)   (a)   *They sprayed paint onto the wall.*
            (b)   *They sprayed the wall with paint.*
      (3)   (a)   *I poured coffee into the cup.*
            (b)   **I poured the cup with coffee.*
      (4)   (a)   **She filled tissues into her pocket.*
            (b)   *She filled her pocket with tissues.*

(ii) Which of the following verbs can be used in both of the (a) and
      (b) structures illustrated in examples (1–4): *attach, cram, glue, ladle, pack,*
      paste, splash, spread?

Discussion topics/projects

I   One way to analyze the semantic structure of sentences is to start with the
    verb as the central element and define the semantic roles required by that
    verb. (This is sometimes called "theta assignment.") For example, a verb like
    kill requires an agent and a theme, as in *The cat* [agent] *killed the mouse*
    [theme]. A verb like *give* requires an agent, a theme and a goal, as in *The*
    girl [agent] *gave the flowers* [theme] *to her mother* [goal]. We can represent
    these observations in the following way:

KILL [Agent _____ Theme]
    GIVE [Agent _____ Theme, Goal]

How would you define the set of semantic roles for the following verbs, using the format illustrated? Are there required roles and optional roles?

break, build, die, eat, fear, kiss, like, occupy, offer, open, put, receive, send, sneeze, steal, taste, teach, understand, want, write

(For background reading, see chapter 10 of Brinton, 2000.)

II The words in the following list are all related in terms of the superordinate form *tableware*. How would you go about determining what the prototype item of "tableware" must be? Is a hierarchical diagram illustrating hyponymous relations useful? Would it be helpful to list some (or all) of the words beside a scale from 5 (= "excellent example of tableware") to 1 (= "not really an example of tableware") and ask people to indicate their choices on the scale? Do you think that the word with the highest score would indicate the prototype?

bowl	*flatware*	*ladle*	*soup spoon*
crockery	*fork*	*mug*	*spoon*
cup	*glass*	*plate*	*teaspoon*
cutlery	*glassware*	*platter*	*tumbler*
dish	*knife*	*saucer*	*wineglass*

(For background reading, see chapter 1 of Ungerer and Schmid, 2006.)

Further reading

Basic treatments

Hurford, J., B. Heasley and M. Smith (2007) *Semantics: A Coursebook* (2nd edition) Cambridge University Press

Radford, A., M. Atkinson, D. Britain, H. Clahsen and A. Spencer (2009) *Linguistics: An Introduction* (chapter 12) (2nd edition) Cambridge University Press

More detailed treatments

Cruse, A. (2004) *Meaning in Language* (2nd edition) Oxford University Press

Saeed, J. (2003) *Semantics* (2nd edition) Blackwell

Conceptual and associative meaning

Aitchison, J. (2003) *Words in the Mind* (3rd edition) Blackwell

Pinker, S. (2007) *The Stuff of Thought* (chapter 1) Viking

Semantic roles

Kroeger, P. (2005) *Analyzing Grammar* (chapter 4) Cambridge University Press

Lexical relations

Murphy, M. (2003) *Semantic Relations and the Lexicon* Cambridge University Press

Antonymy

Jones, S. (2002) *Antonymy* Routledge

Prototypes

Taylor, J. (2003) *Linguistic Categorization* (3rd edition) Oxford University Press

Collocation and corpus linguistics

Meyer, C. (2002) *English Corpus Linguistics* Cambridge University Press

Stubbs, M. (2001) *Words and Phrases* Blackwell

Other references

Brinton, L. (2000) *The Structure of Modern English* John Benjamins

Sinclair, J. (2003) *Reading Concordances* Pearson

Ungerer, F. and H-J. Schmid (2006) *An Introduction to Cognitive Linguistics* (2nd edition) Pearson

10 Pragmatics

In the late 1960s, two elderly American tourists who had been touring Scotland reported that, in their travels, they had come to a Scottish town in which there was a great ruined cathedral. As they stood in the ruins, they saw a small boy and they asked him when the cathedral had been so badly damaged. He replied *in the war*. Their immediate interpretation, in the 1960s, was that he must be referring to the Second World War which had ended only twenty years earlier. But then they thought that the ruins looked as if they had been in their dilapidated state for much longer than that, so they asked the boy which war he meant. He replied *the war with the English*, which, they eventually discovered, had formally ended in 1745.   Brown (1998)

In the previous chapter, we focused on conceptual meaning and the relationships between words. There are other aspects of meaning that depend more on context and the communicative intentions of speakers. In Gill Brown's story, the American tourists and the Scottish boy seem to be using the word *war* with essentially the same basic meaning. However, the boy was using the word to refer to something the tourists didn't expect, hence the initial misunderstanding. Communication clearly depends on not only recognizing the meaning of words in an utterance, but recognizing what speakers mean by their utterances. The study of what speakers mean, or "speaker meaning," is called **pragmatics**.

Pragmatics

In many ways, pragmatics is the study of "invisible" meaning, or how we recognize what is meant even when it isn't actually said or written. In order for that to happen, speakers (or writers) must be able to depend on a lot of shared assumptions and expectations when they try to communicate. The investigation of those assumptions and expectations provides us with some insights into how more is always being communicated than is said.

Driving by a parking garage, you may see a large sign like the one in the picture. You read the sign, knowing what each of the words means and what the sign as a whole means. However, you don't normally think that the sign is advertising a place where you can park your "heated attendant." (You take an attendant, you heat him/her up, and this is where you can park him/her.) Alternatively, the sign may indicate a place where parking will be carried out by attendants who have been heated.

The words in the sign may allow these interpretations, but we would normally understand that we can park a car in this place, that it's a heated area, and that there

Figure 10.1

Figure 10.2

will be an attendant to look after the car. So, how do we decide that the sign means this when the sign doesn't even have the word *car* on it? We must use the meanings of the words, the context in which they occur, and some pre-existing knowledge of what would be a likely message as we work toward a reasonable interpretation of what the producer of the sign intended it to convey. Our interpretation of the "meaning" of the sign is not based solely on the words, but on what we think the writer intended to communicate.

In the other picture, assuming things are normal and this store has not gone into the business of selling young children, we can recognize an advertisement for a sale of clothes for those babies and toddlers. The word *clothes* doesn't appear in the message, but we can bring that idea to our interpretation of the message as we work out what the advertiser intended us to understand. We are actively involved in creating an interpretation of what we read and hear.

Context

In our discussion of the last two examples, we emphasized the influence of context. There are different kinds of context. One kind is described as **linguistic context**, also known as **co-text**. The co-text of a word is the set of other words used in the same phrase or sentence. The surrounding co-text has a strong effect on what we think the word probably means. In the last chapter, we identified the word *bank* as a homonym, a single form with more than one meaning. How do we usually know which meaning is intended in a particular sentence? We normally do so on the basis of linguistic context.

If the word *bank* is used in a sentence together with words like *steep* or *overgrown*, we have no problem deciding which type of *bank* is meant. Or, if we hear someone say that she has to *get to the bank to withdraw some cash*, we know from this linguistic context which type of *bank* is intended.

More generally, we know how to interpret words on the basis of **physical context**. If we see the word *BANK* on the wall of a building in a city, the physical location will influence our interpretation. While this may seem rather obvious, we should keep in mind that it is not the actual physical situation "out there" that constitutes "the context" for interpreting words or sentences. The relevant context is our mental representation of those aspects of what is physically out there that we use in arriving at an interpretation. Our understanding of much of what we read and hear is tied to this processing of aspects of the physical context, particularly the time and place, in which we encounter linguistic expressions.

Deixis

There are some very common words in our language that can't be interpreted at all if we don't know the context, especially the physical context of the speaker. These are words such as *here* and *there*, *this* or *that*, *now* and *then*, *yesterday*, *today* or *tomorrow*, as well as pronouns such as *you*, *me*, *she*, *him*, *it*, *them*. Some sentences of English are virtually impossible to understand if we don't know who is speaking, about whom, where and when. For example: *You'll have to bring it back tomorrow because she isn't here today.*

Out of context, this sentence is really vague. It contains a large number of expressions (*you*, *it*, *tomorrow*, *she*, *here*, *today*) that rely on knowledge of the immediate physical context for their interpretation (i.e. that the delivery driver will have to return on February 15 to 660 College Drive with the long box labeled "flowers, handle with care" addressed to Lisa Landry). Expressions such as *tomorrow* and *here* are obvious examples of bits of language that we can only understand in terms of the speaker's intended meaning. They are technically known as **deictic** (/daɪktɪk/) **expressions**, from the Greek word **deixis**, which means "pointing" via language.

We use deixis to point to things (*it*, *this*, *these boxes*) and people (*him*, *them*, *those idiots*), sometimes called **person deixis**. Words and phrases used to point to a location (*here*, *there*, *near that*) are examples of **spatial deixis**, and those used to point to a time (*now*, *then*, *last week*) are examples of **temporal deixis**.

All these deictic expressions have to be interpreted in terms of which person, place or time the speaker has in mind. We make a broad distinction between what is marked as close to the speaker (*this*, *here*, *now*) and what is distant (*that*, *there*, *then*). We can also indicate whether movement is away from the speaker's location (*go*) or toward the speaker's location (*come*). If you're looking for someone and she appears, moving toward you, you can say *Here she comes!*. If, however, she is moving away from you in the distance, you're more likely to say *There she goes!*. The same deictic effect explains the different situations in which you would tell someone to *Go to bed* versus *Come to bed*.

People can actually use deixis to have some fun. The bar owner who puts up a big sign that reads *Free Beer Tomorrow* (to get you to return to the bar) can always claim that you are just one day too early for the free drink.

Reference

In discussing deixis, we assumed that the use of words to refer to people, places and times was a simple matter. However, words themselves don't refer to anything. People refer. We have to define **reference** as an act by which a speaker (or writer) uses language to enable a listener (or reader) to identify something. To perform an act of reference, we can use proper nouns (*Chomsky, Jennifer, Whiskas*), other nouns in phrases (*a writer, my friend, the cat*) or pronouns (*he, she, it*). We sometimes assume that these words identify someone or something uniquely, but it is more accurate to say that, for each word or phrase, there is a "range of reference." The words *Jennifer* or *friend* or *she* can be used to refer to many entities in the world. As we observed earlier, an expression such as *the war* doesn't directly identify anything by itself, because its reference depends on who is using it.

We can also refer to things when we're not sure what to call them. We can use expressions such as *the blue thing* and *that icky stuff* and we can even invent names. For instance, there was a man who always drove his motorcycle fast and loud through my neighborhood and was locally referred to as *Mr. Kawasaki*. In this case, a brand name for a motorcycle is being used to refer to a person.

Inference

As in the "Mr. Kawasaki" example, a successful act of reference depends more on the listener's ability to recognize what we mean than on the listener's "dictionary" knowledge of a word we use. For example, in a restaurant, one waiter can ask another, *Where's the spinach salad sitting?* and receive the reply, *He's sitting by the door*. If you're studying linguistics, you might ask someone, *Can I look at your Chomsky?* and get the response, *Sure, it's on the shelf over there*. These examples make it clear that we can use names associated with things (*salad*) to refer to people, and use names of people (*Chomsky*) to refer to things. The key process here is called **inference**. An inference is additional information used by the listener to create a connection between what is said and what must be meant. In the last example, the listener has to operate with the inference: "if X is the name of the writer of a book, then X can be used to identify a copy of a book by that writer." Similar types of inferences are necessary to understand someone who says that *Picasso is in the museum* or *We saw Shakespeare in London* or *Jennifer is wearing Calvin Klein*.

Anaphora

We usually make a distinction between introducing new referents (*a puppy*) and referring back to them (*the puppy, it*).

*We saw a funny home video about a boy washing **a puppy** in a small bath.*
***The puppy** started struggling and shaking and the boy got really wet.*
*When he let go, **it** jumped out of the bath and ran away.*

In this type of referential relationship, the second (or subsequent) referring expression is an example of **anaphora** ("referring back"). The first mention is called the **antecedent**. So, in our example, *a boy*, *a puppy* and *a small bath* are antecedents and *The puppy*, *the boy*, *he*, *it* and *the bath* are anaphoric expressions.

Anaphora can be defined as subsequent reference to an already introduced entity. Mostly we use anaphora in texts to maintain reference. The connection between an antecedent and an anaphoric expression is created by use of a pronoun (*it*), or a phrase with *the* plus the antecedent noun (*the puppy*), or another noun that is related to the antecedent in some way (***The little dog** ran out of the room*). The connection between antecedents and anaphoric expressions is often based on inference, as in these examples.

*We found **a house** to rent, but **the kitchen** was very small.*
*I caught **a bus** and asked **the driver** if it went near the downtown area.*

In the first example, we must make an inference like "if X is a house, then X has a kitchen" in order to interpret the connection between antecedent *a house* and anaphoric expression *the kitchen*. In the second example, we must make an inference like "if X is a bus, then X has a driver" in order to make the connection between *a bus* and *the driver*.

We have used the term "inference" here to describe what the listener (or reader) does. When we talk about an assumption made by the speaker (or writer), we usually talk about a "presupposition."

Presupposition

When we use a referring expression like *this*, *he* or *Shakespeare*, we usually assume that our listeners can recognize which referent is intended. In a more general way, we design our linguistic messages on the basis of large-scale assumptions about what our listeners already know. Some of these assumptions may be mistaken, of course, but mostly they're appropriate. What a speaker (or writer) assumes is true or known by a listener (or reader) can be described as a **presupposition**.

If someone tells you *Your brother is waiting outside*, there is an obvious presupposition that you have a brother. If you are asked *Why did you arrive late?*, there is a presupposition that you did arrive late. And if you are asked the question *When did you stop smoking?*, there are at least two presuppositions involved. In asking this question, the speaker presupposes that you used to smoke and that you no longer do so. Questions like this, with built-in presuppositions, are very useful devices for interrogators or trial lawyers. If the defendant is asked by the prosecutor, *Okay, Mr. Buckingham, how fast were you going when you ran the red light?*, there is a presupposition that Mr. Buckingham did in fact run the red light. If he simply answers the *How fast* part of the question, by giving a speed, he is behaving as if the presupposition is correct.

One of the tests used to check for the presuppositions underlying sentences involves negating a sentence with a particular presupposition and checking if the presupposition remains true. Whether you say *My car is a wreck* or the negative version *My car is not a wreck*, the underlying presupposition (*I have a car*) remains true despite the fact that the two sentences have opposite meanings. This is called the "constancy under negation" test for identifying a presupposition. If someone says, *I used to regret marrying him, but I don't regret marrying him now*, the presupposition (*I married him*) remains constant even though the verb *regret* changes from affirmative to negative.

Speech acts

We have been considering ways in which we interpret the meaning of an utterance in terms of what the speaker intended to convey. We have not yet considered the fact that we usually know how the speaker intends us to "take" (or "interpret the function of") what is said. In very general terms, we can usually recognize the type of "action" performed by a speaker with the utterance. We use the term **speech act** to describe actions such as "requesting," "commanding," "questioning" or "informing." We can define a speech act as the action performed by a speaker with an utterance. If you say, *I'll be there at six*, you are not just speaking, you seem to be performing the speech act of "promising."

Direct and indirect speech acts

We usually use certain syntactic structures with the functions listed beside them in the following table.

	Structures	Functions
Did you eat the pizza?	Interrogative	Question
Eat the pizza (please)!	Imperative	Command (Request)
You ate the pizza.	Declarative	Statement

When an interrogative structure such as *Did you…?*, *Are they…?* or *Can we…?* is used with the function of a question, it is described as a **direct speech act**. For example, when we don't know something and we ask someone to provide the information, we usually produce a direct speech act such as *Can you ride a bicycle?*.

Compare that utterance with *Can you pass the salt?*. In this second example, we are not really asking a question about someone's ability. In fact, we don't normally use this structure as a question at all. We normally use it to make a request. That is, we are using a syntactic structure associated with the function of a question, but in this case with the function of a request. This is an example of an **indirect speech act**. Whenever one of the structures in the set above is used to perform a function other than the one listed beside it on the same line, the result is an indirect speech act.

The utterance *You left the door open* has a declarative structure and, as a direct speech act, would be used to make a statement. However, if you say this to someone who has just come in (and it's really cold outside), you would probably want that person to close the door. You are not using the imperative structure. You are using a declarative structure to make a request. It's another example of an indirect speech act.

It is possible to have strange effects if one person fails to recognize another person's indirect speech act. Consider the following scene. A visitor to a city, carrying his luggage, looking lost, stops a passer-by.

VISITOR: *Excuse me. Do you know where the Ambassador Hotel is?*
PASSER-BY: *Oh sure, I know where it is.* (and walks away)

In this scene, the visitor uses a form normally associated with a question (*Do you know…?*), and the passer-by answers that question literally (*I know…*). That is, the passer-by is acting as if the utterance was a direct speech act instead of an indirect speech act used as a request for directions.

The main reason we use indirect speech acts seems to be that actions such as requests, presented in an indirect way (*Could you open that door for me?*), are generally considered to be more gentle or more polite in our society than direct speech acts (*Open that door for me!*). Exactly why they are considered to be more polite is based on some complex social assumptions.

Politeness

We can think of politeness in general terms as having to do with ideas like being tactful, modest and nice to other people. In the study of linguistic politeness, the most relevant concept is "face." Your **face**, in pragmatics, is your public self-image. This is the emotional and social sense of self that everyone has and expects everyone else to recognize. **Politeness** can be defined as showing awareness and consideration of another person's face.

If you say something that represents a threat to another person's self-image, that is called a **face-threatening act**. For example, if you use a direct speech act to get someone to do something (*Give me that paper!*), you are behaving as if you have more social power than the other person. If you don't actually have that social power (e.g. you're not a military officer or prison warden), then you are performing a face-threatening act. An indirect speech act, in the form associated with a question (*Could you pass me that paper?*), removes the assumption of social power. You're only asking if it's possible. This makes your request less threatening to the other person's face. Whenever you say something that lessens the possible threat to another's face, it can be described as a **face-saving act**.

Negative and positive face

We have both a negative face and a positive face. (Note that "negative" doesn't mean "bad" here, it's simply the opposite of "positive.") **Negative face** is the need to be independent and free from imposition. **Positive face** is the need to be connected, to belong, to be a member of the group. So, a face-saving act that emphasizes a person's negative face will show concern about imposition (*I'm sorry to bother you…*; *I know you're busy, but…*). A face-saving act that emphasizes a person's positive face will show solidarity and draw attention to a common goal (*Let's do this together…*; *You and I have the same problem, so…*).

Ideas about the appropriate language to mark politeness differ substantially from one culture to the next. If you have grown up in a culture that has directness as a valued way of showing solidarity, and you use direct speech acts (*Give me that chair!*) to people whose culture is more oriented to indirectness and avoiding direct imposition, then you will be considered impolite. You, in turn, may think of the others as vague and unsure of whether they really want something or are just asking about it (*Are you using this chair?*). In either case, it is the pragmatics that is misunderstood and, unfortunately, more will be communicated than is said.

Understanding how successful communication works is actually a process of interpreting not just what speakers say, but what they "intend to mean." We'll explore other aspects of this process in the next chapter.

Study questions

1   What kinds of deictic expressions are used in this utterance (e.g. *I* = person deixis)?

   I'm busy now so you can't stay here. Come back later.

2   What are the anaphoric expressions in this sentence?

   Dr. Foster gave Andy some medicine after he told her about his headaches and she advised him to take the pills three times a day until the pain went away.

3   What kind of inference is involved in interpreting each of these utterances?
   (a)   Teacher: *You can borrow my Shakespeare.*
   (b)   Waiter: *The ham sandwich left without paying.*
   (c)   Nurse: *The hernia in room 5 wants to talk to the doctor.*
   (d)   Dentist: *My eleven-thirty canceled so I had an early lunch.*

4   What is one obvious presupposition of a speaker who says:
   (a)   *Your clock isn't working.*
   (b)   *Where did he find the money?*
   (c)   *We regret buying that car.*
   (d)   *The king of France is bald.*

5   Someone stands between you and the TV set you're watching, so you decide to say one of the following. Identify which would be direct or indirect speech acts.
   (a) *Move!*   (c) *Could you please sit down?*
   (b) *You're in the way.*   (d) *Please get out of the way.*

6   In these examples, is the speaker appealing to positive or negative face?
   (a)   *If you're free, there's going to be a party at Yuri's place on Saturday.*
   (b)   *Let's go to the party at Yuri's place on Saturday. Everyone's invited.*

Tasks

A   What do you think is meant by the statement: "A context is a psychological construct" (Sperber and Wilson, 1995)?

B   Why is the concept of "deictic projection" necessary for the analysis of the following deictic expressions?
   (1)   On a telephone answering machine: *I am not here now.*
   (2)   On a map/directory: YOU ARE HERE
   (3)   Watching a horse race: *Oh, no. I'm in last place.*

(4)   In a car that won't start: *Maybe I'm out of gas.*

(5)   Pointing to an empty chair in class: *Where is she today?*

C   Which of these utterances contain "performative verbs" and how did you decide?

(1)   *I apologize.*

(2)   *He said he was sorry.*

(3)   *I bet you $20.*

(4)   *She won the bet.*

(5)   *I drive a Mercedes.*

(6)   *You must have a lot of money.*

D   What is metapragmatics? What aspects of the following utterance illustrate metapragmatic awareness?

I know that Justin said, "I'll help you, darling," but he wasn't actually promising anything, I'm sure.

E   Using these examples, and any others you think are appropriate, try to decide if euphemisms and proverbs should be studied as part of pragmatics. Are they, for example, similar to indirect speech acts?

(1)   *She's got a bun in the oven.*

(2)   *He's gone to a better place.*

(3)   *Unfortunately, there was some collateral damage.*

(4)   *The grass is always greener on the other side of the fence.*

(5)   *If wishes were horses, beggars would ride.*

(6)   *People who live in glass houses shouldn't throw stones.*

F   The following phrases were all on signs advertising sales. What is being sold in each case and (if you know) what other words would you add to the description to make it clearer? What is the underlying structure of each phrase? For example, *Furniture Sale* might have the structure: "someone is selling furniture." Would the same structure be appropriate for *Garage Sale* and the others?

Back-to-School Sale	*Dollar Sale*	*One Cent Sale*
Bake Sale	*Foundation Sale*	*Plant Sale*
Big Screen Sale	*Furniture Sale*	*Sidewalk Sale*
Clearance Sale	*Garage Sale*	*Spring Sale*
Close-out Sale	*Labor Day Sale*	*Tent Sale*
Colorful White Sale	*Liquidation Sale*	*Yard Sale*

Discussion topics/projects

I   Let's imagine you were in a situation where you had to ask your parents if you could go out to a dance and you received one of these two responses. Do you think that these responses have the same or different "meanings"?

"Yes, of course, go."   *"If you want, you can go."*

Next, consider this situation, described in Tannen (1986).

A Greek woman explained how she and her father (and later her husband) communicated. If she wanted to do something, like go to a dance, she had to ask her father for permission. He never said no. But she could tell from the way he said yes whether or not he meant it. If he said something like "Yes, of course, go," then she knew he thought it was a good idea. If he said something like "If you want, you can go," then she understood that he didn't think it was a good idea, and she wouldn't go.

Why do you think "he never said no" (when he was communicating "No")?
How would you analyze the two speech acts reported as responses in this passage?
Are you familiar with any other comparable situations where "more is communicated than is said"?
(For background reading, see chapter 4 of Tannen, 1986.)

II   What counts as polite behavior can differ substantially from one group or culture to the next. Below are some basic descriptions from Lakoff (1990) of three types of politeness, called distance politeness, deference politeness and camaraderie politeness. As you read these descriptions, try to decide which type you are most familiar with and whether you have encountered the others on any occasion. What kind of language do you think is characteristic of these different types of politeness?

  • "Distance politeness is the civilized human analogue to the territorial strategies of other animals. An animal sets up physical boundary markers (the dog and the hydrant) to signal its fellows: My turf, stay out. We, being symbol-using creatures, create symbolic fences."
  • "Distancing cultures weave remoteness into their language."
  • "Another culture might avoid the danger of conflict by adopting a strategy of deferential politeness. If a participant decides that whatever is to happen in a conversation – both what is said and what it is to mean – is up to the other person, conflict can easily be avoided."

- "Where distance politeness more or less assumes equality between participants, deference works by debasing one or both."
- "While distance politeness has been characteristic of the middle and upper classes in most of Europe for a very long time, deference has been typical in many Asian societies. But it is also the preferred model of interaction for women in the majority of societies, either always or only when talking to men."
- "A third strategy (camaraderie) that has recently emerged in this culture makes a different assumption: that interaction and connection are good in themselves, that openness is the greatest sign of courtesy."
- "In a camaraderie system, the appearance of openness and niceness is to be sought above all else. There is no holding back, nothing is too terrible to say."

(For background reading, see chapter 2 of Lakoff, 1990.)

Further reading

Basic treatments

Peccei, J. (1999) *Pragmatics* Routledge

Yule, G. (1996) *Pragmatics* Oxford University Press

More detailed treatments

Grundy, P. (2008) *Doing Pragmatics* (3rd edition) Hodder

Verschueren, J. (1999) *Understanding Pragmatics* Arnold

Context

Malmkjaer, K. and J. Williams (eds.) (1998) *Context in Language Learning and Language Understanding* Cambridge University Press

Reference and deixis

Cruse, A. (2004) *Meaning in Language* (part 4) (2nd edition) Oxford University Press

Anaphora

Huang, Y. (2000) *Anaphora: A Cross-Linguistic Approach* Oxford University Press

Presupposition

Levinson, S. (1983) *Pragmatics* (chapter 4) Cambridge University Press

Speech acts

Thomas, J. (1995) *Meaning in Interaction* (chapter 2) Longman

Politeness

Watts, R. (2003) *Politeness* Cambridge University Press

Face

Brown, P. and S. Levinson (1987) *Politeness: Some Universals in Language Usage* Cambridge University Press

Other references

Lakoff, R. (1990) *Talking Power* Basic Books

Sperber, D. and D. Wilson (1995) *Relevance* (2nd edition) Blackwell

Tannen, D. (1986) *Conversational Style* Ablex

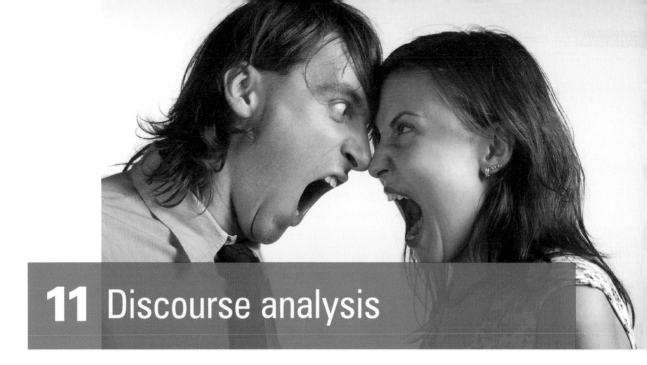

11 Discourse analysis

There's two types of favors, the big favor and the small favor. You can measure the size of the favor by the pause that a person takes after they ask you to "Do me a favor." Small favor – small pause. "Can you do me a favor, hand me that pencil." No pause at all. Big favors are, "Could you do me a favor …" Eight seconds go by. "Yeah? What?"

"… well." The longer it takes them to get to it, the bigger the pain it's going to be.

Humans are the only species that do favors. Animals don't do favors. A lizard doesn't go up to a cockroach and say, "Could you do me a favor and hold still, I'd like to eat you alive." That's a big favor even with no pause.

Seinfeld (1993)

In the study of language, some of the most interesting observations are made, not in terms of the components of language, but in terms of the way language is used, even how pauses are used, as in comedian Jerry Seinfeld's commentary. We have already considered some of the features of language in use when we discussed pragmatics in the preceding chapter. We were, in effect, asking how it is that language-users successfully interpret what other language-users intend to convey. When we carry this investigation further and ask how we make sense of what we read, how we can recognize well-constructed texts as opposed to those that are jumbled or incoherent, how we understand speakers who communicate more than they say, and how we successfully take part in that complex activity called conversation, we are undertaking what is known as **discourse analysis**.

Discourse analysis

The word "discourse" is usually defined as "language beyond the sentence" and so the analysis of discourse is typically concerned with the study of language in texts and conversation. In many of the preceding chapters, when we were concentrating on linguistic description, we were concerned with the accurate representation of the forms and structures. However, as language-users, we are capable of more than simply recognizing correct versus incorrect forms and structures. We can cope with fragments in newspaper headlines such as *Trains collide, two die*, and know that what happened in the first part was the cause of what happened in the second part. We can also make sense of notices like *No shoes, no service*, on shop windows in summer, understanding that a conditional relation exists between the two parts ("If you are wearing no shoes, you will receive no service"). We have the ability to create complex discourse interpretations of fragmentary linguistic messages.

Interpreting discourse

We can even cope with texts, written in English, which we couldn't produce ourselves and which appear to break a lot of the rules of the English language. Yet we can build an interpretation. The following example, provided by Eric Nelson, is from an essay by a student learning English and contains all kinds of errors, yet it can be understood.

> *My Town*
> *My natal was in a small town, very close to Riyadh capital of Saudi Arabia. The distant between my town and Riyadh 7 miles exactly. The name of this Almasani that means in English Factories. It takes this name from the peopl's carrer. In my childhood I remmeber the people live. It was very simple. Most the people was farmer.*

This example may serve to illustrate a simple point about the way we react to language that contains ungrammatical forms. Rather than simply reject the text as ungrammatical, we try to make sense of it. That is, we attempt to arrive at a reasonable interpretation of what the writer intended to convey. (Most people say they understand the "My Town" text quite easily.)

It is this effort to interpret (or to be interpreted), and how we accomplish it, that are the key elements investigated in the study of discourse. To arrive at an interpretation, and to make our messages interpretable, we certainly rely on what we know about linguistic form and structure. But, as language-users, we have more knowledge than that.

Cohesion

We know, for example, that texts must have a certain structure that depends on factors quite different from those required in the structure of a single sentence. Some of those factors are described in terms of **cohesion**, or the ties and connections that exist within texts. A number of those types of **cohesive ties** can be identified in the following paragraph.

> *My father once bought a Lincoln convertible. He did it by saving every penny he could. That car would be worth a fortune nowadays. However, he sold it to help pay for my college education. Sometimes I think I'd rather have the convertible.*

There are connections present here in the use of words to maintain reference to the same people and things throughout: *father – he – he – he*; *my – my – I*; *Lincoln – it*. There are connections between phrases such as: *a Lincoln convertible – that car – the convertible*. There are more general connections created by a number of terms that share a common element of meaning, such as "money" (*bought – saving – penny – worth a fortune – sold – pay*) and "time" (*once – nowadays – sometimes*). There is also a connector (*However*) that marks the relationship of what follows to what went before. The verb tenses in the first four sentences are all in the past, creating a connection between those events, and a different time is indicated by the present tense of the final sentence.

Analysis of these cohesive ties within a text gives us some insight into how writers structure what they want to say. An appropriate number of cohesive ties may be a crucial factor in our judgments on whether something is well written or not. It has also been noted that the conventions of cohesive structure differ from one language to the next and may be one of the sources of difficulty encountered in translating texts.

However, by itself, cohesion would not be sufficient to enable us to make sense of what we read. It is quite easy to create a highly cohesive text that has a lot of connections between the sentences, but is very difficult to interpret. Note that the following text has connections such as *Lincoln – the car*, *red – that color*, *her – she*, *letters – a letter*, and so on.

> *My father bought a Lincoln convertible. The car driven by the police was red. That color doesn't suit her. She consists of three letters. However, a letter isn't as fast as a telephone call.*

It becomes clear from this type of example that the "connectedness" we experience in our interpretation of normal texts is not simply based on connections between the words. There must be some other factor that leads us to distinguish connected texts that make sense from those that do not. This factor is usually described as "coherence."

Coherence

The key to the concept of **coherence** ("everything fitting together well") is not something that exists in words or structures, but something that exists in people. It is people who "make sense" of what they read and hear. They try to arrive at an interpretation that is in line with their experience of the way the world is. Indeed, our ability to make sense of what we read is probably only a small part of that general ability we have to make sense of what we perceive or experience in the world. You may have found when you were reading the last example (of oddly constructed text) that you kept trying to make the text fit some situation or experience that would accommodate all the details (involving a red car, a woman and a letter). If you work at it long enough, you may indeed find a way to incorporate all those disparate elements into a single coherent interpretation. In doing so, you would necessarily be involved in a process of filling in a lot of gaps that exist in the text. You would have to create meaningful connections that are not actually expressed by the words and sentences. This process is not restricted to trying to understand "odd" texts. In one way or another, it seems to be involved in our interpretation of all discourse.

It is certainly present in the interpretation of casual conversation. We are continually taking part in conversational interactions where a great deal of what is meant is not actually present in what is said. Perhaps it is the ease with which we ordinarily anticipate each other's intentions that makes this whole complex process seem so unremarkable. Here is a good example, adapted from Widdowson (1978).

HER: *That's the telephone.*
HIM: *I'm in the bath.*
HER: *O.K.*

There are certainly no cohesive ties within this fragment of discourse. How does each of these people manage to make sense of what the other says? They do use the information contained in the sentences expressed, but there must be something else involved in the interpretation. It has been suggested that exchanges of this type are best understood in terms of the conventional actions performed by the speakers in such interactions. Drawing on concepts derived from the study of speech acts (introduced in Chapter 10), we can characterize the brief conversation in the following way.

She makes a request of him to perform action.
He states reason why he cannot comply with request.
She undertakes to perform action.

If this is a reasonable analysis of what took place in the conversation, then it is clear that language-users must have a lot of knowledge of how conversation works that is not simply "linguistic" knowledge.

Speech events

In exploring what it is we know about taking part in conversation, or any other speech event (e.g. debate, interview, various types of discussions), we quickly realize that there is enormous variation in what people say and do in different circumstances. In order to begin to describe the sources of that variation, we would have to take account of a number of criteria. For example, we would have to specify the roles of speaker and hearer (or hearers) and their relationship(s), whether they were friends, strangers, men, women, young, old, of equal or unequal status, and many other factors. All of these factors will have an influence on what is said and how it is said. We would have to describe what the topic of conversation was and in what setting it took place. Some of the effects of these factors on the way language is used are explored in greater detail in Chapters 19 and 20. Yet, even when we have described all these factors, we will still not have analyzed the actual structure of the conversation itself. As language-users, in a particular culture, we clearly have quite sophisticated knowledge of how conversation works.

Conversation analysis

In simple terms, English conversation can be described as an activity in which, for the most part, two or more people take **turns** at speaking. Typically, only one person speaks at a time and there tends to be an avoidance of silence between speaking turns. (This is not true in all situations or societies.) If more than one participant tries to talk at the same time, one of them usually stops, as in the following example, where A stops until B has finished.

A: *Didn't you [know wh-*
B: *[But he must've been there by two*
A: *Yes but you knew where he was going*

(A small square bracket [is conventionally used to indicate a place where simultaneous or overlapping speech occurs.)

For the most part, participants wait until one speaker indicates that he or she has finished, usually by signaling a **completion point**. Speakers can mark their turns as complete in a number of ways: by asking a question, for example, or by pausing at the end of a completed syntactic structure like a phrase or sentence. Other participants can indicate that they want to take the speaking turn, also in a number of ways. They can start to make short sounds, usually repeated, while the speaker is talking, and often use body shifts or facial expressions to signal that they have something to say.

Turn-taking

There are different expectations of conversational style and different strategies of participation in conversation. Some of these strategies seem to be the source of what is sometimes described by participants as "rudeness" (if one speaker cuts in on another speaker) or "shyness" (if one speaker keeps waiting for an opportunity to take a turn and none seems to occur). The participants characterized as "rude" or "shy" in this way may simply be adhering to slightly different conventions of **turn-taking**.

One strategy, which may be overused by "long-winded" speakers or those who are used to "holding the floor," is designed to avoid having normal completion points occur. We all use this strategy to some extent, usually in situations where we have to work out what we are trying to say while actually saying it. If the normal expectation is that completion points are marked by the end of a sentence and a pause, then one way to "keep the turn" is to avoid having those two markers occur together. That is, don't pause at the end of sentences; make your sentences run on by using connectors like *and, and then, so, but*; place your pauses at points where the message is clearly incomplete; and preferably "fill" the pause with a hesitation marker such as *er, em, uh, ah*.

In the following example, note how the pauses (marked by …) are placed before and after verbs rather than at the end of sentences, making it difficult to get a clear sense of what this person is saying until we hear the part after each pause.

A: *that's their favorite restaurant because they … enjoy French food and when they were … in France they couldn't believe it that … you know that they had … that they had had better meals back home*

In the next example, speaker X produces **filled pauses** (with *em, er, you know*) after having almost lost the turn at his first brief hesitation.

X: *well that film really was … [wasn't what he was good at*
Y: *[when di-*

X: *I mean his other … em his later films were much more … er really more in the*
   romantic style and that was more what what he was … you know … em best at doing
Y: *so when did he make that one*

These types of strategies, by themselves, should not be considered undesirable or dom-ineering. They are present in the conversational speech of most people and they are part of what makes conversation work. We recognize these subtle indicators as ways of organiz-ing our turns and negotiating the intricate business of social interaction via language. In fact, one of the most noticeable features of conversational discourse is that it is generally very "co-operative." This observation has been formulated as a principle of conversation.

The co-operative principle

An underlying assumption in most conversational exchanges seems to be that the participants are co-operating with each other. This principle, together with four maxims that we expect our conversational partners to obey, was first described by the philosopher Paul Grice. The **co-operative principle** is stated in the following way: "Make your conversational contribution such as is required, at the stage at which it occurs, by the accepted purpose or direction of the talk exchange in which you are engaged" (Grice, 1975: 45). Supporting this principle are four maxims, often called the "Gricean maxims."

The Quantity maxim: Make your contribution as informative as is required, but not more, or less, than is required.
The Quality maxim: Do not say that which you believe to be false or for which you lack adequate evidence.
The Relation maxim: Be relevant.
The Manner maxim: Be clear, brief and orderly.

It is certainly true that, on occasion, we can experience conversational exchanges in which the co-operative principle may not seem to be in operation. However, this general description of the normal expectations we have in conversation helps to explain a number of regular features in the way people say things. For example, during their lunch break, one woman asks another how she likes the sandwich she is eating and receives the following answer.

   Oh, a sandwich is a sandwich.

In logical terms, this reply appears to have no communicative value since it states something obvious and doesn't seem to be informative at all. However, if the woman is being co-operative and adhering to the Quantity maxim about being "as informative as is required," then the listener must assume that her friend is communicating something. Given the opportunity to evaluate the sandwich, her friend has responded without an explicit evaluation, thereby implying that she has no opinion, good or bad, to express. That is, her friend has essentially communicated that the sandwich isn't worth talking about.

Hedges

We use certain types of expressions, called **hedges**, to show that we are concerned about following the maxims while being co-operative participants in conversation. Hedges can be defined as words or phrases used to indicate that we're not really sure that what we're saying is sufficiently correct or complete. We can use *sort of* or *kind of* as hedges on the accuracy of our statements, as in descriptions such as *His hair was kind of long* or *The book cover is sort of yellow* (rather than *It is yellow*). These are examples of hedges on the Quality maxim. Other examples would include the expressions listed below that people sometimes put at the beginning of their conversational contributions.

> *As far as I know …,*
> *Now, correct me if I'm wrong, but …*
> *I'm not absolutely sure, but ….*

We also take care to indicate that what we report is something we *think* or *feel* (not *know*), is *possible* or *likely* (not *certain*), and *may* or *could* (not *must*) happen. Hence the difference between saying *Jackson is guilty* and *I think it's possible that Jackson may be guilty*. In the first version, we will be assumed to have very good evidence for the statement.

Implicatures

When we try to analyze how hedges work, we usually talk about speakers implying something that is not said. Similarly, in considering what the woman meant by *a sandwich is a sandwich*, we decided that she was implying that the sandwich wasn't worth talking about. With the co-operative principle and the maxims as guides, we can start to work out how people actually decide that someone is "implying" something in conversation. Consider the following example.

CAROL: *Are you coming to the party tonight?*
LARA: *I've got an exam tomorrow.*

On the face of it, Lara's statement is not an answer to Carol's question. Lara doesn't say *Yes* or *No*. Yet Carol will immediately interpret the statement as meaning "No" or "Probably not." How can we account for this ability to grasp one meaning from a sentence that, in a literal sense, means something else? It seems to depend, at least partially, on the assumption that Lara is being relevant and informative, adhering to the maxims of Relation and Quantity. (To appreciate this point, try to imagine Carol's reaction if Lara had said something like *Roses are red, you know*.) Given that Lara's original answer contains relevant information, Carol can work out that "exam tomorrow" conventionally involves "study tonight," and "study tonight" precludes "party tonight." Thus, Lara's answer is not simply a statement about tomorrow's activities, it contains an **implicature** (an additional conveyed meaning) concerning tonight's activities.

It is noticeable that, in order to describe the conversational implicature involved in Lara's statement, we had to appeal to some background knowledge (about exams, studying and partying) that must be shared by the conversational participants. Investigating how we use our background knowledge to arrive at interpretations of what we hear and read is a critical part of doing discourse analysis.

Background knowledge

A particularly good example of the processes involved in using background knowledge was provided by Sanford and Garrod (1981), who presented readers with a short text, one sentence at a time. Their text begins with the following two sentences.

> *John was on his way to school last Friday.*
> *He was really worried about the math lesson.*

Most people who are asked to read these sentences report that they think John is probably a schoolboy. Since this piece of information is not directly stated in the text, it must be an inference. Other inferences, for different readers, are that John is walking or that he is on a bus. These inferences are clearly derived from our conventional knowledge, in our culture, about "going to school," and no reader has ever suggested that John is swimming or on a boat, though both are physically possible, if unlikely, interpretations.

An interesting aspect of the reported inferences is that they are treated as likely or possible interpretations that readers will quickly abandon if they do not fit in with some subsequent information. Here is the next sentence in the text.

> *Last week he had been unable to control the class.*

On encountering this sentence, most readers decide that John is, in fact, a teacher and that he is not very happy. Many report that he is probably driving a car to school. Then the next sentence is presented.

It was unfair of the math teacher to leave him in charge.

Suddenly, John reverts to his schoolboy status, and the inference that he is a teacher is quickly abandoned. The final sentence of the text contains a surprise.

After all, it is not a normal part of a janitor's duties.

This type of text and manner of presentation, one sentence at a time, is rather artificial, of course. Yet the exercise involved does provide us with some insight into the ways in which we "build" interpretations of what we read by using a lot more information than is presented in the words on the page. That is, we actually create what the text is about, based on our expectations of what normally happens. In attempting to describe this phenomenon, researchers often use the concept of a "schema" or a "script."

Schemas and scripts

A **schema** is a general term for a conventional knowledge structure that exists in memory. We were using our conventional knowledge of what a school classroom is like, or a "classroom schema," as we tried to make sense of the previous example. We have many schemas (or schemata) that are used in the interpretation of what we experience and what we hear or read about. If you hear someone describe what happened during a visit to a supermarket, you don't have to be told what is normally found in a supermarket. You already have a "supermarket schema" (food displayed on shelves, arranged in aisles, shopping carts and baskets, check-out counter, and other conventional features) as part of your background knowledge.

Similar in many ways to a schema is a **script**. A script is essentially a dynamic schema. That is, instead of the set of typical fixed features in a schema, a script has a series of conventional actions that take place. You have a script for "Going to the dentist" and another script for "Going to the movies." We all have versions of an "Eating in a restaurant" script, which we can activate to make sense of this short text.

Trying not to be out of the office for long, Suzy went into the nearest place, sat down and ordered an avocado sandwich. It was quite crowded, but the service was fast, so she left a good tip. Back in the office, things were not going well.

On the basis of our restaurant script, we would be able to say a number of things about the scene and events briefly described in this short text. For example, although the text doesn't have this information, we would assume that Suzy opened a door to get into the restaurant, that there were tables there, that she ate the sandwich, then she paid for it, and so on. The fact that information of this type can turn up in people's attempts to remember the text is further evidence of the existence of scripts. It is also a good indication of the fact that our understanding of what we read doesn't come directly from what words and sentences are on the page, but the interpretations we create, in our minds, of what we read.

Indeed, crucial information is sometimes omitted from important instructions on the assumption that everybody knows the script. Think carefully about the following instructions from a bottle of cough syrup.

> *Fill measure cup to line*
> *and repeat every 2 to 3 hours.*

No, you've not just to keep filling the measure cup every 2 to 3 hours. Nor have you to rub the cough syrup on your neck or in your hair. You are expected to know the script and *drink* the stuff from the measure cup every 2 or 3 hours.

Clearly, our understanding of what we read is not only based on what we see on the page (language structures), but also on other things that we have in mind (knowledge structures). To understand more about the connection between these two things, we have to take a close look at the workings of the human brain.

Study questions

1 How is the word "discourse" usually defined?
2 What is the basic difference between cohesion and coherence?
3 How do speakers mark completion points at the end of a turn?
4 What are hedges in discourse?
5 Which maxim does this speaker seem to be particularly careful about?

   I may be mistaken, but I thought I saw a wedding ring on his finger.

6 In the study of discourse understanding, what are scripts?

Tasks

A In the analysis of discourse, what is "intertextuality"?
B In conversation analysis, what is the difference between a "preferred" response and a "dispreferred" response? How would you characterize the responses by *She* in these two examples?

   (i) HE: *How about going for some coffee?*
        SHE: *Oh … eh … I'd love to … but you see … I … I'm supposed to get this thing finished … you know.*
   (ii) HE: *I think she's really sexy.*
        SHE: *Well … er … I'm not sure … you may be right … but you see … other people probably don't go for all that … you know … all that make-up … so em sorry but I don't think so.*

C The following extract is from a conversation between two women chatting about people they both knew in high school (Overstreet, 1999: 112–113). The phrase *or something* is used twice by Crystal in this extract. Is she adhering to the Co-operative Principle and the Quality maxim or not? How did you decide?

   JULIE: *I can't remember any ge- guys in our grade that were gay.*
   CRYSTAL: *Larry Brown an' an' John Murphy. I – huh I dunno, I heard John Murphy was dressed – was like a transvestite or something.*
   JULIE: *You're kidding.*
   CRYSTAL: *I – I dunno. That was a – an old rumor, I don't even know if it was true.*
   JULIE: *That's funny.*
   CRYSTAL: *Or cross-dresser or something.*
   JULIE: *Larry – Larry Brown is gay?*

D (i) Identify the main cohesive ties in this first paragraph of a novel (Faulkner, 1929).

   (ii) What do you think "they" were hitting?

Through the fence, between the curling flower spaces, I could see them hitting. They were coming toward where the flag was and I went along the fence. Luster was hunting in the grass by the flower tree. They took the flag out, and they were hitting. Then they put the flag back and they went to the table, and he hit and the other hit. They went on, and I went along the fence. Luster came away from the flower tree and we went along the fence and they stopped and we stopped and I looked through the fence while Luster was hunting in the grass.

E This is a version of a story described in Widdowson (2007). When most people first read this story, they find it confusing. Can you identify the source of this confusion in terms of background knowledge or assumptions?

A man and his son were crossing the street one day when a car suddenly came towards them and hit the boy, knocking him down. In less than ten minutes an ambulance came and took the boy to the nearest hospital. As the boy was being taken into the emergency room, one of the surgeons saw him and cried out, "Oh no. This is my son!"

F (i) What is Critical Discourse Analysis?

   (ii) How might the following text be analyzed using that approach? This text originally appeared in the British newspaper the *Sun* (February 2, 1989) and is cited in van Dijk (1996: 98) and Cameron (2001: 127).

BRITAIN INVADED BY ARMY OF ILLEGALS

Britain is being swamped by a tide of illegal immigrants so desperate for a job that they will work for a pittance in our restaurants, cafés and nightclubs.

Immigration officers are being overwhelmed with work. Last year, 2191 "illegals" were nabbed and sent back home. But there were tens of thousands more, slaving behind bars, cleaning hotel rooms and working in kitchens …

Illegals sneak in by:

- DECEIVING immigration officers when they are quizzed at airports
- DISAPPEARING after their entry visas run out
- FORGING work permits and other documents
- RUNNING AWAY from immigration detention centres

Discussion topics/projects

I   In the study of discourse, a distinction is often made between "new information" (treated as new for the reader or listener) and "given information" (treated as already known by the reader or listener). Read through the following recipe for bread sauce and identify the ways in which given information is presented. (Try to think carefully about carrying out the instructions in the Method section and how many unmentioned things you are assumed to have and use.)

Ingredients: *1 small onion*   *3 oz. fresh breadcrumbs*
                   2 cloves   *1 oz. butter*
                   1 cup of milk   *pepper and salt*

Method: Peel the onion and push cloves into it. Simmer gently with the milk and butter for at least twenty minutes. Remove the onion, pour the milk over the breadcrumbs. Let this stand to thicken and reheat before serving.

(For background reading, see chapter 5 of Brown and Yule, 1983.)

II   According to Deborah Schiffrin, "the analysis of discourse markers is part of the more general analysis of discourse coherence" (1987: 49). Looking at the use of discourse markers (in bold) in the following extract from conversation, do you think that they help to make this discourse more coherent? If any of them were omitted, would it become less coherent? Given these examples, how would you define discourse markers? Do you think the word *like* (used twice here) should be treated as a discourse marker?

*I believe in that. Whatever's gonna happen is gonna happen. I believe … that … **y'know** it's fate. It really is. **Because** eh my husband has a brother, that was killed in an automobile accident, **and** at the same time there was another fellow, in there, that walked away with not even a scratch on him. **And** I really fee- I don't feel y'can push fate, **and** I think a lot of people do. **But** I feel that you were put here for so many, years or whatever the case is, **and** that's how it was meant to be. **Because** like when we got married, we were supposed t'get married uh like about five months later. My husband got a notice t'go into the service **and** we moved it up. **And** my father died the week … after we got married. While we were on our honeymoon. **And** I just felt, that move was meant to be, **because** if not, he wouldn't have been there. **So** eh **y'know** it just s- seems that that's how things work.*

(For background reading, see chapter 3 of Schiffrin, 1987.)

Further reading

Basic treatments

Cutting, J. (2008) *Pragmatics and Discourse* (2nd edition) Routledge

Widdowson, H. (2007) *Discourse Analysis* Oxford University Press

More detailed treatments

Paltridge, B. (2006) *Discourse Analysis* Continuum

Renkema, J. (2004) *Introduction to Discourse Studies* (2nd edition) John Benjamins

Specifically on spoken discourse

Cameron, D. (2001) *Working with Spoken Discourse* Sage

Conversation analysis

Have, P. (2007) *Doing Conversation Analysis* (2nd edition) Sage

Psathas, G. (1995) *Conversation Analysis* Sage

The Gricean maxims

Chapman, S. (2005) *Paul Grice: Philosopher and Linguist* Palgrave Macmillan

Grice, P. (1989) *Studies in the Way of Words* Harvard University Press

Schemas and scripts

Brown, G. and G. Yule (1983) *Discourse Analysis* (chapter 7) Cambridge University Press

Other references

Grice, P. (1975) "Logic and conversation" In P. Cole and J. Morgan (eds.) *Syntax and Semantics 3: Speech Acts* (41–58) Academic Press

Faulkner, W. (1929) *The Sound and the Fury* Jonathan Cape

Overstreet, M. (1999) *Whales, Candlelight and Stuff Like That: General Extenders in English Discourse* Oxford University Press

Sanford, A. and S. Garrod (1981) *Understanding Written Language* Wiley

Schiffrin, D. (1987) *Discourse Markers* Cambridge University Press

van Dijk, T. (1996) "Discourse, power and access" In C. Caldas-Coulthard and M. Coulthard (eds.) *Texts and Practices: Readings in Critical Discourse Analysis* (84–104) Routledge

Widdowson, H. (1978) *Teaching Language as Communication* Oxford University Press

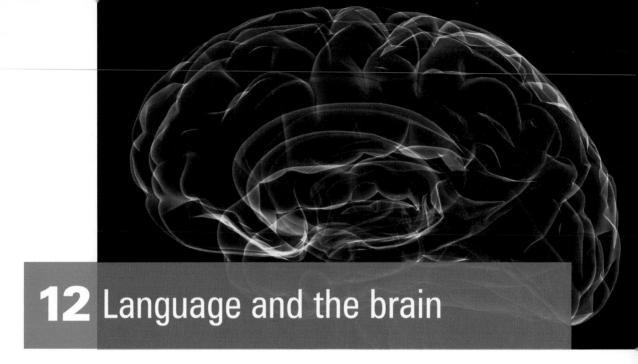

12 Language and the brain

I once had a patient who suffered a right hemisphere stroke and fell to the ground, unable to walk because of a paralyzed left leg. She lay on the floor for two days, not because no one came to her aid, but because she kept blithely reassuring her husband that she was fine, that there was nothing wrong with her leg. Only on the third day did he bring her in for treatment. When I asked her why she could not move her left leg, and held it up for her to see, she said indifferently that it was someone else's leg.

Flaherty (2004)

In the preceding chapters we have reviewed in some detail the various features of language that people use to produce and understand linguistic messages. Where is this ability to use language located? The obvious answer is "in the brain." However, it can't be just anywhere in the brain. For example, it can't be where damage was done to the right hemisphere of the patient's brain in Alice Flaherty's description. The woman could no longer recognize her own leg, but she could still talk about it. The ability to talk was unimpaired and hence clearly located somewhere else in her brain.

Neurolinguistics

The study of the relationship between language and the brain is called **neurolinguistics**. Although this is a relatively recent term, the field of study dates back to the nineteenth century. Establishing the location of language in the brain was an early challenge, but one event incidentally provided a clue.

In September 1848, near Cavendish, Vermont, a construction foreman called Phineas P. Gage was in charge of a construction crew blasting away rocks to lay a new stretch of railway line. As Mr. Gage pushed an iron tamping rod into the blasting hole in a rock, some gunpowder accidentally exploded and sent the three-and-a-half-foot long tamping rod up through his upper left cheek and out from the top of his forehead. The rod landed about fifty yards away. Mr. Gage suffered the type of injury from which, it was assumed, no one could recover. However, a month later, he was up and about, with no apparent damage to his senses or his speech.

The medical evidence was clear. A huge metal rod had gone through the front part of Mr. Gage's brain, but his language abilities were unaffected. He was a medical marvel. The point of this rather amazing tale is that, while language may be located in the brain, it clearly is not situated right at the front.

Language areas in the brain

Since that time, a number of discoveries have been made about the specific parts in the brain that are related to language functions. We now know that the most important parts are in areas above the left ear. In order to describe them in greater detail, we need to look more closely at some of the gray matter. So, take a head, remove hair, scalp, skull, then disconnect the brain stem (connecting the brain to the spinal cord) and cut the corpus callosum (connecting the two hemispheres). If we disregard a certain amount of other material, we will basically be left with two parts, the left hemisphere and the right hemisphere. If we put the right hemisphere aside for now, and place the left hemisphere down so that we have a side view, we'll be looking at something close to the accompanying illustration (adapted from Geschwind, 1991).

The shaded areas in this illustration indicate the general locations of those language functions involved in speaking and listening. We have come to know that these areas exist largely through the examination, in autopsies, of the brains of people who, in life, were known to have specific language disabilities. That is, we have tried to determine where language abilities for normal users must be by finding areas with specific damage in the brains of people who had identifiable language disabilities.

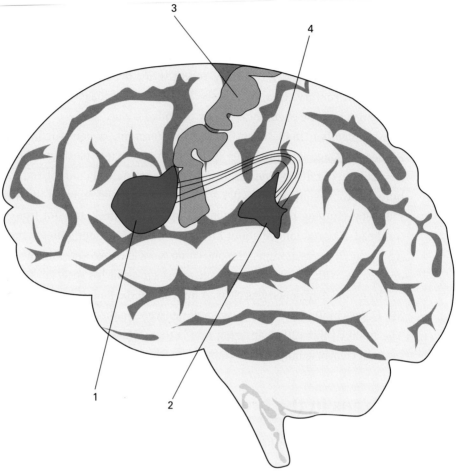

Figure 12.1

Broca's area

The part shown as (1) in the illustration is technically described as the "anterior speech cortex" or, more usually, as **Broca's area**. Paul Broca, a French surgeon, reported in the 1860s that damage to this specific part of the brain was related to extreme difficulty in producing speech. It was noted that damage to the corresponding area on the right hemisphere had no such effect. This finding was first used to argue that language ability must be located in the left hemisphere and since then has been treated as an indication that Broca's area is crucially involved in the production of speech.

Wernicke's area

The part shown as (2) in the illustration is the "posterior speech cortex," or **Wernicke's area**. Carl Wernicke was a German doctor who, in the 1870s, reported that damage to this part of the brain was found among patients who had speech comprehension difficulties. This finding confirmed the left hemisphere location of language ability and led to the view that Wernicke's area is part of the brain crucially involved in the understanding of speech.

The motor cortex and the arcuate fasciculus

The part shown as (3) in the illustration is the **motor cortex**, an area that generally controls movement of the muscles (for moving hands, feet, arms, etc.). Close to Broca's area is the part of the motor cortex that controls the articulatory muscles of the face, jaw, tongue and larynx. Evidence that this area is involved in the physical articulation of speech comes from work reported in the 1950s by two neurosurgeons, Penfield and Roberts (1959). These researchers found that, by applying small amounts of electrical current to specific areas of the brain, they could identify those areas where the electrical stimulation would interfere with normal speech production.

The part shown as (4) in the illustration is a bundle of nerve fibers called the **arcuate fasciculus**. This was also one of Wernicke's discoveries and is now known to form a crucial connection between Wernicke's and Broca's areas.

The localization view

Having identified these four components, it is tempting to conclude that specific aspects of language ability can be accorded specific locations in the brain. This is called the **localization view** and it has been used to suggest that the brain activity involved in hearing a word, understanding it, then saying it, would follow a definite pattern. The word is heard and comprehended via Wernicke's area. This signal is then transferred via the arcuate fasciculus to Broca's area where preparations are made to produce it. A signal is then sent to part of the motor cortex to physically articulate the word.

This is certainly an oversimplified version of what may actually take place, but it is consistent with much of what we understand about simple language processing in the brain. It is probably best to think of any proposal concerning processing pathways in the brain as some form of metaphor that may turn out to be inadequate once we learn more about how the brain functions. The "pathway" metaphor seems quite appealing in an electronic age when we're familiar with the process of sending signals through electrical circuits. In an earlier age, dominated more by mechanical technology, Sigmund Freud subtly employed a "steam engine" metaphor to account for aspects of the brain's activity when he wrote of the effects of repression "building up pressure" to the point of "sudden release." In an even earlier age, Aristotle's metaphor was of the brain as a cold sponge that functioned to keep the blood cool.

In a sense, we are forced to use metaphors mainly because we cannot obtain direct physical evidence of linguistic processes in the brain. Because we have no direct access, we generally have to rely on what we can discover through indirect methods. Most of these methods involve attempts to work out how the system is working from clues picked up when the system has problems or malfunctions.

Tongue tips and slips

We have all experienced difficulty, on some occasion(s), in getting brain and speech production to work together smoothly. (Some days are worse than others, of course.) Minor production difficulties of this sort may provide possible clues to how our linguistic knowledge is organized within the brain.

The tip of the tongue phenomenon

There is, for example, the **tip of the tongue** phenomenon in which we feel that some word is just eluding us, that we know the word, but it just won't come to the surface. Studies of this phenomenon have shown that speakers generally have an accurate phonological outline of the word, can get the initial sound correct and mostly know the number of syllables in the word. This experience also mainly occurs with uncommon words and names. It suggests that our "word-storage" system may be partially organized on the basis of some phonological information and that some words in the store are more easily retrieved than others.

When we make mistakes in this retrieval process, there are often strong phonological similarities between the target word we're trying to say and the mistake we actually produce. For example, speakers produced *secant*, *sextet* and *sexton* when asked to name a particular type of navigational instrument (*sextant*). Other examples are *fire distinguisher* (for "extinguisher") and *transcendental medication* (instead of "meditation"). Mistakes of this type are sometimes referred to as **malapropisms** after a character called Mrs. Malaprop (in a play by Sheridan) who consistently produced "near-misses" for words, with great comic effect. Another comic character in a TV program who was known for his malapropisms was Archie Bunker, who once suggested that *We need a few laughs to break up the monogamy.*

Slips of the tongue

Another type of speech error is commonly described as a **slip of the tongue**. This produces expressions such as *make a long shory stort* (instead of "make a long story short"), *use the door to open the key*, and *a fifty-pound dog of bag food*. Slips of this type are sometimes called **spoonerisms** after William Spooner, an Anglican clergyman at Oxford University, who was renowned for his tongue-slips. Most of the slips attributed to him involve the interchange of two initial sounds, as when he addressed a rural group as *noble tons of soil*, or described God as *a shoving leopard to his flock*, or in this complaint to a student who had been absent from classes: *You have hissed all my mystery lectures*.

Most everyday slips of the tongue, however, are not as entertaining. They are often simply the result of a sound being carried over from one word to the next, as in *black bloxes* (for "black boxes"), or a sound used in one word in anticipation of its occurrence in the next word, as in *noman numeral* (for "roman numeral"), or *a tup of tea* ("cup"), or *the most highly played player* ("paid"). The last example is close to the reversal type of slip, illustrated by *shu flots*, which may not make you *beel fetter* if you're suffering from a *stick neff*, and it's always better to *loop before you leak*. The last two examples involve the interchange of word-final sounds and are much less common than word-initial slips.

It has been argued that slips of this type are never random, that they never produce a phonologically unacceptable sequence, and that they indicate the existence of different stages in the articulation of linguistic expressions. Although the slips are mostly treated as errors of articulation, it has been suggested that they may result from "slips of the brain" as it tries to organize linguistic messages.

Slips of the ear

One other type of slip may provide some clues to how the brain tries to make sense of the auditory signal it receives. These have been called **slips of the ear** and can result, for example, in our hearing *great ape* and wondering why someone should be looking for one in his office. (The speaker actually said "gray tape.") A similar type of misunderstanding seems to be behind the child's report that in Sunday school, everyone was singing about a bear called "Gladly" who was cross-eyed. The source of this slip turned out to be a line from a religious song that went *Gladly the cross I'd bear*. It may also be the case that some malapropisms (e.g. *transcendental medication*) originate as slips of the ear.

Some of these humorous examples of slips may give us a clue to the normal workings of the human brain as it copes with language. However, some problems with language production and comprehension are the result of much more serious disorders in brain function.

Aphasia

If you have experienced any of those "slips" on occasion, then you will have some hint of the types of experience that some people live with constantly. Those people suffer from different types of language disorders, generally described as "aphasia." **Aphasia** is defined as an impairment of language function due to localized brain damage that leads to difficulty in understanding and/or producing linguistic forms.

The most common cause of aphasia is a stroke (when a blood vessel in the brain is blocked or bursts), though traumatic head injuries from violence or an accident may have similar effects. Those effects can range from mild to severe reduction in the ability to use language. Someone who is aphasic often has interrelated language disorders, in that difficulties in understanding can lead to difficulties in production, for example. Consequently, the classification of different types of aphasia is usually based on the primary symptoms of someone having difficulties with language.

Broca's aphasia

The serious language disorder known as **Broca's aphasia** (also called "motor aphasia") is characterized by a substantially reduced amount of speech, distorted articulation and slow, often effortful speech. What is said often consists almost entirely of lexical morphemes (e.g. nouns, verbs). The frequent omission of functional morphemes (e.g. articles, prepositions) and inflections (e.g. plural -*s*, past tense -*ed*) has led to the characterization of this type of aphasic speech as "agrammatic." In **agrammatic** speech, the grammatical markers are missing.

An example of speech produced by someone whose aphasia was not severe is the following answer to a question regarding what the speaker had for breakfast:

I eggs and eat and drink coffee breakfast

However, this type of disorder can be quite severe and result in speech with lots of hesitations and really long pauses (marked by ...): *my cheek ... very annoyance ... main is my shoulder ... achin' all round here*. Some patients can also have lots of difficulty in articulating single words, as in this attempt to say "steamship": *a stail ... you know what I mean ... tal ... stail*. In Broca's aphasia, comprehension is typically much better than production.

Wernicke's aphasia

The type of language disorder that results in difficulties in auditory comprehension is sometimes called "sensory aphasia," but is more commonly known as **Wernicke's aphasia**. Someone suffering from this disorder can actually produce very fluent speech which is, however, often difficult to make sense of. Very general terms are used, even in response to specific requests for information, as in this sample: *I can't talk all of the things I do, and part of the part I can go alright, but I can't tell from the other people.*

Difficulty in finding the correct word, sometimes referred to as **anomia**, also happens in Wernicke's aphasia. To overcome their word-finding difficulties, speakers use different strategies such as trying to describe objects or talking about their purpose, as in *the thing to put cigarettes in* (for "ashtray"). In the following example (from Lesser & Milroy, 1993), the speaker tries a range of strategies when he can't come up with the word ("kite") for an object in a picture.

> *it's blowing, on the right, and er there's four letters in it, and I think it begins with a C – goes – when you start it then goes right up in the air – I would I would have to keep racking my brain how I would spell that word – that flies, that that doesn't fly, you pull it round, it goes up in the air*

Conduction aphasia

One other, much less common, type of aphasia has been associated with damage to the arcuate fasciculus and is called **conduction aphasia**. Individuals suffering from this disorder sometimes mispronounce words, but typically do not have articulation problems. They are fluent, but may have disrupted rhythm because of pauses and hesitations. Comprehension of spoken words is normally good. However, the task of repeating a word or phrase (spoken by someone else) creates major difficulty, with forms such as *vaysse* and *fosh* being reported as attempted repetitions of the words "base" and "wash." What the speaker hears and understands can't be transferred very successfully to the speech production area.

It should be emphasized that many of these symptoms (e.g. word-finding difficulty) can occur in all types of aphasia. They can also occur in more general disorders resulting from brain disease, as in dementia and Alzheimer's disease. Difficulties in speaking can also be accompanied by difficulties in writing. Impairment of auditory comprehension tends to be accompanied by reading difficulties. Language disorders of the type we have described are almost always the result of injury to the left hemisphere. This left hemisphere dominance for language has also been demonstrated by another approach to the investigation of language and the brain.

Dichotic listening

An experimental technique that has demonstrated a left hemisphere dominance for syllable and word processing is called the **dichotic listening test**. This technique uses the generally established fact that anything experienced on the right-hand side of the body is processed in the left hemisphere, and anything on the left side is processed in the right hemisphere. As illustrated in Flaherty's (2004) description at the beginning of this chapter, a stroke in the right hemisphere resulted in paralysis of the left leg. So, a basic assumption would be that a signal coming in the right ear will go to the left hemisphere and a signal coming in the left ear will go to the right hemisphere.

With this information, an experiment is possible in which a subject sits with a set of earphones on and is given two different sound signals simultaneously, one through each earphone. For example, through one earphone comes the syllable *ga* or the word *dog*, and through the other earphone at exactly the same time comes *da* or *cat*. When asked to say what was heard, the subject more often correctly identifies the sound that

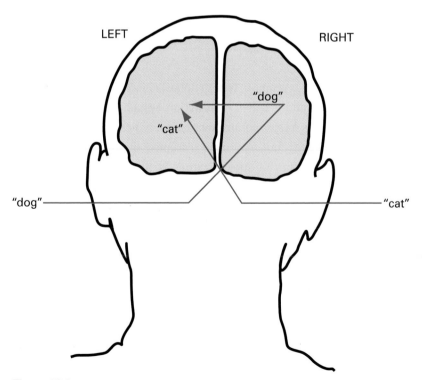

Figure 12.2

came via the right ear. This is known as the **right ear advantage** for linguistic sounds. The process involved is best understood with the help of the accompanying illustration. (You're looking at the back of this head.)

In this process, the language signal received through the left ear is first sent to the right hemisphere and then has to be sent to the left hemisphere (language center) for processing. This non-direct route takes longer than a linguistic signal received through the right ear and going directly to the left hemisphere. First signal to get processed wins.

The right hemisphere appears to have primary responsibility for processing a lot of other incoming signals that are non-linguistic. In the dichotic listening test, it can be shown that non-verbal sounds (e.g. music, coughs, traffic noises, birds singing) are recognized more often via the left ear, meaning they are processed faster via the right hemisphere. So, among the specializations of the human brain, the right hemisphere is first choice for non-language sounds (among other things) and the left hemisphere specializes in language sounds (among other things too).

These specializations may actually have more to do with the type of processing, rather than the type of material, that is handled best by each of the two hemispheres. The essential distinction seems to be between analytic processing, such as recognizing the smaller details of sounds, words and phrase structures in rapid sequence, done with the "left brain," and holistic processing, such as identifying more general structures in language and experience, done with the "right brain."

The critical period

The apparent specialization of the left hemisphere for language is usually described in terms of lateral dominance or **lateralization** (one-sidedness). Since the human child does not emerge from the womb as a fully articulate language-user, it is generally thought that the lateralization process begins in early childhood. It coincides with the period during which language acquisition takes place. During childhood, there is a period when the human brain is most ready to receive input and learn a particular language. This is sometimes called the "sensitive period" for language acquisition, but is more generally known as **the critical period**.

Though some think it may start earlier, the general view is that the critical period for first language acquisition lasts from birth until puberty. If a child does not acquire language during this period, for any one of a number of reasons, then he or she will find it almost impossible to learn language later on. In one unfortunate but well-documented case, we have gained some insight into what happens when the critical period passes without adequate linguistic input.

Genie

In 1970, a girl who became known as "Genie" was admitted to a children's hospital in Los Angeles. She was thirteen years old and had spent most of her life tied to a chair in a small closed room. Her father was intolerant of any kind of noise and had beaten her whenever she made a sound as a child. There had been no radio or television, and Genie's only other human contact was with her mother who was forbidden to spend more than a few minutes with the child to feed her. Genie had spent her whole life in a state of physical, sensory, social and emotional deprivation.

As might be expected, Genie was unable to use language when she was first brought into care. However, within a short period of time, she began to respond to the speech of others, to try to imitate sounds and to communicate. Her syntax remained very simple. The fact that she went on to develop some speaking ability and understand a fairly large number of English words provides some evidence against the notion that language cannot be acquired at all after the critical period. Yet her diminished capacity to develop grammatically complex speech does seem to support the idea that part of the left hemisphere of the brain is open to accept a language program during childhood and, if no program is provided, as in Genie's case, then the facility is closed down.

In Genie's case, tests demonstrated that she had no left hemisphere language facility. So, how was she able to learn any part of language, even in a limited way? Those same tests appeared to indicate the quite remarkable fact that Genie was using the right hemisphere of her brain for language functions. In dichotic listening tests, she showed a very strong left ear advantage for verbal as well as non-verbal signals. Such a finding, supported by other studies of right brain function, raises the possibility that our capacity for language is not limited to only one or two specific areas, but is based on more complex connections extending throughout the whole brain.

When Genie was beginning to use speech, it was noted that she went through some of the same early "stages" found in normal child language acquisition. In the next chapter, we will investigate what these normal stages are.

Study questions

1   What is a more common name for the posterior speech cortex?
2   Is the use of "fire distinguisher" instead of "fire extinguisher" a spoonerism or a malapropism?
3   What is aphasia?
4   Which type of aphasia is characterized by speech like this: *speech … two times … read … wr … ripe, er, rike, er, write … ?*
5   What happens in a dichotic listening test?
6   What is the critical period?

Tasks

A   We made no distinction between the left and right hemispheres in terms of shape or size, assuming they were symmetrical. However, on closer inspection, there is some asymmetry in the lateralization of the brain. What seems to be the main source of this difference between the physiology of the two hemispheres? Should this difference be treated as support for the phrenology model of human brain function?

B   What is meant by the "bathtub effect" in descriptions of features of speech errors? Do any examples of speech errors in this chapter illustrate this effect?

C   In this chapter we focused on the left hemisphere and how it is affected by impairments. What happens to the language of an individual after damage in the right hemisphere?

D   How would you go about analyzing the following extract from Radford *et al.* (2009) as more likely to be indicative of agrammatism or paragrammatism? (The speaker is trying to talk about a lady's shoe.)

Now there there I remember. I have you there what I thought was the … a lady one. Another. With a very short. Very very clever done. Do that the one two. Go. But there's the liver. And there is the new. And so on.

E   The following extract from Buckingham and Kertesz (1976: 21) is discussed in Obler and Gjerlow (1999: 59) as an illustration of "neologistic jargon aphasia." Can you identify any characteristics of this condition that show up in the language used by this speaker? Is the syntax badly impaired? Are morphological features such as inflections used normally or not? Does the speaker have word-finding difficulties? Would you say that this aphasia is more likely to be associated with Broca's area or Wernicke's area? (The speaker is responding to the question, "Who is running the store now?")

I don't know. Yes, the bick, uh, yes I would say that the mick daysis nosis or chpickters. Course, I have also missed on the carfter teck. Do you know what that is? I've, uh, token to ingish. They have been toast sosilly. They'd have been put to myafa and made palis and, uh, myadakal senda you. That is me alordisdus. That makes anacronous senda.

F   What happens in "brain imaging" procedures such as CAT scans, fMRI scans and PET scans that might help in the study of language and the brain?

Discussion topics/projects

I   One aphasia patient was asked to read aloud the written words on the left below and, in each case, actually said the words on the right. Is there any pattern to be found in these errors? Does this type of phenomenon provide any clues to the way words may be stored and accessed in the brain?

ambition	→ career	commerce	→ business
anecdote	→ narrator	mishap	→ accident
applause	→ audience	parachute	→ balloon
apricot	→ peach	thermometer	→ temperature
arithmetic	→ mathematics	victory	→ triumph

(For background reading, see Allport, 1983, the source of these examples.)

II   The story of Genie is full of remarkable episodes. The following extract is from Rymer (1993), quoting Susan Curtiss, a linguist who worked with Genie for many years. How would you explain events like this?

"Genie was the most powerful nonverbal communicator I've ever come across," Curtiss told me. "The most extreme example of this that comes to mind: Because of her obsession, she would notice and covet anything plastic that anyone had. One day we were walking – I think we were in Hollywood. I would act like an idiot, sing operatically, to get her to release some of that tension she always had. We reached the corner of this very busy intersection, and the light turned red, and we stopped. Suddenly, I heard the sound – it's a sound you can't mistake – of a purse being spilled. A woman in a car that had stopped at the intersection was emptying her purse, and she got out of the car and ran over and gave it to Genie and then ran back to the car. A plastic purse. Genie hadn't said a word."

(For background reading, see chapter 17 of Rymer, 1993.)

Further reading

Basic treatments

Heilman, K. (2002) *Matter of Mind* (chapter 2) Oxford University Press

Obler, L. and K. Gjerlow (1999) *Language and the Brain* Cambridge University Press

More detailed treatments

Caplan, D. (1996) *Language: Structure, Processing and Disorders* MIT Press

Ingram, J. (2007) *Neurolinguistics* Cambridge University Press

On Phineas Gage

Damasio, A. (1994) *Descartes' Error* Putnam

Brain structure

Springer, S. and G. Deutsch (2001) *Left Brain, Right Brain* (6th edition) W. H. Freeman

Slips

Bond, Z. (1999) *Slips of the Ear* Academic Press

Poulisse, N. (1999) *Slips of the Tongue* John Benjamins

Aphasia

Goodglass, H., E. Kaplan and B. Barresi (2001) *The Assessment of Aphasia and Related Disorders* (3rd edition) Lippincott, Williams and Wilkins

Lesser, R. and L. Milroy (1993) *Linguistics and Aphasia* Longman

Dichotic listening

Hugdahl, K. and R. Davidson (2004) *The Asymmetrical Brain* (441–476) MIT Press

The critical period

Singleton, D. and L. Ryan (2004) *Language Acquisition: The Age Factor* (2nd edition) Multilingual Matters

Genie

Curtiss, S. (1977) *Genie: A Psycholinguistic Study of a Modern-day Wild Child* Academic Press

Rymer, R. (1993) *Genie* HarperCollins

Other references

Allport, G. (1983) "Language and cognition" In R. Harris (ed.) *Approaches to Language* (80–94) Pergamon Press

Buckingham, H. and A. Kertesz (1976) *Neologistic Jargon Aphasia* Swets and Zeitlinger

Geschwind, N. (1991) "Specializations of the Human Brain" In W. Wang (ed.) *The Emergence of Language* (72–87) W. H. Freeman

Penfield, W. and L. Roberts (1959) *Speech and Brain Mechanisms* Princeton University Press

Radford, A., M. Atkinson, D. Britain, H. Clahsen and A. Spencer (2009) *Linguistics: An Introduction* (2nd edition) Cambridge University Press

13 First language acquisition

CHILD:	Want other one spoon, Daddy.
FATHER:	You mean, you want the other spoon.
CHILD:	Yes, I want other one spoon, please Daddy.
FATHER:	Can you say "the other spoon"?
CHILD:	Other ... one ... spoon.
FATHER:	Say "other."
CHILD:	Other.
FATHER:	"Spoon."
CHILD:	Spoon.
FATHER:	"Other spoon."
CHILD:	Other ... spoon. Now give me other one spoon?

Braine (1971)

First language acquisition is remarkable for the speed with which it takes place. Long before a child starts school, he or she has become an extremely sophisticated language-user, operating a system for self-expression and communication that no other creature, or computer, comes close to matching. In addition to the speed of acquisition, the fact that it generally occurs, without overt instruction, for all children, regardless of great differences in their circumstances, provides strong support for the idea that there is an innate predisposition in the human infant to acquire language. We can think of this as a special capacity for language with which each newborn child is endowed. By itself, however, this inborn language capacity is not enough.

Acquisition

The process of language acquisition has some basic requirements. During the first two or three years of development, a child requires interaction with other language-users in order to bring the general language capacity into contact with a particular language such as English. We have already seen, in the case of Genie (Chapter 12), that a child who does not hear or is not allowed to use language will learn no language. We have also identified the importance of cultural transmission (Chapter 2), meaning that the particular language a child learns is not genetically inherited, but is acquired in a particular language-using environment.

The child must also be physically capable of sending and receiving sound signals in a language. All infants make "cooing" and "babbling" noises during their first year, but congenitally deaf infants stop after about six months. So, in order to speak a language, a child must be able to hear that language being used. By itself, however, hearing language sounds is not enough. One case, reported by Moskowitz (1991), demonstrated that, with deaf parents who gave their normal-hearing son ample exposure to television and radio programs, the boy did not acquire an ability to speak or understand English. What he did learn very effectively, by the age of three, was the use of American Sign Language, that is, the language he used to interact with his parents. A crucial requirement appears to be the opportunity to interact with others via language.

Input

Under normal circumstances, human infants are certainly helped in their language acquisition by the typical behavior of older children and adults in the home environment who provide language samples, or **input**, for the child. Adults such as mom, dad and the grandparents tend not to address the little creature before them as if they are involved in normal adult-to-adult conversation. There is not much of this: *Well, John Junior, shall we invest in blue chip industrials, or would grain futures offer better short-term prospects?* However, there does seem to be a lot of this: *Oh, goody, now Daddy push choo-choo?* The characteristically simplified speech style adopted by someone who spends a lot of time interacting with a young child is called **caregiver speech**.

Salient features of this type of speech (also called "motherese" or "child-directed speech") are the frequent use of questions, often using exaggerated intonation, extra loudness and a slower tempo with longer pauses. In the early stages, this type of speech also incorporates a lot of forms associated with "babytalk." These are either simplified words (*tummy*, *nana*) or alternative forms, with repeated simple sounds and syllables, for things in the child's environment (*choo-choo*, *poo-poo*, *pee-pee*, *wa-wa*).

Built into a lot of caregiver speech is a type of conversational structure that seems to assign an interactive role to the young child even before he or she becomes a speaking participant. If we look at an extract from the speech of a mother to her child (aged 1 year 1 month) as if it were a two-party conversation, then this type of structuring becomes apparent. Notice how the mother reacts to the child's actions and vocalizations as if they were turns in the conversation. (This example is from Brunner, 1983.)

MOTHER: *Look!*
CHILD: (touches pictures)
MOTHER: *What are those?*
CHILD: (vocalizes a babble string and smiles)
MOTHER: *Yes, there are rabbits.*
CHILD: (vocalizes, smiles, looks up at mother)
MOTHER: (laughs) *Yes, rabbit.*
CHILD: (vocalizes, smiles)
MOTHER: *Yes.* (laughs)

Caregiver speech is also characterized by simple sentence structures and a lot of repetition. If the child is indeed in the process of working out a system of putting sounds and words together, then these simplified models produced by the interacting adult may serve as good clues to the basic structural organization involved. Moreover, it has generally been observed that the speech of those regularly interacting with very young children changes and becomes more elaborate as the child begins using more and more language. Several stages in the early acquisition process have been identified.

The acquisition schedule

All normal children develop language at roughly the same time, along much the same schedule. Since we could say the same thing for sitting up, crawling, standing, walking, using the hands and many other physical activities, it would seem that the language acquisition schedule has the same basis as the biologically determined development of motor skills. This biological schedule is tied very much to the maturation of the infant's brain.

We could think of the child as having the biological capacity to cope with distinguishing certain aspects of linguistic input at different stages during the early years of life. Long before children begin to talk, they have been actively processing what they hear. We can identify what very young children are paying attention to by the way they increase or decrease "sucking behavior" in response to speech sounds or turn their heads in the direction of those sounds. At one month, for example, an infant is capable of distinguishing between sounds such as [ba] and [pa]. During the first three months, the child develops a range of crying styles, with different patterns for different needs, produces big smiles in response to a speaking face, and starts to create distinct vocalizations.

Cooing and babbling

The earliest use of speech-like sounds has been described as **cooing**. During the first few months of life, the child gradually becomes capable of producing sequences of vowel-like sounds, particularly high vowels similar to [i] and [u]. By four months of age, the developing ability to bring the back of the tongue into regular contact with the back of the palate allows the infant to create sounds similar to the velar consonants [k] and [g], hence the common description as "cooing" or "gooing" for this type of production. Speech perception studies have shown that by the time they are five months old, babies can already hear the difference between the vowels [i] and [a] and discriminate between syllables like [ba] and [ga].

Between six and eight months, the child is sitting up and producing a number of different vowels and consonants, as well as combinations such as *ba-ba-ba* and *ga-ga-ga*. This type of sound production is described as **babbling** In the later babbling stage, around nine to ten months, there are recognizable intonation patterns to the consonant and vowel combinations being produced, as well as variation in the combinations such as *ba-ba-da-da*. Nasal sounds also become more common and certain syllable sequences such as *ma-ma-ma* and *da-da-da* are inevitably interpreted by parents as versions of "mama" and "dada" and repeated back to the child.

As children begin to pull themselves into a standing position during the tenth and eleventh months, they become capable of using their vocalizations to express emotions and emphasis. This late babbling stage is characterized by more complex syllable combinations (*ma-da-ga-ba*), a lot of sound-play and attempted imitations. This "pre-language" use of sound provides the child with some experience of the social role of speech because adults tend to react to the babbling, however incoherent, as if it is actually the child's contribution to social interaction.

One note of caution should be sounded at this point. Child language researchers certainly report very carefully on the age of any child whose language they study. However, they are also very careful to point out that there is substantial variation among children in terms of the age at which particular features of linguistic development occur. So, we should always treat statements concerning development stages such as "by six months" or "by the age of two" as approximate and subject to variation in individual children.

The one-word stage

Between twelve and eighteen months, children begin to produce a variety of recogniz-able single-unit utterances. This period, traditionally called the **one-word stage**, is characterized by speech in which single terms are uttered for everyday objects such as "milk," "cookie," "cat," "cup" and "spoon" (usually pronounced [pun]). Other forms such as [ʌsæ] may occur in circumstances that suggest the child is producing a version of *What's that*, so the label "one-word" for this stage may be misleading and a term such as "single-unit" would be more accurate. We sometimes use the term **holophras-tic** (meaning a single form functioning as a phrase or sentence) to describe an utterance that could be analyzed as a word, a phrase, or a sentence.

While many of these holophrastic utterances seem to be used to name objects, they may also be produced in circumstances that suggest the child is already extending their use. An empty bed may elicit the name of a sister who normally sleeps in the bed, even in the absence of the person named. During this stage, then, the child may be capable of referring to *Karen* and *bed*, but is not yet ready to put the forms together to produce a more complex phrase. Well, it is a lot to expect from someone who can only walk with a stagger and has to come down stairs backwards.

The two-word stage

Depending on what we count as an occurrence of two distinct words used together, the **two-word stage** can begin around eighteen to twenty months, as the child's vocabulary moves beyond fifty words. By the time the child is two years old, a variety of combinations, similar to *baby chair*, *mommy eat*, *cat bad*, will usually have appeared. The adult interpretation of such combinations is, of course, very much tied to the context of their utterance. The phrase *baby chair* may be taken as an expression of possession (= this is baby's chair), or as a request (= put baby in chair), or as a statement (= baby is in the chair), depending on different circumstances.

Whatever it is that the child actually intends to communicate through such expres-sions, the significant functional consequences are that the adult behaves as if commu-nication is taking place. That is, the child not only produces speech, but also receives feedback confirming that the utterance worked as a contribution to the interaction. Moreover, by the age of two, whether the child is producing 200 or 300 distinct "words," he or she will be capable of understanding five times as many, and will typically be treated as an entertaining conversational partner by the principal caregiver.

Telegraphic speech

Between two and two-and-a-half years old, the child begins producing a large number of utterances that could be classified as "multiple-word" speech. The salient feature of these utterances ceases to be the number of words, but the variation in word forms that begins to appear. Before we investigate this development, we should note a stage that is described as **telegraphic speech**. This is characterized by strings of words (lexical morphemes) in phrases or sentences such as *this shoe all wet*, *cat drink milk* and *daddy go bye-bye*. The child has clearly developed some sentence-building capacity by this stage and can get the word order correct. While this type of telegram-format speech is being produced, a number of grammatical inflections begin to appear in some of the word forms and simple prepositions (*in*, *on*) are also used.

By the age of two-and-a-half, the child's vocabulary is expanding rapidly and the child is initiating more talk while increased physical activity includes running and jumping. By three, the vocabulary has grown to hundreds of words and pronunciation has become closer to the form of adult language. At this point, it is worth considering what kind of influence the adults have in the development of the child's speech.

The acquisition process

As the linguistic repertoire of the child increases, it is often assumed that the child is, in some sense, being "taught" the language. This idea is not really supported by what the child actually does. For the vast majority of children, no one provides any instruction on how to speak the language. Nor should we picture a little empty head gradually being filled with words and phrases. A more accurate view would have the children actively constructing, from what is said to them, possible ways of using the language. The child's linguistic production appears to be mostly a matter of trying out constructions and testing whether they work or not.

It is simply not possible that the child is acquiring the language principally through a process of imitating adult speech. Certainly, children can be heard to repeat versions of what adults say on occasion and they are clearly in the process of adopting a lot of vocabulary from the speech they hear. However, adults simply do not produce many of the expressions that turn up in children's speech. Notice how, in the following extract (from Clark, 1993), the child creates a totally new verb (*to Woodstock*) in the context.

NOAH: (*picking up a toy dog*) *This is Woodstock.*
    (He bobs the toy in Adam's face)
ADAM: *Hey Woodstock, don't do that.*
    (Noah persists)
ADAM: *I'm going home so you won't Woodstock me.*

It is also unlikely that adult "corrections" are a very effective determiner of how the child speaks. A lot of very amusing conversational snippets, involving an adult's attempt to correct a child's speech, seem to demonstrate the hopelessness of the task. One example (*other one spoon*) was quoted at the beginning of the chapter. Even when the correction is attempted in a more subtle manner, the child will continue to use a personally constructed form, despite the adult's repetition of what the correct form should be. Note that in the following dialog (quoted in Cazden, 1972) the child, a four-year-old, is neither imitating the adult's speech nor accepting the adult's correction.

CHILD: *My teacher **holded** the baby rabbits and we patted them.*
MOTHER: *Did you say your teacher **held** the baby rabbits?*
CHILD: *Yes.*
MOTHER: *What did you say she did?*
CHILD: *She **holded** the baby rabbits and we patted them.*
MOTHER: *Did you say she **held** them tightly?*
CHILD: *No, she **holded** them loosely.*

One factor that seems to be important in the child's acquisition process is the actual use of sound and word combinations, either in interaction with others or in wordplay, alone. One two-year-old, described in Weir (1966), was tape-recorded as he lay in bed alone and could be heard playing with words and phrases, *I go dis way … way bay … baby do dis bib … all bib … bib … dere.* Word play of this type seems to be an important element in the development of the child's linguistic repertoire. The details of this development beyond the telegraphic stage have been traced through the linguistic features that begin to turn up on a regular basis in the steady stream of speech emerging from the little chatterbox.

Developing morphology

By the time a child is two-and-a-half years old, he or she is going beyond telegraphic speech forms and incorporating some of the inflectional morphemes that indicate the grammatical function of the nouns and verbs used. The first to appear is usually the *-ing* form in expressions such as *cat sitting* and *mommy reading book.*

The next morphological development is typically the marking of regular plurals with the -s form, as in *boys* and *cats*. The acquisition of the plural marker is often accompanied by a process of **overgeneralization**. The child overgeneralizes the apparent rule of adding -s to form plurals and will talk about *foots* and *mans*. When the alternative pronunciation of the plural morpheme used in *houses* (i.e. ending in [-əz]) comes into use, it too is given an overgeneralized application and forms such as *boyses* or *footses* can be heard. At the same time as this overgeneralization is taking place, some children also begin using irregular plurals such as *men* quite appropriately for a while, but then try out the general rule on the forms, producing expressions like *some mens* and *two feets*, or even *two feetses*. Not long after, the use of the possessive inflection -'s occurs in expressions such as *girl's dog* and *Mummy's book*.

At about the same time, different forms of the verb "to be," such as *are* and *was*, begin to be used. The appearance of forms such as *was* and, at about the same time, *went* and *came* should be noted. These are irregular past-tense forms that we would not expect to hear before the more regular forms. However, they do typically precede the appearance of the -ed inflection. Once the regular past-tense forms (*walked*, *played*) begin appearing in the child's speech, the irregular forms may disappear for a while, replaced by overgeneralized versions such as *goed* and *comed*. For a period, the -ed inflection may be added to everything, producing such oddities as *walkeded* and *wented*. As with the plural forms, the child works out (usually after the age of four) which forms are regular and which are not.

Finally, the regular -s marker on third person singular present-tense verbs appears. It occurs first with full verbs (*comes*, *looks*) and then with auxiliaries (*does*, *has*).

Throughout this sequence there is a great deal of variability. Individual children may produce "good" forms one day and "odd" forms the next. The evidence suggests that the child is working out how to use the linguistic system while focused on communication and interaction rather than correctness. For the child, the use of forms such as *goed* and *foots* is simply a means of trying to say what he or she means during a particular stage of development. Those embarrassed parents who insist that the child didn't hear such things at home are implicitly recognizing that "imitation" is not the primary force in first language acquisition.

Developing syntax

Similar evidence against "imitation" as the basis of the child's speech production has been found in studies of the syntactic structures used by young children. One child, specifically asked to repeat what she heard, would listen to an adult say forms such as *the owl who eats candy runs fast* and then repeat them in the form *owl eat candy and he run fast*. It is clear that the child understands what the adult is saying. She just has her own way of expressing it.

There have been numerous studies of the development of syntax in children's speech. We will look at the development of two structures that seem to be acquired in a regular way by most English-speaking children. In the formation of questions and the use of negatives, there appear to be three identifiable stages. The ages at which children go through these stages can vary quite a bit, but the general pattern seems to be that Stage 1 occurs between 18 and 26 months, Stage 2 between 22 and 30 months, and Stage 3 between 24 and 40 months. (The overlap in the periods during which children go through these stages is a natural effect of the different rates at which different children normally develop these and other structures.)

Forming questions

In forming questions, the child's first stage has two procedures. Simply add a Wh-form (*Where, Who*) to the beginning of the expression or utter the expression with a rise in intonation towards the end, as in these examples:

Where kitty?   *Doggie?*
Where horse go?   *Sit chair?*

In the second stage, more complex expressions can be formed, but the rising intonation strategy continues to be used. It is noticeable that more Wh-forms come into use, as in these examples:

What book name?   *You want eat?*
Why you smiling? *See my doggie?*

In the third stage, the required movement of the auxiliary in English questions (*I can have* … ⇒ *Can I have* …?) becomes evident in the child's speech, but doesn't automatically spread to all Wh-question types. In fact, some children beginning school in their fifth or sixth year may still prefer to form Wh-questions (especially with negatives) without the type of inversion found in adult speech (e.g. *Why kitty can't* …? instead of *Why can't kitty* …?). Apart from these problems with Wh-questions and continuing trouble with the morphology of verbs (e.g. *Did I caught* …? instead of *Did I catch* … ?), Stage 3 questions are generally quite close to the adult model, as in these examples:

Can I have a piece?   *Did I caught it?*
Will you help me?   *How that opened?*
What did you do?   *Why kitty can't stand up?*

Forming negatives

In the case of negatives, Stage 1 seems to involve a simple strategy of putting *No* or *Not* at the beginning, as in these examples:

no mitten   *not a teddy bear*   *no fall*   *no sit there*

In the second stage, the additional negative forms *don't* and *can't* appear, and with *no* and *not*, are increasingly used in front of the verb rather than at the beginning of the sentence, as in these examples:

He no bite you   *I don't want it*
That not touch   *You can't dance*

The third stage sees the incorporation of other auxiliary forms such as *didn't* and *won't* while the typical Stage 1 forms disappear. A very late acquisition is the negative form *isn't*, with the result that some Stage 2 forms (with *not* instead of *isn't*) continue to be used for quite a long time, as in the examples:

I didn't caught it   *He not taking it*
She won't let go   *This not ice cream*

The study of the developing use of negative forms has produced some delightful examples of children operating their own rules for negative sentences. One famous example (from McNeill, 1966) also shows the futility of overt adult "correction" of children's speech.

CHILD: *Nobody don't like me.*
MOTHER: *No, say "nobody likes me."*
CHILD: *Nobody don't like me.*
   (Eight repetitions of this dialog)
MOTHER: *No, now listen carefully; say "nobody likes me."*
CHILD: *Oh! Nobody don't likes me.*

Developing semantics

The anecdotes that parents retell about their child's early speech (to the intense embarrassment of the grown-up child) usually involve examples of the strange use of words. Having been warned that flies bring germs into the house, one child was asked what "germs" were and the answer was "something the flies play with." It is not always possible to determine so precisely the meanings that children attach to the words they use.

It seems that during the holophrastic stage many children use their limited vocabulary to refer to a large number of unrelated objects. One child first used *bow-wow* to refer to a dog and then to a fur piece with glass eyes, a set of cufflinks and even a bath thermometer. The word *bow-wow* seemed to have a meaning like "object with shiny bits." Other children often extend *bow-wow* to refer to cats, cows and horses.

This process is called **overextension** and the most common pattern is for the child to overextend the meaning of a word on the basis of similarities of shape, sound and size, and, to a lesser extent, movement and texture. Thus the word *ball* is extended to all kinds of round objects, including a lampshade, a doorknob and the moon. Or, a *tick-tock* is initially used for a watch, but can also be used for a bathroom scale with a round dial. On the basis of size, presumably, the word *fly* was first used for the insect and then came to be used for specks of dirt and even crumbs of bread. Apparently due to similarities of texture, the expression *sizo* was first used by one child for scissors, and then extended to all metal objects. The semantic development in a child's use of words is usually a process of overextension initially, followed by a gradual process of narrowing down the application of each term as more words are learned.

Although overextension has been well-documented in children's speech production, it isn't necessarily used in speech comprehension. One two-year-old used *apple*, in speaking, to refer to a number of other round objects like a tomato and a ball, but had no difficulty picking out *the apple*, when asked, from a set of round objects including a ball and a tomato.

One interesting feature of the young child's semantics is the way certain lexical relations are treated. In terms of hyponymy, the child will almost always use the "middle"-level term in a hyponymous set such as *animal – dog – poodle*. It would seem more logical to learn the most general term (*animal*), but all evidence indicates that children first use *dog* with an overextended meaning close to the meaning of "animal." This may be connected to a similar tendency in adults, when talking to young children, to refer to *flowers* (not the more general *plants*, or the more specific *tulips*).

It also seems that antonymous relations are acquired fairly late (after the age of five). In one study, a large number of kindergarten children pointed to the same heavily laden apple tree when asked *Which tree has more apples?* and also when asked *Which tree has less apples?*. They just seem to think the correct response will be the larger one, disregarding the difference between *more* and *less*. The distinctions between a number of other pairs such as *before/after* and *buy/sell* also seem to be later acquisitions.

Despite the fact that the child is still to acquire a large number of other aspects of his or her first language through the later years of childhood, it is normally assumed that, by the age of five, the child has completed the greater part of the basic language acquisition process. According to some, the child is then in a good position to start learning a second (or foreign) language. However, most people don't start trying to learn another language until much later. The question that always arises is: if first language acquisition was so straightforward and largely automatic, why is learning a second language so difficult? We will try to answer that question in the next chapter.

Study questions

1 Can you describe four typical features of caregiver speech?
2 Why are some of the infant's first sounds described as "cooing"?
3 During which stage do children typically first produce syllable sequences similar to "mama" and "dada" and how old are they?
4 At about what age do children typically begin producing varied syllable combinations such as *ma-da-ga-ba*?
5 Which of these two utterances was produced by the older child and why?

   (a) *I not hurt him*
   (b) *No the sun shining*

6 What is the term used to describe the process involved when a child uses one word like *ball* to refer to an apple, an egg, a grape and a ball?

Tasks

A The "sucking behavior" of infants was mentioned in this chapter in connection with early speech perception. How can it be measured and what can we learn from these measurements?

B There is a typical sequence in the acquisition of some functional and inflectional morphemes by English-speaking children. This sequence was documented in Brown (1973) and is summarized in O'Grady (2005: 94).

   Try to create a chart, with stages 1–10, showing the typical sequence of acquisition of English morphemes (*-ing*), alongside appropriate examples (*cat sitting*), using the following examples from children's speech:

   a cat, boys, cats, cat sitting, he came, he walked, in bag, it comes, it opened, it went away, Karen's bed, mommy reading book, mommy's book, not in that, on bed, she knows, that on top, the dog, this is no, you are look

C What is meant by MLU ("Mean Length of Utterance") in child language studies? Can you work out the MLU of this small sample of utterances: *no big box, daddy eat red apple, daddy eats apples, no eating that, that mommy's book.*

D The following examples are from the speech of three children. Identify which child is at the earliest stage, which is next in order, and which is at the most advanced stage. Describe those features in the examples from each child's speech that support your ordering.

   CHILD X: *You want eat?*
   I can't see my book.
   Why you waking me up?

CHILD Y: *Where those dogs goed?*

You didn't eat supper.

Does lions walk?

CHILD Z: *No picture in there.*

Where momma boot?

Have some?

E   Do boys and girls develop language differently in the early stages? Have any differences been documented in how they speak and how they are spoken to?

F   There are two distinct theoretical perspectives on how first language acquisition takes place, generally labeled the "rational" perspective and the "empirical" perspective. We can characterize each perspective with a number of tenets or principles, as illustrated in the following statements. Divide these statements into two sets, one representing the rational perspective and the other representing the empirical perspective. Which perspective do you prefer?

   (a)   Acquisition proceeds in a piecemeal fashion, building on what is already acquired.
   (b)   Acquisition takes places along a predetermined path.
   (c)   Children begin life with some knowledge of the possible units of language.
   (d)   Children learn to say things unrelated to input.
   (e)   General learning mechanisms account for language learning.
   (f)   It takes time to integrate new linguistic information with existing knowledge.
   (g)   Language learning is independent of other kinds of learning.
   (h)   New linguistic knowledge is acquired very quickly.
   (i)   Speech is perceived from the start as distinct from any other physical stimuli.
   (j)   There are only a few fixed possibilities of language structures to learn.
   (k)   There are many possible language structures to be learned.
   (l)   There is no initial distinction between speech and any other physical stimuli.
   (m)   There is no pre-programmed knowledge of language.
   (n)   What children learn to say is directly related to input.

Discussion topics/projects

I   In our discussion of developing semantics, we focused mainly on the use of nouns. In the following examples, a young child (age shown as year; month) seems to be using verbs in a way that is not based on typical adult uses and hence unlikely to be "imitations." Is there any consistent pattern in these examples? Can you suggest an explanation for this child's choice of words for the kinds of actions being described?

(2;3) *I come it closer so it won't fall* (= bring it closer)

(2;6) *Mommy, can you stay this open?* (= keep this open)

(2;8) *Daddy, go me round* (= make me go round)

(2;9) *I'm gonna fall this on her* (= drop this on her)

(2;11) *How would you flat it?* (= flatten it)

(3;1) *I'm singing him* (= making him sing)

(For background reading, see chapter 6 of Clark, 2009.)

II　Which of these three metaphors of first language acquisition (from Valian, 1999) would you agree with and why?

　(i)　According to the copy metaphor, "the child gradually aligns her speech with that of her language community" and "the focus is on an active role for input."

　(ii)　According to the hypothesis testing metaphor, "the child forms and tests hypotheses about what structures exist in the language" and "the child is not copying the input."

　(iii)　According to the trigger metaphor, "the child neither copies the input nor evaluates it" and "a given piece of input triggers the correct parametric value," assuming the child has innate knowledge of a small set of possible parametric values.

(For background reading, see Valian, 1999.)

Further reading

Basic treatments

Apel, K. and J. Masterson (2001) *Beyond Baby Talk* Three Rivers Press

O'Grady, W. (2005) *How Children Learn Language* Cambridge University Press

More detailed treatments

Clark, E. (2009) *First Language Acquisition* (2nd edition) Cambridge University Press

Lust, B. (2006) *Child Language* Cambridge University Press

Speech perception in infants

Jusczyk, P. (1997) *The Discovery of Spoken Language* MIT Press

Babbling

Oller, D. (2000) *The Emergence of the Speech Capacity* Lawrence Erlbaum

Morphological development

Moskowitz, B. (1991) "The acquisition of language" In W. Wang (ed.) *The Emergence of Language* (131–149) W. H. Freeman

Syntactic development

O'Grady, W. (1997) *Syntactic Development* University of Chicago Press

Semantic development

Bloom, P. (2002) *How Children Learn the Meanings of Words* MIT Press

Rational and empirical perspectives (in that order)

Pinker, S. (1994) *The Language Instinct* William Morrow

Tomasello, M. (2003) *Constructing a Language* Harvard University Press

Other references

Brown, R. (1973) *A First Language* Harvard University Press

Bruner, J. (1983) *Child's Talk: Learning to Use Language* Norton

Cazden, C. (1972) *Child Language and Education* Holt

Clark, E. (1993) *The Lexicon in Acquisition* Cambridge University Press

McNeill, D. (1966) "Developmental psycholinguistics" In F. Smith and G. Miller (eds.) *The Genesis of Language* (15–84) MIT Press

Valian, V. (1999) "Input and language acquisition" In W. Ritchie and T. Bhatia (eds.) *Handbook of Child Language Acquisition* (497–530) Academic Press

Weir, R. (1966) "Questions on the learning of phonology" In F. Smith and G. Miller (eds.) *The Genesis of Language* (153–168) MIT Press

14 Second language acquisition/learning

"Easter is a party for to eat of the lamb," the Italian nanny explained. "One too may eat of the chocolate."

"And who brings the chocolate?" the teacher asked.

I knew the word, so I raised my hand, saying, "The rabbit of Easter. He bring of the chocolate."

"A rabbit?" The teacher, assuming I'd used the wrong word, positioned her index fingers on top of her head, wriggling them as though they were ears. "You mean one of these? A *rabbit* rabbit?"

"Well, sure," I said. "He come in the night when one sleep on a bed. With a hand he have a basket and foods."

The teacher sighed and shook her head. As far as she was concerned, I had just explained everything that was wrong with my country. "No, no," she said. "Here in France the chocolate is brought by a big bell that flies in from Rome."

I called for a time-out. "But how do the bell know where you live?"

"Well," she said, "how does a rabbit?"

Sedaris (2000)

Some children grow up in a social environment where more than one language is used and are able to acquire a second language in circumstances similar to those of first language acquisition. Those fortunate individuals are bilingual (see Chapter 18). However, most of us are not exposed to a second language until much later and, like David Sedaris, our ability to use a second language, even after years of study, rarely matches ability in our first language. There is something of an enigma in this, since there is apparently no other system of "knowledge" that we can learn better at two or three years of age than at thirteen or thirty. A number of reasons have been suggested to account for this enigma, and a number of different approaches have been proposed to help learners become as effective communicating in a second language (L2) as they are in their first language (L1).

Second language learning

A distinction is sometimes made between learning in a "foreign language" setting (learning a language that is not generally spoken in the surrounding community) and a "second language" setting (learning a language that is spoken in the surrounding community). That is, Japanese students in an English class in Japan are learning English as a foreign language (EFL) and, if those same students were in an English class in the USA, they would be learning English as a second language (ESL). In either case, they are simply trying to learn another language, so the expression **second language learning** is used more generally to describe both situations.

Acquisition and learning

A more significant distinction is made between acquisition and learning. The term **acquisition** is used to refer to the gradual development of ability in a language by using it naturally in communicative situations with others who know the language. The term **learning**, however, applies to a more conscious process of accumulating knowledge of the features, such as vocabulary and grammar, of a language, typically in an institutional setting. (Mathematics, for example, is learned, not acquired.)

Activities associated with learning have traditionally been used in language teaching in schools and have a tendency, when successful, to result in more knowledge "about" the language (as demonstrated in tests) than fluency in actually using the language (as demonstrated in social interaction). Activities associated with acquisition are those experienced by the young child and, by analogy, those who "pick up" a second language from long periods spent in interaction, constantly using the language, with native speakers of the language. Those individuals whose L2 exposure is primarily a learning type of experience tend not to develop the same kind of general proficiency as those who have had more of an acquisition type of experience.

Acquisition barriers

For most people, the experience with an L2 is fundamentally different from their L1 experience and it is hardly conducive to acquisition. They usually encounter the L2 during their teenage or adult years, in a few hours each week of school time (rather than via the constant interaction experienced as a child), with a lot of other things going on (young children have little else to do), and with an already known language available for most of their daily communicative requirements. Despite the fact that insufficient time, focus and incentive undermine many L2 learning attempts, there are some individuals who seem to be able to overcome the difficulties and develop an ability to use the L2 quite effectively, though not usually sounding like a native speaker (i.e. someone for whom it is an L1).

However, even in ideal acquisition situations, very few adults seem to reach native-like proficiency in using an L2. There are individuals who can achieve great expertise in the written language, but not the spoken language. One example is Joseph Conrad, who wrote novels in English that became classics of English literature, but whose English speech retained the strong Polish accent of his L1. This might suggest that some features of an L2, such as vocabulary and grammar, are easier to learn than others such as pronunciation. Indeed, without early experience using the sounds and intonation of the L2, even highly fluent adult learners are likely to be perceived as having an "accent" of some kind.

This type of observation is sometimes taken as evidence that, after the critical period for language acquisition has passed, around the time of puberty, it becomes very difficult to acquire another language fully (see Chapter 12). We might think of this process in terms of our inherent capacity for language being strongly taken over by features of the L1, with a resulting loss of flexibility or openness to receive the features of another language.

Against this view, it has been demonstrated that students in their early teens are quicker and more effective L2 learners in the classroom than, for example, seven-year-olds. It may be, of course, that the effective learning of an L2 (even with a trace of an accent) requires a combination of factors. The optimum age for learning may be during the years from about ten to sixteen when the flexibility of our inherent capacity for language has not been completely lost, and the maturation of cognitive skills allows a more effective analysis of the regular features of the L2 being learned.

Affective factors

Yet even during this proposed optimum age for L2 learning, there may exist an acquisition barrier of quite a different kind. Teenagers are typically much more self-conscious than younger children. If there is a strong element of unwillingness or embarrassment in attempting to produce the different sounds of another language, then it may override whatever physical and cognitive abilities there are. If this self-consciousness is accompanied by a lack of empathy with the other culture (for example, feeling no identification with its speakers or their customs), then the subtle effects of not really wanting to sound like a Russian or a German or an American may strongly inhibit the learning process.

This type of emotional reaction, or "affect," may also be caused by dull textbooks, unpleasant classroom surroundings or an exhausting schedule of study and/or work.

All these negative feelings or experiences are **affective factors** that can create a barrier to acquisition. Basically, if we are stressed, uncomfortable, self-conscious or unmotivated, we are unlikely to learn very much.

Children seem to be less constrained by affective factors. Descriptions of L2 acquisition in childhood are full of instances where young children quickly overcome their inhibitions as they try to use new words and phrases. Adults can sometimes overcome their inhibitions too. In one intriguing study, a group of adult L2 learners volunteered to have their self-consciousness levels reduced by having their alcohol levels gradually increased. Up to a certain point, the pronunciation of the L2 noticeably improved, but after a certain number of drinks, as we might expect, pronunciations deteriorated rapidly. Courses introducing "French with cognac" or "Russian with vodka" may provide a partial solution, but the inhibitions are likely to return with sobriety.

Focus on method

Despite all these barriers, the need for instruction in other languages has led to a variety of educational approaches and methods aimed at fostering L2 learning. As long ago as 1483, William Caxton used his newly established printing press to produce a book of *Right good lernyng for to lerne shortly frenssh and englyssh*. He was not the first to compile exercise material for L2 learners and his phrase-book format with customary greetings (*Syre, god you kepe. I haue not seen you in longe tyme*) has many modern counterparts. More recent approaches designed to promote L2 learning have tended to reflect different theoretical views on how an L2 might best be learned.

The grammar–translation method

The most traditional approach is to treat L2 learning in the same way as any other academic subject. Vocabulary lists and sets of grammar rules are used to define the target of learning, memorization is encouraged, and written language rather than spoken language is emphasized. This method has its roots in the traditional teaching of Latin and is described as the **grammar–translation method**. This label has actually been applied to the approach by its detractors, who have pointed out that its emphasis on learning about the L2 often leaves students quite ignorant of how the language might be used in everyday conversation. Although this method clearly produced many successful L2 users over the centuries, it is sometimes claimed that students can leave school, having achieved high grades in French class via this method, yet find themselves at a loss when confronted by the way the French in France actually use their language.

The audiolingual method

A very different approach, emphasizing the spoken language, became popular in the middle of the twentieth century. It involved a systematic presentation of the structures of the L2, moving from the simple to the more complex, in the form of drills that the student had to repeat. This approach, called the **audiolingual method**, was strongly influenced by a belief that the fluent use of a language was essentially a set of "habits" that could be developed with a lot of practice. Much of this practice involved hours spent in a language laboratory repeating oral drills. Versions of this approach are still used in language teaching, but its critics have pointed out that isolated practice in drilling language patterns bears no resemblance to the interactional nature of actual spoken language use. Moreover, it can be incredibly boring.

Communicative approaches

More recent revisions of the L2 learning experience can best be described as **communicative approaches**. They are partially a reaction against the artificiality of "pattern-practice" and also against the belief that consciously learning the grammar rules of a language will necessarily result in an ability to use the language. Although there are many different versions of how to create communicative experiences for L2 learners, they are all based on a belief that the functions of language (what it is used for) should be emphasized rather than the forms of the language (correct grammatical or phonological structures). Classroom lessons are likely to be organized around concepts such as "asking for things" in different social settings, rather than "the forms of the past tense" in different sentences. These changes have coincided with attempts to provide more appropriate materials for L2 learning that has a specific purpose, as in "English for medical personnel" or "Japanese for business people."

Focus on the learner

The most fundamental change in the area of L2 learning in recent years has been a shift from concern with the teacher, the textbook and the method to an interest in the learner and the acquisition process. For example, one radical feature of most communicative approaches is the toleration of "errors" produced by students. Traditionally, "errors" were regarded negatively and had to be avoided or eradicated. The more recent acceptance of such errors in learners' use of the L2 is based on a fundamental shift in perspective from the more traditional view of how L2 learning takes place.

Rather than consider a Spanish (L1) speaker's production of *in the room there are three womens* as simply a failure to learn correct English (which can be remedied through extra practice of the correct form), we can look at this utterance as an indication of the natural L2 acquisition process in action. An "error," then, is not something that hinders a student's progress, but is probably a clue to the active learning progress being made by the student as he or she tries out ways of communicating in the new language. Just as children acquiring their L1 produce certain types of ungrammatical forms at times, so we might expect the L2 learner to produce similar forms at certain stages (see Chapter 13). The example of *womens* might be seen as a type of overgeneralization (of -*s* as the plural marker), used by the learner in accordance with the most common way of making plural forms in English.

Transfer

Of course, some errors may be due to "transfer" (also called "crosslinguistic influence"). **Transfer** means using sounds, expressions or structures from the L1 when performing in the L2. For example, a Spanish (L1) speaker who produces *take it from the side inferior* may be trying to use the Spanish adjective *inferior* (= *lower* in English) and placing it after the noun, as is typical in Spanish constructions. If the L1 and L2 have similar features (e.g. marking plural on the ends of nouns), then the learner may be able to benefit from the **positive transfer** of L1 knowledge to the L2. On the other hand, transferring an L1 feature that is really different from the L2 (e.g. putting the adjective after the noun) results in **negative transfer** and it may make the L2 expression difficult to understand. We should remember that negative transfer (sometimes called "interference") is more common in the early stages of L2 learning and often decreases as the learner develops familiarity with the L2.

Interlanguage

On close inspection, the language produced by L2 learners contains a large number of "errors" that seem to have no connection to the forms of either the L1 or L2. For example, the Spanish L1 speaker who says in English *She name is Maria* is producing a form that is not used by adult speakers of English, does not occur in English L1 acquisition by children, and is not based on a structure in Spanish. Evidence of this sort suggests that there is some in-between system used in the L2 acquisition process that certainly contains aspects of the L1 and L2, but which is an inherently variable system with rules of its own. This system is called an **interlanguage** and it is now considered to be the basis of all L2 production.

If some learners develop a fairly fixed repertoire of L2 expressions, containing many forms that do not match the target language, and seem not to be progressing any further, their interlanguage is said to have "fossilized." The process of **fossilization** in L2 pronunciation seems to be the most likely basis of what is perceived as a foreign accent. However, an interlanguage is not designed to fossilize. It will naturally develop and become a more effective means of L2 communication given appropriate conditions. Discovering just what count as the appropriate conditions for successful L2 learning is an ongoing area of investigation.

Motivation

There are several factors that combine in a profile of a successful L2 learner. Obviously, the motivation to learn is important. Many learners have an **instrumental motivation**. That is, they want to learn the L2 in order to achieve some other goal, such as completing a school graduation requirement or being able to read scientific publications, but not really for any social purposes. In contrast, those learners with an **integrative motivation** want to learn the L2 for social purposes, in order to take part in the social life of a community using that language and to become an accepted member of that community.

It is also worth noting that those who experience some success in L2 communication are among the most motivated to learn. So, motivation may be as much a result of success as a cause. A language-learning situation that provides support and encourages students to try to use whatever L2 skills they have in order to communicate successfully must consequently be more helpful than one that dwells on errors, corrections and a failure to be perfectly accurate. Indeed, the learner who is willing to guess, risks making mistakes and tries to communicate in the L2 will tend, given the opportunity, to be more successful. An important part of that opportunity is the availability of "input."

Input and output

The term **input** is used, as in L1 acquisition (see Chapter 13), to describe the language that the learner is exposed to. To be beneficial for L2 learning, that input has to be comprehensible, because we can't process what we don't understand. Input can be made comprehensible by being simpler in structure and vocabulary, as in the variety of speech called **foreigner talk**. Native speakers of English may try to ask an international student *How are you getting on in your studies?*, but, if not understood, may switch to *English class, you like it?* This type of foreigner talk may be beneficial, not only for immediate communicative success, but also for providing the beginning learner with clearer and comprehensible examples of the basic structure of the L2 as input.

As the learner's interlanguage develops, however, there is a need for more interaction and the kind of "negotiated input" that arises in conversation. **Negotiated input** is L2 material that the learner can acquire in interaction through requests for clarification while active attention is being focused on what is said. In the following interaction (from Pica *et al.*, 1991), notice how the learner, a non-native speaker (NNS) of English, and the English native speaker (NS) negotiate meaning together. The comprehensible input (i.e. using the word *triangle* to describe a shape) is provided at a point where the learner needs it and is paying attention to the meaning in context.

NS: *like part of a triangle?*
NNS: *what is triangle?*
NS: *a triangle is a shape um it has three sides*
NNS: *a peak?*
NS: *three straight sides*
NNS: *a peak?*
NS: *yes it does look like a mountain peak, yes*
NNS: *only line only line?*
NS: *okay two of them, right? one on each side? a line on each side?*
NNS: *yes*
NS: *little lines on each side?*
NNS: *yes*
NS: *like a mountain?*
NNS: *yes*

In this type of interaction, the learner experiences the benefits of both receiving input (hearing the L2) and producing output (speaking the L2). The opportunity to produce comprehensible **output** in meaningful interaction seems to be another important element in the learner's development of L2 ability, yet it is one of the most difficult things to provide in large L2 classes. One solution has been to create different types of tasks and activities in which learners have to interact with each other, usually in small groups or pairs, to exchange information or solve problems. Despite fears that learners will simply learn each other's "mistakes," the results of such **task-based learning** provide overwhelming evidence of more and better L2 use by learners. The goal of such activities is not that the learners will know more about the L2, but that they will develop communicative competence in the L2.

Communicative competence

Communicative competence can be defined as the general ability to use language accurately, appropriately, and flexibly. The first component is **grammatical competence**, which involves the accurate use of words and structures. Concentration on grammatical competence only, however, will not provide the learner with the ability to interpret or produce L2 expressions appropriately.

The ability to use appropriate language is the second component, called **sociolinguistic competence**. It enables the learner to know when to say *Can I have some water?* versus *Give me some water!* according to the social context. Much of what was discussed in terms of pragmatics (see Chapter 10) has to become familiar in the cultural context of the L2 if the learner is to develop sociolinguistic competence.

The third component is called **strategic competence**. This is the ability to organize a message effectively and to compensate, via strategies, for any difficulties. In L2 use, learners inevitably experience moments when there is a gap between communicative intent and their ability to express that intent. Some learners may just stop talking (bad idea), whereas others will try to express themselves using a **communication strategy** (good idea). For example, a Dutch L1 speaker wanted to refer to *een hoefijzer* in English, but didn't know the English word. So, she used a communication strategy. She created a way of referring to the object by using vocabulary she already knew, saying *the things that horses wear under their feet, the iron things* and the listener understood immediately what she meant (*horseshoes*). This flexibility in L2 use is a key element in communicative success. In essence, strategic competence is the ability to overcome potential communication problems in interaction.

Applied linguistics

In attempting to investigate the complex nature of L2 learning, we have to appeal to ideas not only from linguistic analysis, but from other fields such as communication studies, education, psychology and sociology. This large-scale endeavor is often described as **applied linguistics**. Because it represents an attempt to deal with a large range of practical issues involving language (not only L2 learning), applied linguistics has created connections with fields as diverse as anthropology (see Chapter 20), neurolinguistics (Chapter 12), social psychology (Chapter 19) and sign language studies (next chapter).

Study questions

1   What do you think "the Joseph Conrad phenomenon" refers to?
2   Why do we say that mathematics is learned, not acquired?
3   What are four typical barriers to acquiring an L2 as an adult compared to L1 acquisition as a child?
4   What is the difference between positive and negative transfer?
5   What happens when an interlanguage fossilizes?
6   What are the three components of communicative competence?

Tasks

A   What is the difference between "input" and "intake" in L2 learning?
B   What arguments are presented in support of "the output hypothesis" in L2 studies?
C   What is meant by a "stylistic continuum" in the study of interlanguage?
D   What is contrastive analysis and how might it help us understand the following types of L2 errors in English produced by students whose L1 is Spanish?

   (a)   *He must wear the tie black.*
   (b)   *My study is modernes languages.*
   (c)   *He no understand you.*
   (d)   *It was the same size as a ball of golf.*
   (e)   *We stayed at home because was raining.*
   (f)   *I eat usually eggs for breakfast.*

E   One feature of interlanguage grammars is the apparent existence of temporary rules that don't match the rules of either the L1 or the L2, as described in Gass and Selinker (2001). The following examples are from a speaker whose L1 was Arabic. Can you describe the rule(s) he seems to be using for the use of plural -*s* in English?

   (a)   *How many brother you have?*
   (b)   *The streets are very wide.*
   (c)   *I finish in a few day.*
   (d)   *Here is a lot of animal in the houses.*
   (e)   *Many people live in villages.*
   (f)   *There are two horses in the picture.*
   (g)   *Both my friend from my town.*
   (h)   *Seven days in a week.*

F   Classroom activities in communicative language teaching create situations in which L2 learners produce different types of communication strategies. Can you match each type of strategy (1–6) with one of the examples (a–f)? How would you rank them from least to most effective?

1 appeal for assistance

2 approximation

3 circumlocution

4 message abandonment

5 mime or gesture

6 sound imitation

(a) *the color is dark and … the size is just as a hand … it is made of …la- leather*
(talking about a glove)

(b) *how do you say in English that word … we say in Spanish "bujía"*
(talking about a candlestick)

(c) *the man he play a … you know … it makes a* [whistles] *like that*
(talking about a small musical pipe)

(d) *the first you … like put together and you … do the next step … I can't … I'm sorry*
(talking about a plunge coffee maker)

(e) *maybe is something like a rope*
(talking about an electrical cord)

(f) *the oval is the big one and the other part is what take to*
[demonstrates holding the handle of a brush]
(talking about a Christmas tree stand)

Discussion topics/projects

I Which of the following statements do you agree with? What reasons would you give to support your opinions?

(i) People with high IQs are good language learners.

(ii) Most mistakes in the L2 are due to interference from the L1.

(iii) L2 learners should not be allowed to hear mistakes or they will learn them.

(iv) Teachers should teach simple L2 structures before complex ones.

(v) Teachers should teach only one L2 grammatical rule at a time and practice it thoroughly before introducing the next rule.

(For background reading, see chapter 7 of Lightbown and Spada, 2006.)

II "Communicative Language Teaching is premised on the assumption that learners do not need to be taught grammar before they can communicate but will acquire it naturally as part of the process of learning to communicate. In some versions of Communicative Language Teaching, then, there is no place at all for the direct teaching of grammar" (Ellis, 1997).

(i) Do you believe that second language learning is possible with only a focus on function ("communication") and no focus on form ("grammar")?

(ii) Why do you think that there are renewed calls for "form-focused instruction" after many years of Communicative Language Teaching?

(For background reading, see chapter 9 of Ellis, 1997.)

Further reading

Basic treatments

Ellis, R. (1997) *Second Language Acquisition* Oxford University Press

Lightbown, P. and N. Spada (2006) *How Languages are Learned* (3rd edition) Oxford University Press

More detailed treaments

Gass, S. and L. Selinker (2001) *Second Language Acquisition* Lawrence Erlbaum

Saville-Troike, M. (2006) *Introducing Second Language Acquisition* Cambridge University Press

Bilingual acquisition

Yip, M. and S. Matthews (2007) *The Bilingual Child* Cambridge University Press

The effects of age

Singleton, D. and L. Ryan (2004) *Language Acquisition: The Age Factor* (2nd edition) Multilingual Matters

Focus on method

Richards, J. and T. Rodgers (2001) *Approaches and Methods in Language Teaching* (2nd edition) Cambridge University Press

Focus on the learner

VanPatten, B. (2003) *From Input to Output: A Teacher's Guide to Second Language Acquisition* McGraw-Hill

Pronunciation with wine

Guiora, A., B. Beit-Hallahmi, R. Brannon, C. Dull and T. Scovel (1972) "The effects of experimentally induced change in ego states on pronunciation ability in a second language: an exploratory study" *Comprehensive Psychiatry* 13: 5–23

The horseshoe example

Kellerman, E., T. Ammerlan, T. Bongaerts and N. Poulisse (1990) "System and hierarchy in L2 compensatory strategies" In R. Scarcella, E. Anderson and S. Krashen (eds.) *Developing Communicative Competence in a Second Language* (163–178) Newbury House

Applied linguistics

Cook, G. (2003) *Applied Linguistics* Oxford University Press

Other references

Pica, T., L. Holliday, N. Lewis, D. Berducci and J. Newman (1991) "Language learning through interaction: what role does gender play?" *Studies in Second Language Acquisition* 11: 63–90

15 Gestures and sign languages

This old lady, in her nineties, but sharp as a pin, would sometimes fall into a peaceful reverie. As she did so, she might have seemed to be knitting, her hands in constant complex motion. But her daughter, also a signer, told me she was not knitting but thinking to herself, thinking in Sign. And even in sleep, I was further informed, the old lady might sketch fragmentary signs on the counterpane. She was dreaming in Sign.   Sacks (1989)

When we considered the process of language acquisition, we concentrated on the fact that what is naturally acquired by most children is speech. Yet this is not the only way that a first language can be acquired. Just as most children of English-speaking or Spanish-speaking parents naturally acquire English or Spanish at a very early age, so the deaf children of deaf parents naturally acquire **Sign** (or **Sign Language**). Later in life, as Oliver Sacks observed, they may even use Sign when they "talk" in their sleep. If those children grow up in American homes, they will typically acquire American Sign Language, also known as Ameslan or **ASL**, as their version of Sign. With a signing population of at least half a million, and perhaps as many as two million, ASL is a widely used language in the United States. The size of this population is quite remarkable since, until relatively recently, the use of ASL was discouraged in most educational institutions for the deaf. In fact, historically, very few teachers of the deaf learned ASL, or even considered it to be a "real" language at all. For many people, Sign wasn't language, it was "merely gestures."

Gestures

Although both Sign and **gestures** involve the use of the hands (with other parts of the body), they are rather different. Sign is like speech and is used instead of speaking, whereas gestures are mostly used while speaking. Examples of gestures are making a downward movement with one hand while talking about not doing very well in a class or making a twisting motion with one hand as you describe trying to open a bottle or jar. The gestures are just part of the way in which meaning is expressed and can be observed while people are speaking and signing.

In the study of non-verbal behavior, a distinction can be drawn between gestures and emblems. **Emblems** are signals such as "thumbs up" (= things are good) or "shush" (= keep quiet) that function like fixed phrases and do not depend on speech. Emblems are conventional and depend on social knowledge (e.g. what is and isn't considered offensive in a particular social world). In Britain, the use of two fingers (the index and middle fingers together) raised in a V-shape traditionally represents one emblem (= victory) when the back of the hand faces the sender and a quite different emblem (= I insult you in a very offensive way) when the back of the hand faces the receiver of the signal. It is important, when visiting different places, not to get the local emblems mixed up.

Types of gestures

Within the set of gestures that accompany speech, we can distinguish between those that echo, in some way, the content of the spoken message and those that indicate something being referred to. **Iconics** are gestures that seem to be a reflection of the meaning of what is said, as when we trace a square in the air with a finger while saying *I'm looking for a small box*. By itself, an iconic gesture doesn't "mean" the same as what is said, but it may add "meaning." In one particularly clear example (from McNeill, 1992), a woman was moving her forearm up and down, with a closed hand, as if holding a weapon, while she was saying *and she chased him out again*. The communicated message, including the weapon (actually an umbrella), was accomplished through speech and gesture combined.

Another common group of gestures can be described as **deictics**. As noted in Chapter 10, the term "deictic" means "pointing" and we often use gestures to point to things or people while talking. We can use deictics in the current context, as when we use a hand to indicate a table (with a cake on it) and ask someone *Would you like some cake?*. We can also use the same gesture and the same table (with cake no longer on it) when we later say *That cake was delicious*. In this case, the gesture and the speech combine to accomplish successful reference to something that only exists in shared memory rather than in the current physical space.

There are other gestures, such as those described as **beats**, which are short quick movements of the hand or fingers. These gestures accompany the rhythm of talk and are often used to emphasize parts of what is being said or to mark a change from describing events in a story to commenting on those events. As with other gestures, these hand movements accompany speech, but are not typically used as a way of speaking. When hand movements are used in order to "speak," we can describe them as part of a sign language.

Types of sign languages

There are two general categories of language involving the use of signs: alternate sign languages and primary sign languages. By definition, an **alternate sign language** is a system of hand signals developed by speakers for limited communication in a specific context where speech cannot be used. In some religious orders where there are rules of silence, restricted alternate sign languages are used (e.g. by monks in a monastery). Among some Australian Aboriginal groups, there are periods (e.g. times of bereavement) when speech is avoided completely and quite elaborate alternate sign languages are used instead. Less elaborate versions are to be found in some special working circumstances (e.g. among bookmakers at British racecourses or traders in commodity exchanges). In all these examples, the users of alternate sign languages have another first language that they can speak.

In contrast, a **primary sign language** is the first language of a group of people who do not use a spoken language with each other. British Sign Language (BSL) and French Sign Language (SLF), as used for everyday communication among members of the deaf communities of Britain and France, are primary sign languages. Contrary to popular belief, these different primary sign languages do not share identical signs and are not mutually intelligible. British Sign Language is also very different from American Sign Language (ASL) which, for historical reasons, has more in common with French Sign Language.

We will focus our attention on ASL in order to describe some features of a primary sign language, but first, we have to account for the fact that, until fairly recently, it was not treated as a possible language at all.

Oralism

It was not until the 1960s that any serious consideration was given to the status of ASL as a natural language, following the work of William Stokoe (1960). Before that, it was genuinely believed by many well-intentioned teachers that the use of sign language by deaf children, perhaps because it was considered too "easy," actually inhibited the acquisition of the English language. Since spoken English was what those teachers believed the children really needed, a teaching method generally known as **oralism** dominated deaf education during most of the twentieth century. This method required that the students practice English speech sounds and develop lip-reading skills. Despite its resounding lack of success, the method was never seriously challenged, perhaps because of an insidious belief among many during this period that, in educational terms, most deaf children could not achieve very much anyway.

Whatever the reasons, the method produced few students who could speak intelligible English (less than 10 percent) and even fewer who could lip-read (around 4 percent). While oralism was failing, the use of ASL was surreptitiously flourishing. Many deaf children of hearing parents actually acquired the banned language at schools for the deaf, not from the teachers, but from other children. Since only one in ten deaf children had deaf parents from whom they acquired sign language, it would seem that the cultural transmission of ASL has been mostly carried out from child to child.

Signed English

Substantial changes in deaf education have taken place in recent years, but there is still an emphasis on the learning of English, written rather than spoken. As a result, many institutions promote the learning of what is known as **Signed English** (also called Manually Coded English or MCE). This is essentially a means of producing signs that correspond to the words in an English sentence, in English word order. In many ways, Signed English is designed to facilitate interaction between the deaf and the hearing community. Its greatest advantage is that it seems to present a much less formidable learning task for the hearing parent of a deaf child and provides the parent with a communication system to use with the child.

For similar reasons, hearing teachers in deaf education can make use of Signed English when they sign at the same time as they speak. It is also easier for those hearing interpreters who produce a simultaneous translation of public speeches or lectures for deaf audiences. Many deaf people actually prefer interpreters to use Signed English because they say there is a higher likelihood of understanding the message. Apparently, when some interpreters try to use ASL, the message seems to suffer, for the simple reason that, unless they learned ASL in childhood, few hearing people are proficient at it.

However, Signed English is neither English nor ASL. When used to produce an exact version of a spoken English sentence, Signed English takes twice as long as the production of that same sentence in either English or ASL. Consequently, in practice, exact versions are rarely produced and a hybrid format emerges, using some word-signs and incomplete English word order. (In many cases, even the word-signs are changed to be more English-like, with a G letter-shape, for example, being used to represent the English word *glad*, rather than the actual ASL sign for this concept.) It's sort of like producing messages with German word order, but containing French nouns, adjectives and verbs. The product is neither French nor German, but (one might argue) it is one way of getting French speakers to learn how German sentences are constructed.

The type of argument just presented is what has been used in support of teaching Signed English in deaf schools because one of the major aims is to prepare students to be able to read and write English. Underlying that aim is the principle that deaf education should be geared towards enabling the deaf, for obvious economic reasons, to take part in the hearing world. The net effect is to make ASL a kind of underground language, used only in deaf–deaf interaction. As such, this natural sign language of the deaf continues to be poorly understood and subject to many of the myths that have existed throughout its history.

Origins of ASL

It would be very surprising if ASL really was "a sort of gestured version of English," as some have claimed. Historically, ASL developed from the French Sign Language used in a Paris school founded in the eighteenth century. Early in the nineteenth century, a teacher from this school, named Laurent Clerc, was brought to the United States by an American minister called Thomas Gallaudet who was trying to establish a school for deaf children. Clerc not only taught deaf children, he also trained other teachers. During the nineteenth century, this imported version of sign language, incorporating features of indigenous natural sign languages used by the American deaf, evolved into what became known as ASL. Such origins help to explain why users of ASL and users of BSL (in Britain) do not share a common sign language.

The structure of signs

As a natural language functioning in the visual mode, ASL is designed for the eyes, not the ears. In producing linguistic forms in ASL, signers use four key aspects of visual information. These are described as the **articulatory parameters** of ASL in terms of shape, orientation, location and movement. We can describe these parameters in the use of the common sign for THANK-YOU.

Figure 15.1

Shape and orientation

To describe the articulation of THANK-YOU in ASL, we start with the **shape**, or configuration of the hand(s), used in forming the sign. The shape may differ in terms of which fingers are used, whether the fingers are extended or bent, and the general configurations of the hand(s). The configuration shown in the illustration is a "flat hand" (not a "fist hand" or a "cupped hand").

The **orientation** of the hand is "palm up" rather than "palm down" when signing THANK-YOU. In other signs, the hand may be oriented in a number of other ways such as the "flat hand, palm towards signer" form used to indicate MINE.

Location and movement

Whatever the shape and orientation of the hand(s), there will also be a **location** (or place of articulation) in relation to the head and upper body of the signer. In THANK-YOU, the sign begins near the mouth and is completed at chest level. Some signs can only be distinguished on the basis of location, as in the difference between signing SUMMER (above the eyes) and UGLY (below the eyes) because hand shape, palm orientation and movement are the same in both of these signs. In some two-handed signs (e.g. MEDICINE, SHIP), one hand acts as the base location while the other hand moves on or above it.

The **movement** element in THANK-YOU is "out and downward" toward the receiver. The difference between faster and slower movement in signing also has an effect on meaning. In a story recounted by Stokoe (2001), the director of public relations at Gallaudet College (for the deaf) happened to notice two employees signing one day about a former president who had been very ill. She saw a sign that she interpreted as DEAD and phoned the *Washington Post*, where an obituary for the ex-president appeared the following day. Rather prematurely, as it turned out, for the same hand movements, used fairly quickly in DEAD, had actually been used by the signer with a much slower rotation to communicate DYING. The difference in type of movement creates a difference in meaning. Clearly, just as there are "slips of the ear" (Chapter 12), there can also be "slips of the eye."

Primes, faces and finger-spelling

The contrasting elements within these four general parameters can be analyzed into sets of features or **primes**. We say that "flat hand" is a prime in terms of shape and "palm up" is a prime in terms of orientation. Identifying each of these primes allows us to create a complete feature analysis of every sign in much the same way as we can analyze the phonological features of spoken language.

In addition to these parameters and primes, there are important functions served by non-manual components such as head movement, eye movement and several specific types of facial expressions. Under normal circumstances, THANK-YOU is articulated with a head nod and a smiling face. If a sentence is functioning as a question, it is typically accompanied by a raising of the eyebrows, widened eyes and a slight leaning forward of the head.

Also, if a new term or name is encountered, signers can use **finger-spelling**, which is a system of hand configurations conventionally used to represent the letters of the alphabet.

From these brief descriptions, it is clear that ASL is a linguistic system designed for the visual medium, in face-to-face interaction. The majority of signs are located around the neck and head. If a sign is made near the chest or waist, it tends to be a two-handed sign. One of the key differences between a system using the visual medium and one using the vocal-auditory channel is that visual messages can incorporate a number of distinct elements simultaneously. Spoken language production is linear, with one sound signal following another in time. In the visual medium, while signs are also produced linearly, multiple components can be produced at the same time in space.

The meaning of signs

The signs of ASL are sometimes mistakenly believed to be simple visual representations or "pictures" of the objects and actions they refer to and the whole language is thought to consist of a limited set of primitive gestures that look like objects or mimic actions in pantomime. Such misconceptions may persist because the hearing world rarely witnesses conversations or technical discussions conducted in ASL, which can range over every imaginable topic, concrete and abstract, and which bear little resemblance to any form of pantomime.

Interestingly, as non-users of ASL, when we are told that a sign is used to refer to a particular object or action, we can often create some symbolic connection that makes the relationship between sign and signified seem more transparent in some sense. We may look at the sign for THANK-YOU and see it as some appropriately symbolic version of the action of "thanking."

However, most of the time, interpretation doesn't work that way in the opposite direction. We normally find it difficult to get the meaning of a sign simply on the basis of what it looks like. Indeed, as when confronted with any unfamiliar language, we may not even be able to identify individual signs (words) in fluent signing. If we can't see the "words," we are hardly likely to be able to identify the "pictures" needed for their interpretation. Most everyday use of ASL signs by fluent ASL-users is not based on identifying symbolic pictures, but on recognizing familiar linguistic forms that have arbitrary status. As an experiment, try to decide what English word would be the translation of the common sign illustrated here.

In use, this sign consists of rotating both hands together with the fingers interlocked in front of the chest. Several different interpretations have been suggested for the source image of this sign. In one, it represents the stripes on a flag, in another, it's a mixing pot, and in yet another it's a coming together. To suggest that any of these images comes into the mind of a signer who uses the sign in conversation to refer to AMERICA is as absurd as proposing that in hearing the word *America*, an English speaker must be thinking about Amerigo Vespucci, the sixteenth-century Italian whose name is

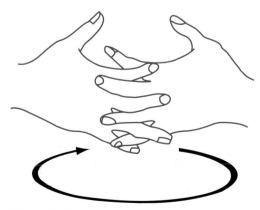

Figure 15.2

reputed to be the source of the modern word. The signs in ASL have their meanings within the system of signs, not through reference to some pictorial image each time they are used.

Representing signs

The fact that a sign language exploits the visual medium in quite subtle ways makes it difficult to represent accurately on the page. As Lou Fant (1977) has observed, "strictly speaking, the only way to write Ameslan is to use motion pictures." One of the major problems is finding a way to incorporate those aspects of facial expression that contribute to the message. A partial solution is to write one line of manually signed words (in capital letters) and then, above this line, to indicate the nature and extent of the facial expression (in some conventional way) that contributes to the message. As illustrated here, the *q* in the transcription is used to show that the facial expression indicated a question function throughout the signing of what would be translated as *Can I borrow the book?*

$$\overline{}\overset{\text{q}}{}$$

ME BORROW BOOK

Other subtle aspects of meaning that can be conveyed by facial expression are still being investigated. In one study, it was observed that a signer, in the middle of telling a story, produced the signed message: MAN FISH [continuous]. The "continuous" element is indicated by sweeping repetitive movement of the hands as they form the verb FISH. The basic translation would be: *The man was fishing.* However, ASL users translated it as *The man was fishing with relaxation and enjoyment.* The source of this extra information was a particular facial expression in which the lips were together and pushed out a little, with the head slightly tilted. This non-manual signal was clearly capable of functioning as the equivalent of an adverb or preposition phrase in English and was an integral part of the message. The notation *mm* was chosen as a way of incorporating this element and so a more accurate transcription of the message might look like this:

$$\overline{}\overset{\text{mm}}{}$$

MAN FISH [continuous]

There are, of course, other notations that have been devised to capture major non-manual elements in ASL communication.

ASL as a natural language

Investigations of ASL from a linguistic point of view are a relatively recent phenom-enon. Yet it has become clear that any feature that is characteristically found in spoken languages has a counterpart in ASL. All those defining properties of human language described in Chapter 2 are present in ASL. There are equivalent levels of phonology and morphology (basic elements), as well as syntax (arrangements of those elements). For example, ASL uses Subject Verb Object (SVO) word order like English, but normally puts adjectives after nouns, unlike English (but like French).

Children acquiring ASL as their first language go through developmental stages similar to children learning spoken language, though the production of signs seems to begin earlier than the production of spoken words. In the hands of witty individuals, ASL is used for a wide range of jokes and "sign-play." There are different ASL dialects in different regions and historical changes in the form of signs can be traced over the past hundred years (older versions are preserved on old films).

In summary, ASL is a natural language that is quite remarkable for its endurance in the face of decades of prejudice and misunderstanding. There is a very old joke among the deaf that begins with the question: *What is the greatest problem facing deaf people?* Perhaps increased knowledge and appreciation of their language among the general population will bring about a change in the old response to that question. The tradi-tional answer was: *Hearing people.*

Study questions

1 In the study of non-verbal behavior, what are emblems?
2 What is the difference between "iconics" and "deictics" in the study of gestures?
3 What is an alternate sign language?
4 What is the major difference between ASL and Signed English?
5 Which articulatory parameters of ASL have "flat hand" and "palm up" as primes?
6 What would be the most likely English translation of:

   (i)

q

    ————————————————

    HAPPEN YESTERDAY NIGHT

  (ii)

      neg   mm

    —— ————————————

    BOY NOT WALK [continuous]

Tasks

A In the chapter, we mentioned deictics or pointing gestures, but didn't explore how they are actually performed. Can you describe in detail the most common pointing gesture? Are there any social constraints on its use? Are there other ways of pointing, using other parts of the body?

B Is gesture tied to self-expression or is it tied to communication with a listener? For example, do we gesture more when a listener is present in person or out of view (e.g. during a phone call)? Do blind people gesture when they're talking?

C What is the connection between deaf education and the invention of the telephone?

D What made people have such a strong commitment to oralism despite its lack of success?

E What is the basis of the distinction between "prelinguistic" and "postlinguistic" hearing impairment?

F Unlike spoken language use where accompanying facial expressions seem to be optional most of the time, ASL is a visual language and facial expressions are an essential part of what is being communicated. What facial expressions would conventionally be associated with signing the following sentences?

  (1) *Are you married?*
  (2) *Where do you work?*

(3)   *You like jazz, I'm surprised.*
(4)   *If I miss the bus, I'll be late for work.*

Discussion topics/projects

I   Which of the following statements do you agree with and what reasons would you give to support your opinion?

(i)   A shrugging gesture always indicates "helplessness" of some kind.
(ii)   The eyebrow flash is used everywhere as a greeting.
(iii) It is easier to learn foreign gestures than foreign words.
(iv)   Brow lowering carries an implication of something negative whereas brow raising implies something positive.
(v)   If a person uses lots of hand movements, such as smoothing the hair or touching the chin while speaking, it's an indication that the person is telling a lie.

(For background reading, see Ekman, 1999.)

II According to Corballis, "there are good reasons to suppose that much of the development of language over the past two million years took place through manual gesture rather than vocalization" (2002: 98).

What do you think of the idea that the origins of language are to be found in manual gestures and that the development of speech comes from the transfer of manual gestures to oral gestures? Is it relevant that the hands of early humans developed well before the capacity for speech? What about the fact that children communicate non-verbally (e.g. pointing) before they produce speech?

(For background reading, see chapter 5 of Corballis, 2002.)

Further reading

Basic treatments
Goldin-Meadow, S. (2003) *Hearing Gesture* Harvard University Press
Lucas, C. and C. Valli (2004) "American Sign Language" In E. Finegan and J. Rickford (eds.) *Language in the USA* (230–244) Cambridge University Press
More detailed treatments
Kendon, A. (2004) *Gesture* Cambridge University Press
Valli, C., C. Lucas and K. Mulrooney (2005) *Linguistics of American Sign Language: An Introduction* (4th edition) Gallaudet University Press
ASL courses
Humphries, T. and C. Padden (2003) *Learning American Sign Language* (plus DVD) (2nd edition) Allyn and Bacon

Stewart, D., E. Stewart and J. Little (2006) *American Sign Language the Easy Way* (2nd edition) Barron's Educational

Australian and British Sign Languages

Johnston, T. and A. Schembri (2007) *Australian Sign Language: An Introduction to Sign Language Linguistics* Cambridge University Press

Sutton-Spence, R. and B. Woll (1999) *The Linguistics of British Sign Language* Cambridge University Press

Alternate sign languages

Kendon, A. (1988) *Sign Languages of Aboriginal Australia* Cambridge University Press

Umiker-Sebeok, D-J. and T. Sebeok (eds.) (1987) *Monastic Sign Languages* Mouton de Gruyter

Other references

Corballis, M. (2002) *From Hand to Mouth* Princeton University Press

Ekman, P. (1999) "Emotional and conversational nonverbal signals" In L. Messing and R. Campbell (eds.) *Gesture, Speech and Sign* (45–55) Oxford University Press

Fant, L. (1977) *Sign Language* Joyce Media

NcNeill, D. (1992) *Hand and Mind* University of Chicago Press

Stokoe, W. (1960) *Sign Language Structure: An Outline of the Visual Communication Systems of the American Deaf* Studies in Linguistics, Occasional Papers 8, University of Buffalo

Stokoe, W. (2001) *Language in Hand* Gallaudet University Press

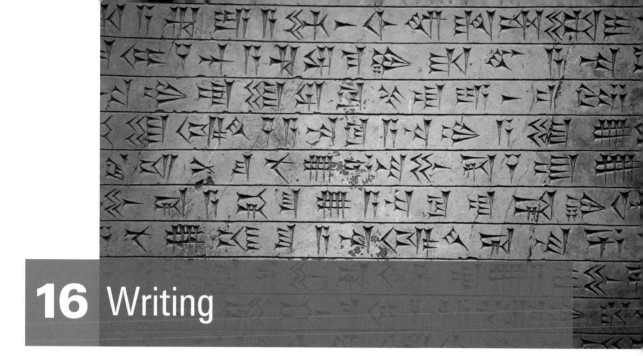

16 Writing

The five-year-old child whose skills in symbolic representation are displayed here seems to be already familiar with some of the basic elements of writing. The sequence of letters goes from left to right, each letter is distinct from the next and generally well formed, and each word is separated from the next by larger spaces. The occasional spelling "mistake," a traditional problem in written English, cannot disguise the fact that this child has already learned how to write.

Figure 16.1

Writing

We can define **writing** as the symbolic representation of language through the use of graphic signs. Unlike speech, it is a system that is not simply acquired, but has to be learned through sustained conscious effort. Not all languages have a written form and, even among people whose language has a well-established writing system, there are large numbers of individuals who cannot use the system.

In terms of human development, writing is a relatively recent phenomenon. We may be able to trace human attempts to represent information visually back to cave drawings made at least 20,000 years ago, or to clay tokens from about 10,000 years ago, which appear to have been an early attempt at bookkeeping, but these artifacts are best described as ancient precursors of writing. The earliest writing for which we have clear evidence is known as "cuneiform," marked on clay tablets about 5,000 years ago. An ancient script that has a more obvious connection to writing systems in use today can be identified in inscriptions dated around 3,000 years ago.

Much of the evidence used in the reconstruction of ancient writing systems comes from inscriptions on stone or tablets. If those ancients were using other elaborate scripts on wood, leather or other perishable materials, we have lost them. But working from the inscriptions we do have, we can trace the development of one writing tradition, lasting a few thousand years, with which humans have sought to create a more permanent record of what was going on.

Pictograms and ideograms

Cave drawings may serve to record some event (e.g. Humans 3, Buffaloes 1), but they are not usually thought of as any type of specifically linguistic message. They are usually treated as part of a tradition of pictorial art. When some of the "pictures" came to represent particular images in a consistent way, we can begin to describe the product as a form of picture-writing, or **pictograms**. In this way, a form such as ☀ might come to be used for the sun. An essential part of this use of a representative symbol is that everyone should use a similar form to convey a roughly similar meaning. That is, a conventional relationship must exist between the symbol and its interpretation.

In time, this picture might develop into a more fixed symbolic form, such as ☉, and come to be used for "heat" and "daytime," as well as for "sun." Note that as the symbol extends from "sun" to "heat," it is moving from something visible to something conceptual (and no longer a picture). This type of symbol is then considered to be part of a system of idea-writing, or **ideograms**. The distinction between pictograms and ideograms is essentially a difference in the relationship between the symbol and the entity it represents. The more "picture-like" forms are pictograms and the more abstract derived forms are ideograms.

A key property of both pictograms and ideograms is that they do not represent words or sounds in a particular language. Modern pictograms, such as those represented in the accompanying illustration, are language-independent and can be understood with much the same basic conventional meaning in a lot of different places where a number of different languages are spoken.

Figure 16.2

It is generally thought that there were pictographic or ideographic origins for a large number of symbols that turn up in later writing systems. For example, in Egyptian hieroglyphics, the symbol ⌓ was used to refer to a house and derived from the diagram-like representation of the floor plan of a house. In Chinese writing, the character 川 was used for a river, and had its origins in the pictorial representation of a stream flowing between two banks. However, it is important to note that neither the Egyptian nor the Chinese written symbols are actually "pictures" of a house or a river. They are more abstract. When we create symbols in a writing system, there is always an abstraction away from the physical world.

When the relationship between the symbol and the entity or idea becomes sufficiently abstract, we can be more confident that the symbol is probably being used to represent words in a language. In early Egyptian writing, the ideogram for water was ≋. Much later, the derived symbol ∿ came to be used for the actual word meaning "water." When symbols are used to represent words in a language, they are described as examples of word-writing, or "logograms."

Logograms

An early example of logographic writing is the system used by the Sumerians, in the southern part of modern Iraq, around 5,000 years ago. Because of the particular shapes used in their symbols, these inscriptions are more generally described as **cuneiform** writing. The term cuneiform means "wedge-shaped" and the inscriptions used by the Sumerians were produced by pressing a wedge-shaped implement into soft clay tablets, resulting in forms such as ⟰⟰ ◁.

The form of this symbol really gives no clue to what type of entity is being referred to. The relationship between the written form and the object it represents has become arbitrary and we have a clear example of word-writing or a **logogram**. The cuneiform symbol above can be compared to a typical pictographic representation of the same fishy entity: ⌀. We can also compare the ideogram for the sun, presented earlier as ⊙, with the logogram used to refer to the same entity found in cuneiform writing: ▸▸⟊.

Contemporary logograms in English are forms such as $, @, 9, &, where each symbol represents one word. A more elaborate writing system that is based, to a certain extent, on the use of logograms can be found in China. Many Chinese written symbols, or **characters**, are used as representations of the meaning of words, or parts of words, and not of the sounds of spoken language. One of the advantages of such a system is that two speakers of very different dialects of Chinese, who might have great difficulty understanding each other's spoken forms, can both read the same written text. Chinese writing, with the longest continuous history of use as a writing system (i.e. 3,000 years), clearly has many other advantages for its users.

One major disadvantage is that quite a large number of different written symbols are required within this type of writing system, although the official "list of modern Chinese characters for everyday use" is limited to 2,500 characters. (Other lists contain up to 50,000 characters.) Remembering large numbers of different composite word-symbols, however, does seem to present a substantial memory load, and the history of most other writing systems illustrates a development away from logographic writing.

To accomplish this, some principled method is needed to go from symbols representing words (i.e. a logographic system) to a set of symbols that represent sounds (i.e. a phonographic system).

Rebus writing

One way of using existing symbols to represent the sounds of language is through a process known as **rebus writing**. In this process, the symbol for one entity is taken over as the symbol for the sound of the spoken word used to refer to the entity. That symbol then comes to be used whenever that sound occurs in any words.

We can create an example, working with the sound of the English word *eye*. We can imagine how the pictogram ◄①► could have developed into the logogram ◇. This logogram is pronounced as *eye* and, with the rebus principle at work, you could then refer to yourself as ◇ ("I"), to one of your friends as ┼◇ ("Crosseye"), combine the form with the logogram for "deaf" to produce "defy," with the logogram for "boat" to produce "bow-tie," and so on.

A similar process is taking place in contemporary English texting where the symbol "2" is used, not only as a number, but as the sound of other words or parts of words, in messages such as "nd2spk2u2nite" ("(I) need to speak to you tonight"). In this message, the letter "u" also illustrates the process of rebus writing, having become the symbol for the sound of the spoken word "you."

Let's take another, non-English, example, in which the ideogram 𝄞 becomes the logogram ﺏ, for the word pronounced *ba* (meaning "boat"). We can then produce a symbol for the word pronounced *baba* (meaning "father") which would be ﺑﺎﺑ. One symbol can thus be used in many different ways, with a range of meanings. What this process accomplishes is a sizeable reduction in the number of symbols needed in a writing system.

Syllabic writing

In the last example, the symbol that is used for the pronunciation of parts of a word represents a unit (*ba*) that consists of a consonant sound (*b*) and a vowel sound (*a*). This unit is one type of syllable. When a writing system employs a set of symbols each one representing the pronunciation of a syllable, it is described as **syllabic writing**.

There are no purely syllabic writing systems in use today, but modern Japanese can be written with a set of single symbols representing spoken syllables and is consequently often described as having a (partially) syllabic writing system, or a **syllabary**.

In the early nineteenth century, a Cherokee named Sequoyah, living in North Carolina, invented a syllabic writing system that was widely used within the Cherokee community to create written messages from the spoken language. In these Cherokee examples, Ᏺ (ho), Ꮓ (sa) and Ꮙ (ge), we can see that the written symbol in each case does not correspond to a single consonant (C) or a vowel (V), but to a syllable (CV).

Both the ancient Egyptian and the Sumerian writing systems evolved to the point where some of the earlier logographic symbols were being used to represent spoken syllables. However, it is not until the time of the Phoenicians, inhabiting what is modern Lebanon between 3,000 and 4,000 years ago, that we find the full use of a syllabic writing system. Many of the symbols that the Phoenicians used were taken from earlier Egyptian writing. The Egyptian form ⌐ (meaning "house") was adopted in a slightly reoriented form as ⅁. After being used logographically for the word pronounced *beth* (still meaning "house"), the symbol came to represent other syllables beginning with a *b* sound. Similarly, the Egyptian form ∿ (meaning "water") turns up as ∿ and is used for syllables beginning with an *m* sound. So, a word that might be pronounced as *muba* could be written as ⅁∿, and the pronunciation *bima* could be written as ∿⅁. Note that the direction of writing is from right to left. By about 3,000 years ago, the Phoenicians had stopped using logograms and had a fully developed syllabic writing system.

Alphabetic writing

If you have a set of symbols being used to represent syllables beginning with, for example, a *b* sound or an *m* sound, then you are actually very close to a situation in which the symbols can be used to represent single sound types in a language. This is, in effect, the basis of alphabetic writing. In principle, an **alphabet** is a set of written symbols, each one representing a single type of sound or phoneme. The situation just described is what seems to have occurred in the development of the writing systems of Semitic languages such as Arabic and Hebrew. Words written in these languages, in everyday use, largely consist of symbols for the consonant sounds in the word, with the appropriate vowel sounds being supplied by the reader (or rdr).

This type of writing system is sometimes called a **consonantal alphabet**. The early version of Semitic alphabetic script, originating in the writing system of the Phoenicians, is the basic source of most other alphabets to be found in the world. Modified versions can be traced to the East into Iranian, Indian and South-East Asian writing systems and to the West through Greek. The basic order of letter symbols, with "A" representing a consonant in the first "ABCD…," was created about three thousand years ago by the Phoenicians and continues to be used as our primary ordering device for lists in everything from dictionaries to telephone books.

The early Greeks took the alphabetizing process a stage further by also using separate symbols to represent the vowel sounds as distinct entities, and so created a remodeled system that included vowels. This change resulted in the Phoenician consonant "alep" becoming a symbol for a vowel sound as *A* (called "alpha") to go with existing symbols for consonant sounds such as *B* (called "beta"), giving us single-sound writing or an "alphabet." In fact, for some writers on the origins of the modern alphabet, it is the Greeks who should be given credit for taking the inherently syllabic system from the Phoenicians and creating a writing system in which the single-symbol to single-sound correspondence was fully realized.

From the Greeks, this revised alphabet passed to the rest of Western Europe through the Romans and, along the way, underwent several modifications to fit the requirements of the spoken languages encountered. As a result, we talk about the Roman alphabet as the writing system used for English. Another line of development took the same basic Greek writing system into Eastern Europe where Slavic languages were spoken. The modified version, called the Cyrillic alphabet (after St. Cyril, a ninth-century Christian missionary), is the basis of the writing system used in Russia today.

The actual form of a number of letters in modern European alphabets can be traced from their origins in Egyptian hieroglyphics. The examples in the accompanying illustration are based on Davies (1987).

Egyptian	Phoenician	Early Greek	Roman
			A
			B
			K
			M
			N
			T
			S

Written English

If indeed the origins of the alphabetic writing system were based on a correspondence between a single symbol and a single sound type, then one might reasonably ask why there is such a frequent mismatch between the forms of written English ("you know") and the sounds of spoken English ("yu no" or /ju noʊ/). Other languages (Italian, Spanish) have writing systems that hold much more closely to the one-sound-one-symbol principle of alphabetic writing. English orthography is not always so consistent.

English orthography

As we noted in Chapter 3, the **orthography** (or spelling) of contemporary English allows for a lot of variation in how each sound is represented. The vowel sound represented by /i/ is written in various ways, as shown in the first two columns on the left below, and the consonant sound represented by /ʃ/ has various spellings, as in the other two columns.

i (*critique*)	ee (*queen*)	s (*sugar*)	ch (*champagne*)
ie (*belief*)	eo (*people*)	ss (*tissue*)	ce (*ocean*)
ei (*receipt*)	ey (*key*)	ssi (*mission*)	ci (*delicious*)
ea (*meat*)	e (*scene*)	sh (*Danish*)	ti (*nation*)

Notice how often in these two lists the single phoneme is actually represented by more than one letter. Part of the reason for this is that the English language is full of words borrowed, often with their spelling, from other languages, as in "ph" for /f/ in the Greek borrowings *alphabet* and *orthography*. Notice again the use of two letters in combination for a single sound. A combination of two letters consistently used for a single sound, as in "ph" /f/ and "sh" /ʃ/ is called a **digraph**.

The English writing system is alphabetic in a very loose sense. Some reasons for this irregular correspondence between sound and symbolic representation may be found in a number of historical influences on the form of written English. The spelling of written English was largely fixed in the form that was used when printing was introduced into fifteenth-century England. At that time, there were a number of conventions regarding the written representation of words that had been derived from forms used in writing other languages, notably Latin and French. For example, "qu" replaced older English "cw" in words like *queen*. Moreover, many of the early printers were native Dutch speakers and could not make consistently accurate decisions about English pronunciations, hence the "h" in *ghost*.

Perhaps more important is the fact that, since the fifteenth century, the pronunciation of spoken English has undergone substantial changes. For example, although we no longer pronounce the initial "k" sound or the internal "gh" sound, we still include letters indicating the older pronunciation in our contemporary spelling of the word *knight*. These are sometimes called "silent letters." They also violate the one-sound-one-symbol principle, but not with as much effect as the "silent" final -*e* of so many English words. Not only do we have to learn that this letter is not pronounced, we also have to know the patterns of influence it has on the preceding vowel, as in the different pronunciations of "a" in the pair *hat/hate* and "o" in *not/note*.

If we then add in the fact that a large number of older written English words were actually "recreated" by sixteenth-century spelling reformers to bring their written forms more into line with what were supposed, sometimes erroneously, to be their Latin origins (e.g. *dette* became *debt*, *doute* became *doubt*, *iland* became *island*), then the sources of the mismatch between written and spoken forms begin to become clear. Even when the revolutionary American spelling reformer Noah Webster was successful (in the USA) in revising a form such as British English *honour*, he only managed to go as far as *honor* (and not *onor*). His proposed revisions of *bred* (for *bread*), *giv* (for *give*) and *laf* (for *laugh*) were in line with the alphabetic principle, and are often the preferred forms of young children learning to write English, but they have obviously not found their way into everyday printed English. In the next chapter we will look more closely at the historical development of English and other ways in which languages change.

Study questions

1 In the study of language, how is writing defined?
2 What is the basic difference between a logographic writing system and a phonographic writing system?
3 What happens in the process known as rebus writing?
4 Is the text message "cu@9" an example of logographic or alphabetic writing?
5 What is the name given to the writing system used for Russian?
6 Where will you find the writing system with the longest history of continuous use?

Tasks

A What is boustrophedon writing and during which period was it used?
B What kind of writing systems are known as abjads and abugidas and what is the basic difference between them?
C What kind of writing system is Hangul, where is it used and how are forms written on the page?
D What kind of writing is used in texting? How would you describe the writing conventions (pictographic, ideographic, logographic, syllabic or alphabetic) that are used in the following text messages?

xlnt msg ("excellent message")   swdyt ("So, what do you think?")
btw ("by the way")   ne1 ("anyone")
b42moro ("before tomorrow")   cul8r ;-) ("see you later, wink")

E Consider the following examples and try to decide in which cases "X" is a symbol with a function, but without meaning, or one with an identifiable general meaning, or one with a very specific meaning. Can any of the uses be considered logographic?

  (1) *The twenty-fourth letter of the English alphabet is X.*
  (2) *On the map was a large X and the words "You are here."*
  (3) *Most of the older men were illiterate at that time and put X where their signature was required.*
  (4) *Indicate your choice by putting X next to only one of the following options.*
  (5) *He wrote X – Y = 6 on the blackboard.*
  (6) *There was an image of a dog with a large X across it.*
  (7) *The teacher put X beside one of my sentences and I don't know why.*
  (8) *We can't take the children with us to see that film because it's rated X.*
  (9) *The witness known as Ms. X testified that she had heard several gunshots.*
 (10) *Aren't there two X chromosomes in the cells of females?*

(11) *At the bottom of the letter, after her signature, she put X three times.*

(12) *In the XXth century, Britain's collapsing empire brought new immigrants.*

F The accompanying illustration is described in Jensen (1969) as a letter from a young woman of the Yukagirs who live in northern Siberia. The woman (c) is sending the letter to "her departing sweetheart" (b). What do you think the letter is communicating? Who are the other figures? What kind of "writing" is this?

a   b   c   d

Figure 16.3

Discussion topics/projects

I According to Florian Coulmas (2003: 201), "the present distribution of scripts testifies to the close link between writing systems and religion." Do you think that the spread of different religions (more than anything else) accounts for the different forms of writing used in the world today? What kind of evidence would you use to argue for or against this idea?

(For background reading, see chapter 10 of Coulmas, 2003.)

II Pictograms may be language-independent, but they do not seem to be culture-independent. In order to interpret many pictographic and ideographic representations, we have to be familiar with cultural assumptions about what the symbols "mean."

(i) As a simple exercise, show the twelve symbols illustrated below to some friends and ask them if they know what each one means. (People may say they have never seen them before, but they should be encouraged to guess.)

(ii) Next, provide them with the following list of "official meanings" and ask them to decide which symbol goes with which meaning.

(a) agitate   (e) lock   (i) open door or lid
(b) blood donors   (f) lost child   (j) press, interview room
(c) dry, heat   (g) registration (k) protection and safety equipment
(d) keep frozen   (h) telegrams   (l) turning basin maneuvring (boats)

(iii) Can you describe what kinds of cultural assumptions are involved in the interpretation of these symbols?

(The symbols are from Ur, 1988.)

Figure 16.4

Further reading

Basic treatments

Hudson, G. (2000) *Essential Introductory Linguistics* (chapters 20–21) Blackwell

Robinson, A. (2007) *The Story of Writing* (2nd edition) Thames & Hudson

More detailed treatments

Coulmas, F. (2003) *Writing Systems* Cambridge University Press

Rogers, H. (2005) *Writing Systems: A Linguistic Approach* Blackwell

A comprehensive review

Daniels, P. and W. Bright (1996) *The World's Writing Systems* Oxford University Press

Precursors of writing

Schmandt-Besserat, D. (1996) *How Writing Came About* University of Texas Press

Ancient languages

Woodard, R. (2003) *The Cambridge Encyclopedia of the World's Ancient Languages* Cambridge University Press

Cuneiform

Glassner, J. (2003) *The Invention of Cuneiform* Johns Hopkins University Press

Egyptian

Allen, J. (2000) *Middle Egyptian: An Introduction to the Language and Culture of Hieroglyphs* Cambridge University Press

Ancient Greek

Jeffery, L. (1990) *The Local Scripts of Archaic Greece* Clarendon Press

The alphabet

Man, J. (2000) *Alpha Beta* Wiley

Written English

Cook, V. (2004) *The English Writing System* Hodder Arnold

Other references

Davies, W. (1987) *Egyptian Hieroglyphics* British Museum/University of California Press

Jensen, H. (1969) *Sign, Symbol and Script* (3rd edition) (translated by G. Unwin) Putnam's

Ur, P. (1988) *Grammar Practice Activities* Cambridge University Press

17 Language history and change

Fæder ure þu þe eart on heofonum,
si þin nama gehalgod.
Tobecume þin rice.
Gewurþe þin willa on eorðan swa swa on heofonum.
Urne gedæghwamlican hlaf syle us to dæg.
And forgyf us ure gyltas,
swa swa we forgyfað urum gyltendum.
And ne gelæd þu us in costnunge,
ac alys us of yfele.

The Lord's Prayer (circa 1000)

This barely recognizable version of the Lord's Prayer from about a thousand years ago provides a rather clear indication that the language of the "Englisc" has gone through substantial changes to become the English we use today. Investigating the features of older languages, and the ways in which they developed into modern languages, involves us in the study of language history and change, also known as **philology**. In the nineteenth century, philology dominated the study of language and one result was the creation of "family trees" to show how languages were related. Before all of that could happen, however, there had to be the discovery that a variety of languages spoken in different parts of the world were actually members of the same family.

Family trees

In 1786, a British government official in India called Sir William Jones made the following observation about Sanskrit, the ancient language of Indian law.

> The Sanskrit language, whatever be its antiquity, is of a wonderful structure; more perfect than the Greek, more copious than the Latin, and more exquisitely refined than either, yet bearing to both of them a stronger affinity, both in the roots of verbs and in the forms of grammar, than could possibly have been produced by accident.

Sir William went on to suggest, in a way that was quite revolutionary for its time, that a number of languages from very different geographical areas must have some common ancestor. It was clear, however, that this common ancestor could not be described from any existing records, but had to be hypothesized on the basis of similar features existing in records of languages that were believed to be descendants.

During the nineteenth century, a term came into use to describe that common ancestor. It incorporated the notion that this was the original form (*Proto*) of a language that was the source of modern languages in the Indian subcontinent (*Indo*) and in Europe (*European*). With **Proto-Indo-European** established as some type of "great-great-grandmother," scholars set out to identify the branches of the Indo-European family tree, tracing the lineage of many modern languages. The accompanying diagram shows a small selection of the Indo-European languages in their family branches.

Indo-European is the language family with the largest population and distribution in the world, but it isn't the only one. There are about thirty such language families containing more than 6,000 different individual languages. According to one reputable source (Ethnologue, 2005), there are actually 6,912 languages in the world. Many of

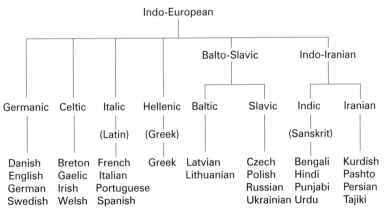

Figure 17.1

these languages are in danger of extinction while a few are expanding. In terms of number of speakers, Chinese has the most native speakers (about 1 billion), while English (about 350 million) is more widely used in different parts of the world.

Family connections

Looking at the Indo-European family tree, we might be puzzled initially by the idea that all these diverse languages are related. After all, two modern languages such as Italian and Hindi would seem to have nothing in common. One way to get a clearer picture of how they are related is through looking at records of an older generation, like Latin and Sanskrit, from which the modern languages evolved. For example, if we use familiar letters to write out the words for *father* and *brother* in Sanskrit, Latin and Ancient Greek, some common features become apparent.

Sanskrit	Latin	Ancient Greek	
pitar	pater	patēr	("father")
bhrātar	frāter	phrāter	("brother")

While these forms have rather clear similarities, it is extremely unlikely that exactly the same words will be found throughout the languages. However, the fact that close similarities occur (especially in the probable pronunciations of the words) is good evidence for proposing a family connection.

Cognates

The process we have just used to establish a possible family connection between different languages involved looking at what are called "cognates." Within groups of related languages, we can often find close similarities in particular sets of words. A **cognate** of a word in one language (e.g. English) is a word in another language (e.g. German) that has a similar form and is or was used with a similar meaning. The English words *mother*, *father* and *friend* are cognates of the German words *Mutter*, *Vater* and *Freund*. On the basis of these cognates, we would imagine that Modern English and Modern German probably have a common ancestor in what has been labeled the Germanic branch of Indo-European. By the same process, we can look at similar sets in Spanish (*madre*, *padre*, *amigo*) and Italian (*madre*, *padre*, *amico*) and conclude that these cognates are good evidence of a common ancestor in the Italic branch of Indo-European.

Comparative reconstruction

Using information from these sets of cognates, we can embark on a procedure called **comparative reconstruction**. The aim of this procedure is to reconstruct what must have been the original or "proto" form in the common ancestral language. In carrying out this procedure, those working on the history of languages operate on the basis of some general principles, two of which are presented here.

The **majority principle** is very straightforward. If, in a cognate set, three words begin with a [p] sound and one word begins with a [b] sound, then our best guess is that the majority have retained the original sound (i.e. [p]).

The **most natural development principle** is based on the fact that certain types of sound change are very common whereas others are extremely unlikely. The direction of change described in each case (1)–(4) has been commonly observed, but the reverse has not.

(1)   Final vowels often disappear (*vino* → *vin*)
(2)   Voiceless sounds become voiced, typically between vowels (*muta* → *muda*)
(3)   Stops become fricatives (*ripa* → *riva*)
(4)   Consonants become voiceless at the end of words (*rizu* → *ris*)

Sound reconstruction

If we were faced with some examples from three languages, as shown below, we could make a start on comparative reconstruction by deciding what was the most likely form of the initial sound in the original source of all three.

Languages			
A	**B**	**C**	
cantare	cantar	chanter	("sing")
catena	cadena	chaîne	("chain")
caro	caro	cher	("dear")
cavallo	caballo	cheval	("horse")

Since the written forms can often be misleading, we check that the initial sounds of the words in languages A and B are all [k] sounds, while in language C the initial sounds are all [ʃ] sounds.

On the evidence presented, the majority principle would suggest that the initial sound [k] in languages A and B is older than the [ʃ] sound in language C. Moreover, the [k] sound is a stop consonant and the [ʃ] sound is a fricative. According to one part of the "most natural development principle," change tends to occur in the direction of stops becoming fricatives, so the [k] sound is more likely to have been the original. Through this type of procedure we have started on the comparative reconstruction of the common origins of some words in Italian (A), Spanish (B) and French (C). In this case, we have a way of checking our reconstruction because the common origin for these three languages is known to be Latin. When we check the Latin cognates of the words listed, we find *cantare, catena, carus* and *caballus*, confirming that [k] was the initial sound.

Word reconstruction

Looking at a non-Indo-European set of examples, we can imagine receiving the following data from a linguist recently returned from an expedition to a remote region of the Amazon. The examples are a set of cognates from three related languages, but what would the proto-forms have looked like?

Languages				
1	**2**	**3**	**Proto-forms**	
mube	mupe	mup	_____	("stream")
abadi	apati	apat	_____	("rock")
agana	akana	akan	_____	("knife")
enugu	enuku	enuk	_____	("diamond")

Using the majority principle, we can suggest that the older forms will most likely be based on language 2 or language 3. If this is correct, then the consonant changes must have been [p] → [b], [t] → [d] and [k] → [g] in order to produce the later forms in language 1. There is a pattern in these changes that follows one part of the "most natural development principle," i.e. voiceless sounds become voiced between vowels. So, the words in languages 2 and 3 must be older forms than those in language 1.

Which of the two lists, 2 or 3, contains the older forms? Remembering one other "most natural development" type of sound change (i.e. final vowels often disappear), we can propose that the words in language 3 have consistently lost the final vowels still present in the words of language 2. Our best guess, then, is that the forms listed for language 2 are closest to what must have been the original proto-forms.

The history of English

The reconstruction of proto-forms is an attempt to determine what a language must have been like before any written records. However, even when we have written records from an older period of a language such as English, they may not bear any resemblance to the written form of the language found in today's newspapers. The version of the Lord's Prayer quoted at the beginning of this chapter provides a good illustration of this point. Even some of the letters seem quite alien. The older letters þ (called "thorn") and ð ("eth") were both replaced by "th" (as in *þu* → *thou*, *eorðan* → *earth*), and æ ("ash") simply became "a" (as in *to dæg* → *today*). To see how one language has undergone substantial changes through time, we can take a brief look at the history of English, which is traditionally divided into four periods.

Old English: before 1100
Middle English: 1100 to 1500
Early Modern English: 1500 to 1700
Modern English: after 1700

Old English

The primary sources for what developed as the English language were the Germanic languages spoken by a group of tribes from northern Europe who moved into the British Isles in the fifth century. In one early account, these tribes of Angles, Saxons and Jutes were described as "God's wrath toward Britain." It is from the names of the first two that we have the term *Anglo-Saxons* to describe these people, and from the name of the first tribe that we get the word for their language *Englisc* and their new home *Engla-land*.

From this early version of *Englisc*, now called **Old English**, we have many of the most basic terms in the language: *mann* ("man"), *wīf* ("woman"), *cild* ("child"), *hūs* ("house"), *mete* ("food"), *etan* ("eat"), *drincan* ("drink") and *feohtan* ("fight"). These pagan settlers also gave us some weekday names, commemorating their gods *Woden* and *Thor*. However, they did not remain pagan for long. From the sixth to the eighth century, there was an extended period during which these Anglo-Saxons were converted to Christianity and a number of terms from Latin (the language of the religion) came into English at that time. The origins of the contemporary English words *angel*, *bishop*, *candle*, *church*, *martyr*, *priest* and *school* all date from this period.

From the eighth century through the ninth and tenth centuries, another group of northern Europeans came first to plunder and then to settle in parts of the coastal regions of Britain. They were the Vikings and it is from their language, Old Norse, that the original forms of *give*, *law*, *leg*, *skin*, *sky*, *take* and *they* were adopted. It is from their winter festival *jól* that we have *Yule* as a term for the Christmas season.

Middle English

The event that marks the end of the Old English period, and the beginning of the **Middle English** period, is the arrival of the Norman French in England, following their victory at Hastings under William the Conqueror in 1066. These French-speaking invaders became the ruling class, so that the language of the nobility, the government, the law and civilized life in England for the next two hundred years was French. It is the source of words like *army*, *court*, *defense*, *faith*, *prison* and *tax*.

Yet the language of the peasants remained English. The peasants worked on the land and reared *sheep*, *cows* and *swine* (words from Old English) while the upper classes talked about *mutton*, *beef* and *pork* (words of French origin). Hence the different terms in modern English to refer to these creatures "on the hoof" as opposed to "on the plate."

Throughout this period, French (or, more accurately, an English version of French) was the prestige language and Chaucer tells us that one of his Canterbury pilgrims could speak it.

She was cleped Madame Eglentyne
Ful wel she song the service dyvyne,
Entuned in her nose ful semely,
And Frenche she spak ful faire and fetisly.

This is an example of Middle English, written in the late fourteenth century. It had changed substantially from Old English, but several changes were yet to take place before the language took on its modern form. Most significantly, the vowel sounds of Chaucer's time were very different from those we hear in similar words today. Chaucer lived in what would have sounded like a "hoos," with his "weef," and "hay" might drink a bottle of "weena" with "heer" by the light of the "mona."

In the two hundred years, from 1400 to 1600, that separated Chaucer and Shakespeare, the sounds of English underwent a substantial change known as the "Great Vowel Shift." The effects of this general raising of long vowel sounds (such as [oː] moving up to [uː], as in *mōna* → *moon*) made the pronunciation of Early Modern English, beginning around 1500, significantly different from earlier periods. The introduction of printing in 1476 brought about significant changes, but because the printers tended to standardize existing pronunciations in the spelling of words (e.g. *knee*, *gnaw*), later pronunciation changes are often not reflected in the way Modern English (after 1700) is written.

Influences from the outside, such as the borrowed words from Norman French or Old Norse that we have already noted, are examples of **external change** in the language. There are also other types of changes that occurred within the historical development of English (and other languages) that don't seem to be caused by outside factors. In the following sections, we will look at some of these processes of **internal change**.

Sound changes

In a number of changes from Middle to Modern English, some sounds disappeared from the pronunciation of certain words, in a process simply described as **sound loss**. The initial [h] of many Old English words was lost, as in *hlud → loud* and *hlaford → lord*. Some words lost sounds, but kept the spelling, resulting in the "silent letters" of contemporary written English. Word-initial velar stops [k] and [g] are no longer pronounced before nasals [n], but we still write the words *knee* and *gnaw* with the remnants of earlier pronunciations.

Another example is a velar fricative [x] that was used in the older pronunciation of *nicht* as [nɪxt] (closer to the Modern German pronunciation of *Nacht*), but is absent in the contemporary form *night*, as [naɪt]. A remnant of this sound is still present in some dialects, as at the end of the Scottish word *loch*, but it is no longer a consonant in Modern English speech.

The sound change known as **metathesis** involves a reversal in position of two sounds in a word. This type of reversal is illustrated in the changed versions of these words from their earlier forms.

acsian → ask   *frist → first*   *brinnan → beornan (burn)*
bridd → bird   *hros → horse*   *wæps → wasp*

The cowboy who pronounces the expression *pretty good* as something close to *purty good* is producing a similar example of metathesis as a dialect variant within Modern English. In some American English dialects, the form *aks*, as in *I aksed him already*, can still be heard instead of *ask*.

The reversal of position in metathesis can sometimes occur between non-adjoining sounds. The Spanish word *palabra* is derived from the Latin *parabola* through the reversal of the [l] and [r] sounds. The pattern is exemplified in the following set.

Latin		Spanish	
miraculum	→	*milagro*	("miracle")
parabola	→	*palabra*	("word")
periculum	→	*peligro*	("danger")

Another type of sound change, known as **epenthesis**, involves the addition of a sound to the middle of a word.

æmtig → empty   *spinel → spindle*   *timr → timber*

The addition of a [p] sound after the nasal [m], as in *empty*, can also be heard in some speakers' pronunciation of *something* as "sumpthing." Anyone who pronounces the word *film* as if it were "filum," or *arithmetic* as "arithametic," is producing examples of epenthesis in Modern English.

One other type of sound change worth noting, though not found in English, occurs in the development of other languages. It involves the addition of a sound to the beginning of a word and is called **prothesis**. It is a common feature in the evolution of some forms from Latin to Spanish, as in these examples.

schola	→	*escuela*	("school")
spiritus	→	*espíritu*	("spirit")

Spanish speakers who are starting to learn English as a second language will sometimes put a prothetic vowel at the beginning of some English words, with the result that words like *strange* and *story* may sound like "estrange" and "estory."

Syntactic changes

Some noticeable differences between the structure of sentences in Old and Modern English involve word order. In Old English texts, we find the Subject-Verb-Object order most common in Modern English, but we can also find a number of different orders that are no longer used. For example, the subject could follow the verb, as in *ferde he* ("he traveled"), and the object could be placed before the verb, as in *he hine geseah* ("he saw him"), or at the beginning of the sentence, as in *him man ne sealde* ("no man gave [any] to him").

In the last example, the use of the negative also differs from Modern English, since the sequence *not gave (*ne sealde*) is no longer grammatical. A "double negative" construction was also possible, as in the following example, where both *ne* ("not") and *næfre* ("never") are used with the same verb. We would now say *You never gave* rather than **You not gave never*.

and	ne	sealdest	þū	me	næfre	ān	ticcen
and	not	gave	you	me	never	a	kid

However, the most sweeping change in the form of English sentences was the loss of a large number of inflectional suffixes from many parts of speech. Notice that, in the previous examples, the forms *sealde* ("he gave") and *sealdest* ("you gave") are differentiated by inflectional suffixes (*-e*, *-est*) that are no longer used in Modern English.

Nouns, adjectives, articles and pronouns all had different inflectional forms according to their grammatical function in the sentence.

Semantic changes

The most obvious way in which Modern English differs from Old English is in the number of borrowed words that have come into the language since the Old English period. (For more on borrowing, see Chapter 5.) Less obviously, many words have ceased to be used. Since we no longer carry swords (most of us, at least), the word *foin*, meaning "the thrust of a sword," is no longer heard. A common Old English word for "man" was *were*, but it has fallen out of use, except in horror films where the compound *werewolf* occasionally appears. A number of expressions such as *lo, verily* or *egad* are immediately recognized as belonging to a much earlier period, along with certain medieval-sounding names such as *Bertha, Egbert* and *Percival.*

Two other processes are described as "broadening" and "narrowing" of meaning. An example of **broadening** of meaning is the change from *holy day* as a religious feast to the very general break from work called a *holiday*. We have broadened the use of *foda* (fodder for animals) to talk about all kinds of *food*. Old English words such as *luflic* ("loving") and *hræd* ("quick") not only went through sound changes, they also developed more complex evaluative meanings ("wonderful" and "preferentially"), as in their modern uses: *That's a lovely idea, but I'd rather have dinner at home tonight.* Another example is the modern use of the word *dog*. We use it very generally to refer to all breeds, but in its older form (Old English *docga*), it was only used for one particular breed.

The reverse process, called **narrowing**, has overtaken the Old English word *hund*, once used for any kind of dog, but now, as *hound*, used only for some specific breeds. Another example is *mete*, once used for any kind of food, which has in its modern form *meat* become restricted to only some specific types. The Old English version of the word *wife* could be used to refer to any woman, but has narrowed in its application nowadays to only married women. A different kind of narrowing can lead to a negative meaning for some words, such as *vulgar* (which used to mean simply "ordinary") and *naughty* (which used to mean "having nothing").

Diachronic and synchronic variation

None of these changes happened overnight. They were gradual and probably difficult to discern while they were in progress. Although some changes can be linked to major social changes caused by wars, invasions and other upheavals, the most pervasive source of change in language seems to be in the continual process of cultural transmission. Each new generation has to find a way of using the language of the previous generation. In this unending process whereby each individual child has to "recreate" the language of the community, there is an unavoidable propensity to pick up some elements exactly and others only approximately. There is also the occasional desire to be different. Given this tenuous transmission process, it should be expected that languages will not remain stable and that change and variation are inevitable.

In this chapter, we have concentrated on variation in language viewed **diachronically**, that is, from the historical perspective of change through time. The type of variation that can be viewed **synchronically**, that is, in terms of differences within one language in different places and among different groups at the same time, is the subject of the next two chapters.

Study questions

1   What are cognates?

2   How would you group the following languages into pairs which are closely related from a historical point of view: Bengali, Breton, Czech, English, French, Kurdish, Pashto, Portuguese, Swedish, Ukrainian, Urdu, Welsh?

3   On the basis of the following data, what are the most likely proto-forms?

Languages				
1	**2**	**3**		
cosa	chose	cosa	_____	("thing")
capo	chef	cabo	_____	("head")
capra	chèvre	cabra	_____	("goat")

4   Which of the following words are likely to be from Old English and which from French: *bacon, beef, calf, deer, ox, pig, veal, venison*?

5   What types of sound changes are illustrated by the following pairs?

(a) *thridda → third*   (b) *scribere → escribir*   (c) *glimsian → glimpse*

(d) *hring → ring*   (e) *slummer → slumber*   (f) *beorht → bright*

6   The Old English verb *steorfan* ("to die, from any cause") is the source of the Modern English verb *starve* ("to die, from lack of food"). What is the technical term used to describe this type of meaning change?

Tasks

A   We can often trace the roots of several different words in Modern English back to a single Indo-European form. Using what you learned in this chapter, can you complete the following chart, using the words provided, to illustrate several English word histories?

corage, coraticum, cord, cordialis, heorte, herton, kardia, kardiakos, kerd

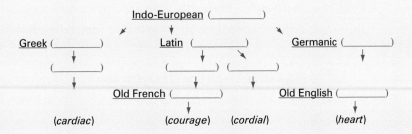

B   Which of these languages cannot be included in the Indo-European family tree? To which other language families do they belong?

Catalan, Chamorro, Faroese, Georgian, Hebrew, Hungarian, Marathi, Serbian, Tamil, Turkish

C   A Danish linguist, Rasmus Rask, and a German writer more famous for fairy tales, Jacob Grimm, both working in the early nineteenth century, are credited with the original insights that became known as "Grimm's Law."
  What is Grimm's Law and how does it account for the different initial sounds in pairs of cognates such as these from French and English (_deux / two, trois / three_) and these from Latin and English (_pater / father, canis / hound, genus / kin_)?

D   What happens in the process of change known as "grammaticalization"? Can you find out how the grammaticalization process made it possible for the English verb forms _go_ and _will_ to be used in sentences such as _I'm gonna be late_ and _I'll be at work until six_?

E   Describe what happened in any documented case of "language death."

F   These four versions of the same biblical event (Matthew 26: 73) are presented in Campbell (2004) as a way of illustrating some changes in the history of English. Can you describe the changes in vocabulary and grammar?

  (i)   Modern English (1961)
        Shortly afterwards the bystanders came up and said to Peter, "Surely you are another of them; your accent gives you away!"

  (ii) Early Modern English (1611)
        And after a while came vnto him they that stood by, and saide to Peter, Surely thou also art one of them, for thy speech bewrayeth thee.

  (iii) Middle English (1395)
        And a litil aftir, thei that stooden camen, and seiden to Petir, treuli thou art of hem; for thi speche makith thee knowun.

  (iv) Old English (1050)
        þa æfter lytlum fyrste genēalæton þa ðe þær stodon, cwædon to petre. Soðlice þu eart of hym, þyn spræc þe gesweotolað.
        (Literally: "then after little first approached they that there stood, said to Peter. Truly thou art of them, thy speech thee makes clear")

Discussion topics/projects

I   A nineteenth-century scholar named Curtius (quoted in Aitchison, 2001) described a major goal of historical linguistics in the following way:

A principal goal of this science is to reconstruct the full, pure forms of an original stage from the variously disfigured and mutilated forms which are attested in the individual languages.

Do you agree that languages decay and become worse ("disfigured and mutilated") through time? What kind of evidence would you use to argue for or against this point of view?
(For background reading, see chapter 17 of Aitchison, 2001.)

II   Using what you have learned about comparative reconstruction, try to recreate the most likely proto-forms for these cognates (from Sihler, 2000: 140).

Languages		
A	**B**	**Proto-forms**
kewo ("red")	*čel* ("red")	_____
kuti ("tree")	*kut* ("wood")	_____
like ("heavy")	*lič* ("morose")	_____
waki ("sister")	*wač* ("sister")	_____
wapo ("hand")	*lap* ("hand")	_____
woli ("beam")	*lol* ("roof")	_____

(For background reading, see sections 96 to 102 of Sihler, 2000.)

Further reading

Basic treatments
Aitchison, J. (2001) *Language Change: Progress or Decay?* (3rd edition) Cambridge University Press
Schendl, H. (2001) *Historical Linguistics* Oxford University Press
More detailed treatments
Campbell, L. (2004) *Historical Linguistics: An Introduction* (2nd edition) MIT Press
Janson, T. (2002) *Speak: A Short History of Languages* Oxford University Press
Language families
Austin, P. (ed.) (2008) *One Thousand Languages* University of California Press
Comrie, B. (ed.) (1987) *The World's Major Languages* Oxford University Press
Language change
Labov, W. (2001) *Principles of Linguistic Change* volume 2: *Social Factors* Blackwell
McMahon, A. (1994) *Understanding Language Change* Cambridge University Press
History of the English language
Barber, C., J. Beal and P. Shaw (2009) *The English Language: A Historical Introduction* (2nd edition) Cambridge University Press

Lerer, S. (2007) *Inventing English: A Portable History of the Language* Columbia University Press

On Sir William Jones

Cannon, G. (1990) *The Life and Mind of Oriental Jones* Cambridge University Press

Broadening and narrowing of meaning

Minkova, D., and R. Stockwell (2009) *English Words: History and Structure* (2nd edition) Cambridge University Press

On "lovely" and "rather"

Adamson, S. (2000) "A lovely little example" In O. Fischer, A. Rosenbach and D. Stein (eds.) *Pathways of Change: Grammaticalization in English* (39–66) John Benjamins

Rissanen, M. (2008) "From 'quickly' to 'fairly': on the history of *rather*" *English Language and Linguistics* 12: 345–359

Other references

Ethnologue (2005) (15th edition) SIL International

Sihler, A. (2000) *Language History: An Introduction* John Benjamins

18 Language and regional variation

Yesterday, I toll my dad, "Buy chocolate kine now, bumbye somebody going egg our house you know, cuz you so chang." He sed, "Sucking kine mo' bettah cuz lass mo' long. Da kids going appreciate cuz …" And befo' he could start his "Back in my days story" I jus sed, "Yeah, yeah, yeah, I undahstand," cuz I nevah like hea da story again ah about how he nevah have candy wen he wuz small and how wuz one TREAT fo' eat da orange peel wit sugar on top. Da orange PEEL you know. Not da actual orange, but da orange PEEL. Strong emphasis on PEEL cuz dey wuz POOR.

Tonouchi (2001)

Throughout this book, we have been talking about languages such as English, Spanish or Swahili as if there was a single variety of each in everyday use. That is, we have largely ignored the fact that every language has a lot of variation, especially in the way it is spoken. If we just look at English, we find widespread variation in the way it is spoken in different countries such as Australia, Britain and the USA. We can also find a range of varieties in different parts of those countries, with Lee Tonouchi's account of "Trick-O-Treat" in Hawai'i as just one example. In this chapter, we investigate aspects of language variation based on where that language is used, as a way of doing **linguistic geography**. First, we should identify the particular variety that we have normally assumed when we referred to a language as English, Spanish or Swahili.

The standard language

When we talked about the words and structures of a language in earlier chapters, we were concentrating on the features of only one variety, usually called the **standard language**. This is actually an idealized variety, because it has no specific region. It is the variety associated with administrative, commercial and educational centers, regardless of region. If we think of Standard English, it is the version we believe is found in printed English in newspapers and books, is widely used in the mass media and is taught in most schools. It is the variety we normally try to teach to those who want to learn English as a second or foreign language. It is clearly associated with education and broadcasting in public contexts and is more easily described in terms of the written language (i.e. vocabulary, spelling, grammar) than the spoken language.

If we are thinking of that general variety used in public broadcasting in the United States, we can refer more specifically to Standard American English or, in Britain, to Standard British English. In other parts of the world, we can talk about other recognized varieties such as Standard Australian English, Standard Canadian English or Standard Indian English.

Accent and dialect

Whether we think we speak a standard variety of English or not, we all speak with an **accent**. It is a myth that some speakers have accents while others do not. We might feel that some speakers have very distinct or easily recognized types of accent while others may have more subtle or less noticeable accents, but every language-user speaks with an accent. Technically, the term "accent" is restricted to the description of aspects of pronunciation that identify where an individual speaker is from, regionally or socially. It is different from the term **dialect**, which is used to describe features of grammar and vocabulary as well as aspects of pronunciation.

We recognize that the sentence *You don't know what you're talking about* will generally "look" the same whether spoken with an American accent or a Scottish accent. Both speakers will be using forms associated with Standard English, but have different pronunciations. However, this next sentence – *Ye dinnae ken whit yer haverin' aboot* – has the same meaning as the first, but has been written out in an approximation of what a person who speaks one dialect of Scottish English might say. There are differences in pronunciation (e.g. *whit, aboot*), but there are also examples of different vocabulary (e.g. *ken, haverin'*) and a different grammatical form (*dinnae*).

While differences in vocabulary are often easily recognized, dialect variations in the meaning of grammatical constructions are less frequently documented. In the following example (from Trudgill, 1983) two British English speaking visitors (B and C) and a local Irish English speaker (A) are involved in a conversation in Donegal, Ireland.

A: *How long are youse here?*
B: *Till after Easter.*
   (Speaker A looks puzzled.)
C: *We came on Sunday.*
A: *Ah. Youse're here a while then.*

It seems that the construction *How long are youse here?*, in speaker A's dialect, is used with a meaning close to the structure "How long have you been here?" referring to past time. Speaker B, however, answers as if the question was referring to future time ("How long are you going to be here?"). When speaker C answers with a past time response (*We came on Sunday*), speaker A acknowledges it and repeats his use of a present tense (*Youse're here*) to refer to past time. Note that the dialect form *youse* (= "you" plural) seems to be understood by the visitors though it is unlikely to be part of their own dialect.

Dialectology

Despite occasional difficulties, there is a general impression of mutual intelligibility among many speakers of different dialects of English. This is one of the criteria used in the study of dialects, or **dialectology**, to distinguish between two different dialects of the same language (whose speakers can usually understand each other) and two different languages (whose speakers can't usually understand each other). This is not the only, or the most reliable, way of identifying dialects, but it is helpful in establishing the fact that each different dialect, like each language, is equally worthy of analysis. It is important to recognize, from a linguistic point of view, that none of the varieties of a language is inherently "better" than any other. They are simply different.

From a social point of view, however, some varieties do become more prestigious. In fact, the variety that develops as the standard language has usually been one socially prestigious dialect, originally associated with a center of economic and political power (e.g. London for British English and Paris for French). Yet, there always continue to be other varieties of a language spoken in different regions.

Regional dialects

The existence of different regional dialects is widely recognized and often the source of some humor for those living in different regions. In the United States, people from the

Brooklyn area of New York may joke about a Southerner's definition of *sex* by telling you that *sex is fo' less than tin*, in their best imitation of someone from the Southern states. In return, Southerners can wonder aloud about what a *tree guy* is in Brooklyn, since they have heard Brooklyn speakers refer to *doze tree guys*. Some regional dialects clearly have stereotyped pronunciations associated with them.

Going beyond stereotypes, those involved in the serious investigation of regional dialects have devoted a lot of survey research to the identification of consistent features of speech found in one geographical area compared to another. These dialect surveys often involve painstaking attention to detail and tend to operate with very specific criteria in identifying acceptable informants. After all, it is important to know if the person whose speech you are recording really is a typical representative of the region's dialect.

Consequently, the informants in the major dialect surveys of the twentieth century tended to be **NORMS** or "non-mobile, older, rural, male speakers." Such speakers were selected because it was believed that they were less likely to have influences from outside the region in their speech. One unfortunate consequence of using such criteria is that the resulting dialect description tends to be more accurate of a period well before the time of investigation. Nevertheless, the detailed information obtained has provided the basis for a number of Linguistic Atlases of whole countries (e.g. England) and regions (e.g. the Upper Midwest area of the United States).

Isoglosses and dialect boundaries

We can look at some examples of regional variation found in a survey that resulted in the Linguistic Atlas of the Upper Midwest of the United States. One of the aims of a survey of this type is to find a number of significant differences in the speech of those living in different areas and to be able to chart where the boundaries are, in dialect terms, between those areas. If it is found, for example, that the vast majority of informants in one area say they carry things home from the store in a *paper bag* while the majority in another area say they use a *paper sack*, then it is usually possible to draw a line across a map separating the two areas, as shown on the accompanying illustration. This line is called an **isogloss** and represents a boundary between the areas with regard to that one particular linguistic item.

If a very similar distribution is found for another two items, such as a preference for *pail* to the north and *bucket* to the south, then another isogloss, probably overlapping the first, can be drawn on the map. When a number of isoglosses come together in this way, a more solid line, indicating a **dialect boundary**, can be drawn.

In the accompanying illustration, a small circle indicates where *paper bag* was used and a plus sign shows where *paper sack* was used. The broken line between

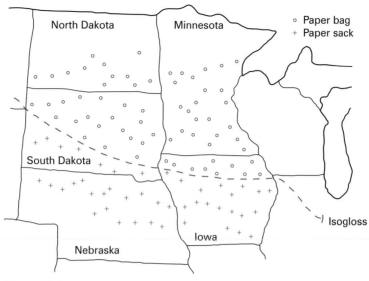

Figure 18.1

the two areas represents an isogloss that roughly coincides with lines separating several other linguistic features. Using this dialect boundary information, we find that in the Upper Midwest of the USA there is a Northern dialect area that includes Minnesota, North Dakota, most of South Dakota and Northern Iowa. The rest of Iowa and Nebraska show characteristics of the Midland dialect. Some of the noticeable pronunciation and vocabulary differences are illustrated here.

	("taught")	("roof")	("creek")	("greasy")
Northern:	[ɔ]	[ʊ]	[ɪ]	[s]
Midland:	[ɑ]	[u]	[i]	[z]

Northern:	*paper bag*	*pail*	*kerosene*	*slippery*	*get sick*
Midland:	*paper sack*	*bucket*	*coal oil*	*slick*	*take sick*

So, if an American English (male) speaker pronounces the word *greasy* as [grizi] and asks for a *bucket* to carry water, then he is not likely to have grown up and spent most of his life in Minnesota. While making this general claim, we shouldn't forget that, although the characteristic forms listed here were found in the speech of a large percentage of those interviewed in the dialect survey, they won't necessarily be used by all speakers currently living in the region.

The dialect continuum

Another note of caution is required with regard to dialect boundaries. The drawing of isoglosses and dialect boundaries is quite useful in establishing a broad view of regional dialects, but it tends to obscure the fact that, at most dialect boundary areas, one dialect or language variety merges into another. Keeping this in mind, we can view regional variation as existing along a **dialect continuum** rather than as having sharp breaks from one region to the next.

A very similar type of continuum can occur with related languages existing on either side of a political border. As you travel from Holland into Germany, you will find concentrations of Dutch speakers giving way to areas near the border where "Dutch" may sound more like "Deutsch" because the Dutch dialects and the German dialects are less clearly differentiated. Then, as you travel into Germany, greater concentrations of distinctly German speakers occur.

Speakers who move back and forth across this border area, using different varieties with some ease, may be described as **bidialectal** (i.e. "speaking two dialects"). Most of us grow up with some form of bidialectalism, speaking one dialect "in the street" among family and friends, and having to learn another dialect "in school." However, in some places, there are different languages used in the street and in school. When we talk about people knowing two distinct languages, we describe them as **bilingual**.

Bilingualism and diglossia

In many countries, regional variation is not simply a matter of two (or more) dialects of a single language, but can involve two (or more) quite distinct and different languages. Canada, for example, is an officially bilingual country, with both French and English as official languages. This recognition of the linguistic rights of the country's French speakers, largely in Quebec, did not come about without a lot of political upheaval. For most of its history, Canada was essentially an English-speaking country, with a French-speaking minority group. In such a situation, **bilingualism** at the level of the individual tends to be a feature of the minority group. In this form of bilingualism, a member of a minority group grows up in one linguistic community, mainly speaking one language (e.g. Welsh in Britain or Spanish in the United States), but learns another language (e.g. English) in order to take part in the larger dominant linguistic community.

Indeed, many members of linguistic minorities can live out their entire lives without ever seeing their native language appear in the public domain. Sometimes political activism can change that. It was only after English notices and signs were frequently defaced, or replaced by scribbled Welsh-language versions, that bilingual

Figure 18.2

(English–Welsh) signs came into widespread use in Wales. Many *henoed* never expected to see their first language on public signs in Wales, as illustrated in the accompanying photograph, though they may wonder why everyone is being warned about them.

Individual bilingualism, however, doesn't have to be the result of political dominance by a group using a different language. It can simply be the result of having two parents who speak different languages. If a child simultaneously acquires the French spoken by her mother and the English spoken by her father, then the distinction between the two languages may not even be noticed by the child. There will simply be two ways of talking according to the person being talked to. However, even in this type of bilingualism, one language tends eventually to become the dominant one, with the other in a subordinate role.

A rather special situation involving two distinct varieties of a language, called **diglossia**, exists in some countries. In diglossia, there is a "low" variety, acquired locally and used for everyday affairs, and a "high" or special variety, learned in school and used for important matters. A type of diglossia exists in Arabic-speaking countries where the high variety (Classical Arabic) is used in formal lectures, serious political events and especially in religious discussions. The low variety is the local version of the language, such as Egyptian Arabic or Lebanese Arabic. Through a long period in European history, a diglossic situation existed with Latin as the high variety and one of the local languages of Europe (early versions of Modern Italian, French and Spanish) as the low variety or "vernacular" (see Chapter 19).

Language planning

Perhaps because bilingualism in contemporary Europe and North America tends to be found mostly among minority groups, many countries are often assumed to be **monolingual**. For many of those residents who are only capable of speaking one language (English), the United States would indeed seem to be a monolingual country. For others, it clearly is not, because they live in large communities where English is not the first language of the home. As one example, the majority of the population in San Antonio, Texas, will be more likely to listen to radio broadcasts in Spanish than in English. This simple fact has quite large repercussions in terms of the organization of local representative government and the educational system. Should elementary school teaching take place in Spanish or English?

Consider a similar question in the context of Guatemala, a country in Central America, where there are twenty-six Mayan languages spoken, as well as Spanish. If, in this situation, Spanish is selected as the language of education, are all those Mayan speakers put at an early educational disadvantage within the society? Questions of this type require answers on the basis of some type of **language planning**. Government, legal and educational organizations in many countries have to plan which variety or varieties of the languages spoken in the country are to be used for official business. In Israel, despite the fact that it was not the most widely used language among the population, Hebrew was chosen as the official government language. In India, the choice was Hindi, yet in many non-Hindi-speaking regions, there were riots against this decision. There were "National Language Wars" in the Philippines before different groups could agree on the name of the national language (Filipino).

The process of language planning may be seen in a better light when the full series of stages is implemented over a number of years. The adoption of Swahili as the national language of Tanzania in East Africa may serve as a good example. There still exist a large number of other languages, as well as the colonial vestiges of English, but the educational, legal and government systems have gradually introduced Swahili as the official language. The process of "selection" (choosing an official language) is followed by "codification," in which basic grammars, dictionaries and written models are used to establish the standard variety. The process of "elaboration" follows, with the standard variety being developed for use in all aspects of social life and the appearance of a body of literary work written in the standard. The process of "implementation" is largely a matter of government attempts to encourage use of the standard, and "acceptance" is the final stage when a substantial majority of the population have come to use the standard and to think of it as the national language, playing a part in not only social, but also national identity.

Pidgins and creoles

In some areas, the standard chosen may be a variety that originally had no native speakers in the country. For example, in Papua New Guinea, a lot of official business is conducted in Tok Pisin. This language is now used by over a million people, but it began many years earlier as a kind of "contact" language called a pidgin. A **pidgin** is a variety of a language that developed for some practical purpose, such as trading, among groups of people who had a lot of contact, but who did not know each other's languages. As such, it would have no native speakers. The origin of the term "pidgin" is thought to be from a Chinese version of the English word "business."

A pidgin is described as an "English pidgin" if English is the **lexifier** language, that is, the main source of words in the pidgin. It doesn't mean that those words will have the same pronunciation or meaning as in the source. For example, the word *gras* has its origins in the English word "grass," but in Tok Pisin it also came to be used for "hair." It is part of *mausgras* ("moustache") and *gras bilong fes* ("beard").

There are several English pidgins still used today. They are characterized by an absence of any complex grammatical morphology and a somewhat limited vocabulary. Inflectional suffixes such as -*s* (plural) and -*'s* (possessive) on nouns in Standard English are rare in pidgins, while structures like *tu buk* ("two books") and *di gyal place* ("the girl's place") are common. Functional morphemes often take the place of inflectional morphemes found in the source language. For example, instead of changing the form of *you* to *your*, as in the English phrase *your book*, English-based pidgins use a form like *bilong*, and change the word order to produce phrases like *buk bilong yu*.

The syntax of pidgins can be quite unlike the languages from which terms were borrowed and modified, as can be seen in this example from an earlier stage of Tok Pisin.

Baimbai	*hed*	*bilongyu*	*i-arrait*	*gain*
by and by	head	belong you	he alright	again

"Your head will soon get well again"

There are believed to be between six and twelve million people still using pidgin languages and between ten and seventeen million using descendants from pidgins called "creoles." When a pidgin develops beyond its role as a trade or contact language and becomes the first language of a social community, it is described as a **creole**. Tok Pisin is now a creole. Although still locally referred to as "Pidgin," the language spoken by a large number of people in Hawai'i is also a creole, technically known as Hawai'i Creole English. A creole initially develops as the first language of children growing up in a pidgin-using community and becomes more complex as it serves more communicative purposes. Thus, unlike pidgins, creoles have large numbers of native speakers and are not restricted at all in their uses. A French creole is spoken by the majority of the population in Haiti and English creoles are used in Jamaica and Sierra Leone.

The separate vocabulary elements of a pidgin can become grammatical elements in a creole. The form *baimbai yu go* ("by and by you go") in early Tok Pisin gradually shortened to *bai yu go*, and finally to *yu bigo*, with a grammatical structure not unlike that of its English translation equivalent, "you will go."

The post-creole continuum

In many contemporary situations where creoles evolved, there is usually evidence of another process at work. Just as there was development from a pidgin to a creole, known as **creolization**, there is now often a retreat from the use of the creole by those who have greater contact with a standard variety of the language. Where education and greater social prestige are associated with a "higher" variety (e.g. British English in Jamaica), a number of speakers will tend to use fewer creole forms and structures. This process, known as **decreolization**, leads at one extreme to a variety that is closer to the external standard model and leaves, at the other extreme, a basic variety with more local creole features. Between these two extremes may be a range of slightly different varieties, some with many and some with fewer creole features. This range of varieties, evolving after (= "post") the creole has come into existence, is called the **post-creole continuum**.

So, in Jamaica, one speaker may say *a fi mi buk dat,* using the basic creole variety, another may put it as *iz mi buk,* using a variety with fewer creole features, and yet another may choose *it's my book,* using a variety with only some pronunciation features of the creole, or a "creole accent." It is also very common for speakers to be able to use a range of varieties in different situations.

We would predict that these differences would be tied very much to social values and social identity. In the course of discussing language varieties in terms of regional differences, we have excluded, in a rather artificial way, the complex social factors that are also at work in determining language variation. In the next chapter, we'll investigate the influence of a number of these social variables.

Study questions

1 Which variety of English would you say is being used in the introductory quotation from Lee Tonouchi?
2 What is the difference between an accent and a dialect?
3 What is one disadvantage of using NORMS in dialect surveys?
4 What does an isogloss represent in a linguistic atlas?
5 What are the first two stages of language planning in the process of adopting a national language?
6 In what specific way is a creole different from a pidgin?

Tasks

A In which areas of the British Isles would we find a Brummie accent, a Geordie accent, a speaker of Scouse, the use of *bairns* (= "children"), *boyo* (= "man"), *fink* (= "think") and *Would you be after wanting some tea?* (= "Do you want some tea?")?
B Two pioneers of dialectology were Georg Wenker and Jules Gilliéron. In what ways were their methods different and which method became the model for later dialect studies?
C Consider the following statements about Standard English and try to decide whether you agree or disagree with them, providing a reason in each case for your decision.

1 Standard English is not a language.
2 Standard English is an accent.
3 Standard English is a speech style.
4 Standard English is a set of rules for correct usage.

D In the study of pidgins, what is meant by a "substrate" and a "superstrate" language? Which of the two is likely to be the source of intonation, syntax and vocabulary?
E The following examples are based on Romaine (1988), quoted in Holmes (2008). Using what you learned about Tok Pisin, can you complete the translations of these examples with the following English words and phrases: *bird's feather, bird's wing, cat's fur, eyebrow, hair, weed*?

gras antap long ai	*gras bilong pisin*	*gras nogut*
gras bilong hed	*gras bilong pusi*	*han bilong pisin*

F The following example of Hawai'i Creole English (from Lum, 1990, quoted in Nichols, 2004) has some characteristic forms and structures. How would you analyze the use of *da, had, one, stay* and *wen* in this extract?

*Had one nudda guy in one tee-shirt was sitting at da table next to us was
watching da Bag Man too. He was eating one plate lunch and afterwards, he
wen take his plate ovah to da Bag Man. Still had little bit everyting on top, even had
bar-ba-que meat left.*

"Bra," da guy tell, "you like help me finish? I stay full awready."

Discussion topics/projects

I   Peter Trudgill has noted that "increased geographical mobility during the course
of the twentieth century led to the disappearance of many dialects and dialect forms
through a process we can call dialect levelling – the levelling out of differences
between one dialect and another" (2000: 155).

  Do you think that "dialect levelling" is continuing in the geographical area you are
most familiar with? Does this mean that there will eventually be only one dialect?
What other forces might be at work that would cause new dialects to emerge?
(For background reading, see chapter 8 of Trudgill, 2000.)

II English is not the official language of the United States, but some insist that it
should be. What are the arguments for and against the "English-Only Movement"?
(For background reading, see Wiley, 2004.)

Further reading

Basic treatments

Crystal, D. (2003) *The Cambridge Encyclopedia of the English Language* (chapter 20) (2nd
    edition) Cambridge University Press

Kretzschmar, W. (2004) "Regional dialects" In E. Finegan and J. Rickford (eds.) *Language in the
    USA* (39–57) Cambridge University Press

More detailed treatments

Chambers, J. and P. Trudgill (1998) *Dialectology* (2nd edition) Cambridge University Press

Wardhaugh, R. (2006) *An Introduction to Sociolinguistics* (5th edition) Blackwell

American English dialects

Wolfram, W. and B. Ward (eds.) (2006) *American Voices: How Dialects Differ from Coast to Coast*
    Blackwell

British English dialects

Hughes, A., P. Trudgill and D. Watt (2005) *English Accents and Dialects* Hodder Arnold

Other varieties of English

Trudgill, P. and J. Hannah (2008) *International English* (5th edition) Arnold

Bilingualism

Myers-Scotton, C. (2006) *Multiple Voices* Blackwell

Pidgins and creoles

Nichols, J. (2004) "Creole languages: forging new identities" In E. Finegan and J. Rickford (eds.)
　　Language in the USA (133–152) Cambridge University Press

Siegel, J. (2008) *The Emergence of Pidgin and Creole Languages* Oxford University Press

The Dutch–German dialect continuum

Barbour, S. and P. Stevenson (1990) *Variation in German* Cambridge University Press

Tok Pisin (baimbai)

Sankoff, G. and S. Laberge (1974) "On the acquisition of native speakers by a language" In
　　D. DeCamp and I. Hancock (eds.) *Pidgins and Creoles* (73–84) Georgetown University Press

Hawai'i Creole English

Sakoda, K. and J. Siegel (2003) *Pidgin Grammar* Bess Press

Other references

Holmes, J. (2008) *An Introduction to Sociolinguistics* (3rd edition) Pearson

Lum, D. (1990) *Pass On, No Pass Back* Bamboo Ridge Press

Romaine, S. (1988) *Pidgin and Creole Languages* Longman

Trudgill, P. (1983) *On Dialect* Blackwell

Trudgill, P. (2000) *Sociolinguistics* (4th edition) Penguin

Wiley, T. (2004) "Language planning, language policy, and the English-Only Movement" In
　　E. Finegan and J. Rickford (eds.) *Language in the USA* (319–338) Cambridge University Press

19 Language and social variation

Admittedly, it is hard to make stylistic judgements on slang from the past, but when we read a seventeenth-century description of someone as a "shite-a-bed scoundrel, a turdy gut, a blockish grutnol and a grouthead gnat-snapper" it's unlikely the writer was using the neutral or "proper" language of the time – I think we can safely assume he was using slang.

Burridge (2004)

In the preceding chapter, we focused on variation in language use found in different geographical areas. However, not everyone in a single geographical area speaks in the same way in every situation. We recognize that certain uses of language, such as the slang in Kate Burridge's description, are more likely to be found in the speech of some individuals in society and not others. We are also aware of the fact that people who live in the same region, but who differ in terms of education and economic status, often speak in quite different ways. Indeed, these differences may be used, implicitly or explicitly, as indications of membership in different social groups or speech communities. A **speech community** is a group of people who share a set of norms and expectations regarding the use of language. The study of the linguistic features that have social relevance for participants in those speech communities is called "sociolinguistics."

Sociolinguistics

The term **sociolinguistics** is used generally for the study of the relationship between language and society. This is a broad area of investigation that developed through the interaction of linguistics with a number of other academic disciplines. It has strong connections with anthropology through the study of language and culture, and with sociology through the investigation of the role language plays in the organization of social groups and institutions. It is also tied to social psychology, particularly with regard to how attitudes and perceptions are expressed and how in-group and out-group behaviors are identified. We use all these connections when we try to analyze language from a social perspective.

Social dialects

Whereas the traditional study of regional dialects tended to concentrate on the speech of people in rural areas, the study of **social dialects** has been mainly concerned with speakers in towns and cities. In the social study of dialect, it is social class that is mainly used to define groups of speakers as having something in common. The two main groups are generally identified as "middle class," those who have more years of education and perform non-manual work, and "working class," those who have fewer years of education and perform manual work of some kind. So, when we refer to "working-class speech," we are talking about a social dialect. The terms "upper" and "lower" are used to further subdivide the groups, mainly on an economic basis, making "upper-middle-class speech" another type of social dialect or **sociolect**.

As in all dialect studies, only certain features of language use are treated as relevant in the analysis of social dialects. These features are pronunciations, words or struc- tures that are regularly used in one form by working-class speakers and in another form by middle-class speakers. In Edinburgh, Scotland, for example, the word *home* is regularly pronounced as [heɪm], as if rhyming with *name*, among lower-working-class speakers, and as [hom], as if rhyming with *foam*, among middle-class speakers. It's a small difference in pronunciation, but it's an indicator of social status. A more familiar example might be the verb *ain't*, as in *I ain't finished yet*, which is generally used more often in working-class speech than in middle-class speech.

When we look for other examples of language use that might be characteristic of a social dialect, we treat class as the **social variable** and the pronunciation or word as the **linguistic variable**. We can then try to investigate the extent to which there is system- atic variation involving the two variables by counting how often speakers in each class use each version of the linguistic variable. This isn't usually an all-or-nothing situation, so studies of social dialects typically report how often speakers in a particular group use a certain form rather than find that only one group or the other uses the form.

Education and occupation

Although the unique circumstances of every life result in each of us having an individual way of speaking, a personal dialect or **idiolect**, we generally tend to sound like others with whom we share similar educational backgrounds and/or occupations.

Among those who leave the educational system at an early age, there is a general pattern of using certain forms that are relatively infrequent in the speech of those who go on to complete college. Expressions such as those contained in *Them boys throwed somethin'* or *It wasn't us what done it* are generally associated with speakers who have spent less time in education. Those who spend more time in the educational system tend to have more features in their spoken language that derive from a lot of time spent with the written language, so that *threw* is more likely than *throwed* and *who* occurs more often than *what* in references to people. The observation that some teacher "talks like a book" is possibly a reflection of an extreme form of this influence from the written language after years in the educational system.

As adults, the outcome of our time in the educational system is usually reflected in our occupation and socio-economic status. The way bank executives, as opposed to window cleaners, talk to each other usually provides linguistic evidence for the significance of these social variables. In the 1960s, sociolinguist William Labov combined elements from place of occupation and socio-economic status by looking at pronunciation differences among salespeople in three New York City department stores (see Labov, 2006). They were Saks Fifth Avenue (with expensive items, upper-middle-class status), Macy's (medium-priced, middle-class status) and Klein's (with cheaper items, working-class status). Labov went into each of these stores and asked salespeople specific questions, such as *Where are the women's shoes?*, in order to elicit answers with the expression *fourth floor*. This expression contains two opportunities for the pronunciation (or not) of **postvocalic** /r/, that is, the /r/ sound after a vowel. Strictly speaking, it is /r/ after a vowel and before a consonant or the end of a word.

In the department stores, there was a regular pattern in the answers. The higher the socio-economic status of the store, the more /r/ sounds were produced, and the lower the status, the fewer /r/ sounds were produced by those who worked there. So, the frequency of occurrence of this linguistic variable (r) could mark the speech samples as upper middle class versus middle class versus working class. Other studies confirmed this regular pattern in the speech of New Yorkers.

In a British study conducted in Reading, about 40 miles west of London, Trudgill (1974) found that the social value associated with the same variable (r) was quite different. Middle-class speakers in Reading pronounced fewer /r/ sounds than working-class speakers. In this particular city, upper-middle-class speakers didn't seem to pronounce postvocalic /r/ at all. They said things like *Oh, that's mahvellous, dahling!*. The results of these two studies are shown in Table 19.1 (from Romaine, 2000).

Table 19.1 Percentages of groups pronouncing postvocalic /r/

Social class	New York City	Reading
upper middle class	32	0
lower middle class	20	28
upper working class	12	44
lower working class	0	49

Social markers

As shown in Table 19.1, the significance of the linguistic variable (r) can be virtually the opposite in terms of social status in two different places, yet in both places the patterns illustrate how the use of this particular speech sound functions as a **social marker**. That is, having this feature occur frequently in your speech (or not) marks you as a member of a particular social group, whether you realize it or not.

There are other pronunciation features that function as social markers. One feature that seems to be a fairly stable indication of lower class and less education, throughout the English-speaking world, is the final pronunciation of *-ing* with [n] rather than [ŋ] at the end of words such as *sitting* and *drinking*. Pronunciations represented by *sittin'* and *drinkin'* are typically associated with working-class speech.

Another social marker is called "[h]-dropping," which makes the words *at* and *hat* sound the same. It occurs at the beginning of words and can result in utterances that sound like *I'm so 'ungry I could eat an 'orse*. In contemporary English, this feature is associated with lower class and less education. It seems to have had a similar association as a social marker for Charles Dickens, writing in the middle of the nineteenth century. He used it as a way of indicating that the character Uriah Heep, in the novel *David Copperfield*, was from a lower class, as in this example (from Mugglestone, 1995).

> "I am well aware that I am the umblest person going," said Uriah Heep, modestly; " ... My mother is likewise a very umble person. We live in a numble abode, Master Copperfield, but we have much to be thankful for. My father's former calling was umble."

Speech style and style-shifting

In his department store study, Labov included another subtle element that allowed him not only to investigate the type of social stratification illustrated in Table 19.1, but also **speech style** as a social feature of language use. The most basic distinction in speech style is between formal uses and informal uses. Formal style is when we pay more careful attention to how we're speaking and informal style is when we pay less attention. They are sometimes described as "careful style" and "casual style." A change from one to the other by an individual is called **style-shifting**.

When Labov initially asked the salespeople where certain items were, he assumed they were answering in an informal manner. After they answered his question, Labov then pretended not to have heard and said, "Excuse me?" in order to elicit a repetition of the same expression, which was pronounced with more attention to being clear. This was taken as a representative sample of the speaker's more careful style. When speakers repeated the phrase *fourth floor*, the frequency of postvocalic /r/ increased in all groups. The most significant increase in frequency was among the Macy's group. In a finding that has been confirmed in other studies, middle-class speakers are much more likely to shift their style of speaking significantly in the direction of the upper middle class when they are using a careful style.

It is possible to use more elaborate elicitation procedures to create more gradation in the category of style. Asking someone to read a short text out loud will result in more attention to speech than simply asking them to answer some questions in an interview. Asking that same individual to read out loud a list of individual words taken from the text will result in even more careful pronunciation of those words and hence a more formal version of the individual's speech style.

When Labov analyzed the way New Yorkers performed in these elicitation proce-dures, he found a general overall increase in postvocalic /r/ in all groups as the task required more attention to speech. Among the lower-middle-class speakers, the increase was so great in the pronunciation of the word lists that their frequency of postvocalic /r/ was actually higher than among upper-middle-class speakers. As other studies have confirmed, when speakers in a middle-status group try to use a prestige form associated with a higher-status group in a formal situation, they have a tendency to overuse the form.

Prestige

In discussing style-shifting, we introduced the idea of a "prestige" form as a way of explaining the direction in which certain individuals change their speech. When that change is in the direction of a form that is more frequent in the speech of those perceived to have higher social status, we are dealing with **overt prestige**, or status that is generally recognized as "better" or more positively valued in the larger community.

There is, however, another phenomenon called **covert prestige**. This "hidden" status of a speech style as having positive value may explain why certain groups do not exhibit style-shifting to the same extent as other groups. For example, we might ask why many lower-working-class speakers do not change their speech style from casual to careful as radically as lower-middle-class speakers. The answer may be that they value the features that mark them as members of their social group and consequently avoid changing them in the direction of features associated with another social group. They may value group solidarity (i.e. sounding like those around them) more than upward mobility (i.e. sounding like those above them).

Among younger speakers in the middle class, there is often covert prestige attached to many features of pronunciation and grammar (*I ain't doin' nuttin'* rather than *I'm not doing anything*) that are more often associated with the speech of lower-status groups.

Speech accommodation

As we look more closely at variation in speech style, we can see that it is not only a function of speakers' social class and attention to speech, but it is also influenced by their perception of their listeners. This type of variation is sometimes described in terms of "audience design," but is more generally known as **speech accommodation**, defined as our ability to modify our speech style toward or away from the perceived style of the person(s) we're talking to.

We can adopt a speech style that attempts to reduce social distance, described as **convergence**, and use forms that are similar to those used by the person we're talking to. In the following examples (from Holmes, 2008), a teenage boy is asking to see some holiday photographs. In the first example, he is talking to his friend, and in the second example, he is talking to his friend's mother. The request is essentially the same, but the style is different as the speaker converges with the perceived speech style of the other.

> *C'mon Tony, gizzalook, gizzalook*
> *Excuse me. Could I have a look at your photos too, Mrs. Hall?*

In contrast, when a speech style is used to emphasize social distance between speakers, the process is called **divergence**. We can make our speech style diverge from another's by using forms that are distinctly different. In the third line of the following example, the Scottish teenager shifts to a speech style with features that differ sub-stantially from the first line.

TEENAGER: *I can't do it, sir.*
TEACHER: *Oh, come on. If I can do it, you can too.*
TEENAGER: *Look, I cannae dae it so …*

The sudden divergence in style seems to be triggered not only by a need to add emphasis to his repeated statement, but also by the "We're the same" claim of his teacher. This teenager is using speech style to mark that they are not the same.

Register and jargon

Another influence on speech style that is tied to social identity derives from **register**. A register is a conventional way of using language that is appropriate in a specific context, which may be identified as situational (e.g. in church), occupational (e.g. among lawyers) or topical (e.g. talking about language). We can recognize specific features that occur in the religious register (*Ye shall be blessed by Him in times of tribulation*), the legal register (*The plaintiff is ready to take the witness stand*) and even the linguistics register (*In the morphology of this dialect there are fewer inflectional suffixes*).

One of the defining features of a register is the use of **jargon**, which is special technical vocabulary (e.g. *plaintiff, suffix*) associated with a specific area of work or interest. In social terms, jargon helps to create and maintain connections among those who see themselves as "insiders" in some way and to exclude "outsiders." This exclusive effect of specialized jargon, as in the medical register (e.g. *Zanoxyn is a nonsteroidal anti-inflammatory drug for arthritis, bursitis and tendonitis*), often leads to complaints about what may seem like "jargonitis."

Slang

Whereas jargon is specialized vocabulary used by those inside established social groups, often defined by professional status (e.g. legal jargon), **slang** is more typically used among those who are outside established higher-status groups. Slang, or "collo-quial speech," describes words or phrases that are used instead of more everyday terms among younger speakers and other groups with special interests. The word *bucks* (for *dollars* or *money*) has been a slang expression for more than a hundred years, but the addition of *mega-* ("a lot of") in *megabucks* is a more recent innovation, along with *dead presidents* (whose pictures are on paper money) and *benjamins* (from Benjamin Franklin, on $100 bills).

Like clothing and music, slang is an aspect of social life that is subject to fashion, especially among adolescents. It can be used by those inside a group who share ideas and attitudes as a way of distinguishing themselves from others. As a marker of group identity during a limited stage of life such as early adolescence, slang expressions can "grow old" rather quickly. Older forms for "really good" such as *groovy*, *hip* and *super* were replaced by *awesome*, *rad* and *wicked* which gave way to *dope*, *kickass* and *phat*. A *hunk* ("physically attractive man") became a *hottie* and instead of something being *the pits* ("really bad"), the next generation thought it was a *bummer* or said, *That sucks!*. The difference in slang use between groups divided into older and younger speakers shows that age is another important factor involved in social variation.

However, the use of slang varies within the younger social group, as illustrated by the use of obscenities or **taboo terms**. Taboo terms are words and phrases that people avoid for reasons related to religion, politeness and prohibited behavior. They are often swear words, typically "bleeped" in public broadcasting (*What the bleep are you doing, you little bleep!*) or "starred" in print (*You stupid f***ing a**hole!*). In a study of the linguistic differences among "Jocks" (higher status) and "Burnouts" (lower status) in Detroit high schools, Eckert (2000) reported the regular use of taboo words among both males and females in the lower-status group. However, among the higher-status group, males used taboo words only with other males, while females didn't seem to use them at all. Social class divisions, at least in the use of slang, are already well established during adolescence.

African American English

In much of the preceding discussion, we have been reviewing research on social variation based mainly on examples from British English and what we might call "European" American English. Labeling one general social variety according to the historical origins of the speakers allows us to put it in contrast with another major variety called **African American English** (**AAE**). Also known as Black English or Ebonics, AAE is a variety used by many (not all) African Americans in many different regions of the USA. It has a number of characteristic features that, taken together, form a distinct set of social markers.

In much the same way as large geographical barriers between groups foster linguistic differences in regional dialects, social barriers such as discrimination and segregation serve to create marked differences between social dialects. In the case of AAE, those different features have often been stigmatized as "bad" language, following a regular pattern whereby the social practices, especially speech, of dominated groups are treated as "abnormal" by those dominant groups who are in charge of defining "normal." Although AAE speakers continue to experience the effects of discrimination, their social dialect often has covert prestige among younger speakers in other social groups, particularly with regard to popular music, and certain features of AAE may be used in expressions of social identity by many who are not African American.

Vernacular language

The form of AAE that has been most studied is usually described as **African American Vernacular English (AAVE)**. The term "vernacular" has been used since the Middle Ages, first to describe local European languages (low prestige) in contrast to Latin (high prestige), then to characterize any non-standard spoken version of a language used by lower status groups. So, the **vernacular** is a general expression for a kind of social dialect, typically spoken by a lower-status group, which is treated as "non-standard" because of marked differences from the "standard" language (see Chapter 18). As the vernacular language of African Americans, AAVE shares a number of features with other non-standard varieties, such as "Chicano English," spoken in some Hispanic American communities. Varieties of what has been called "Asian American English" are also characterized by some of the pronunciation features described in studies of this vernacular.

The sounds of a vernacular

A pervasive phonological feature in AAVE and other English vernaculars is the tendency to reduce final consonant clusters, so that words ending in two consonants (*left hand*) are often pronounced as if there is only one (*lef han*). This can affect the pronunciation of past tense *-ed* forms in certain contexts, with expressions such as *iced tea* and *I passed the test* sounding like *ice tea* and *I pass the tess*. Initial dental consonants (*think, that*) are frequently pronounced as alveolar stops (*tink, dat*), with the result that the definite article (*the*) is heard as [də], as in *You da man!*. Other morphological features, such as possessive *-'s* (*John's girlfriend*) and third person singular *-s* (*she loves him*), are not typically used (*John girlfriend, she love him*). Also, when a phrase contains an obvious indication of plural number, the plural *-s* marker (*guys, friends*) is usually not included (*two guy, one of my friend*).

The grammar of a vernacular

It is typically in aspects of grammar that AAVE and other vernaculars are most stigmatized as being "illogical" or "sloppy." One frequently criticized element is the double negative construction, as in *He don't know nothin* or *I ain't afraid of no ghosts*. Because the negative is expressed twice, these structures have been condemned as "illogical" (since one negative supposedly cancels the other). Yet, this feature of AAVE can be found in many other English dialects and in other languages such as French: *il ne sait rien* (literally, "he not knows nothing"). It was also common in Old English: *Ic naht singan ne cuðe* (literally, "I not sing not could"). There is nothing inherently illogical about these structures, which can extend to multiple negatives, allowing greater emphasis on the negative aspect of the message, as in *He don't never do nothin*.

The "sloppy" criticism focuses on the frequent absence of forms of the verb "to be" (*are, is*) in AAVE expressions such as *You crazy* or *She workin now*. It may be more accurate to say that wherever *are* and *is* can be contracted in the casual style of other varieties (*You're, She's*), they are not articulated in AAVE. Formal styles of Standard English require *are* and *is* in such expressions, but many regional varieties do not. Nor do many other languages such as Arabic and Russian require forms of "to be" in similar contexts. This feature of AAVE speech can't be "sloppy" any more than it would be "sloppy" in normal Arabic or Russian speech.

While AAVE speakers don't include the auxiliary verb *is* in expressions such as *She workin now*, to describe what is happening currently, they can use *be* (not *is*), as in *She be workin downtown now*, as a way of expressing habitual action. That is, the presence or absence of *be* distinguishes between what is a recurring activity or state and what is currently happening. To talk about a habitual action that started or happened in the past, AAVE uses *bin* (typically stressed), not *was*, as in *She bin workin there*. In effect, the use of habitual *be* or *bin*, and the absence of forms of "to be" in present state expressions, are all consistent features in the grammar of AAVE. The negative versions of these verbs are formed with *don't* (not *doesn't*) and the verb is not used with a contracted negative. So, in AAVE, *She don't be workin* is grammatical, whereas **She doesn't be workin* and **She ben't workin* would be considered ungrammatical.

In this discussion, we have focused on the linguistic features of social dialects. Yet, the groups who use those dialects are not only distinguished by the language they use, but by more general factors such as beliefs and assumptions about the world and their experience of it. This is usually discussed in terms of "culture," the subject of the next chapter.

Study questions

1 How would you define a "speech community"?
2 What is the difference between an idiolect and a sociolect?
3 Why did Labov try to elicit answers with the expression *fourth floor*?
4 In what way can the pronunciation of *-ing* be a social marker?
5 What is meant by a "register"?
6 In AAVE, what is communicated by the use of *be* in *He don't be smokin now*?

Tasks

A How does "micro-sociolinguistics" differ from "macro-sociolinguistics"?
B In the study of social dialects, what is "the observer's paradox" and how can it be overcome?
C What is the difference between style-shifting and code-switching?
D What is the origin of the term "Ebonics" and how has its meaning changed?
E Variation in language use according to social status is evident in those languages that have a system of honorifics. What are honorifics and in which languages are they most commonly used?

   Using what you discover about honorifics, try to decide which speaker (A or B, C or D) in the following dialogues has superior status within the business organization in which they both work (from Shibatani, 2001: 556).

   A: *Konban nomi ni ikoo ka*
      (tonight drink to go question)
   B: *Ee, iki-masyoo*
      (yes, go-honorific)
   C: *Konban nomi ni iki-masyoo ka*
      (tonight drink to go-honorific question)
   D: *Un, ikoo*
      (yes, let's go)

F According to Fought (2003), Chicano English is spoken in the southwestern region of the USA (from Texas to California), mainly by individuals of Mexican-American heritage. Consider the following statements about Chicano English and try to decide whether you agree or disagree with them, providing a reason in each case for your decision.
   1 Chicano English is a dialect of American English.
   2 Chicano English is another term for "Spanglish."

3   Chicano English is simply ungrammatical or "broken" English, as exemplified by sentences such as *Everybody knew the Cowboys was gonna win again* and *She don't know Brenda*.
4   Chicano English is the second language learner's English of people from countries where Spanish is spoken.
5   There are no native speakers of Chicano English.

Discussion topics/projects

I   According to Brown and Attardo (2005):

> If children move to an area before the age of nine, they are able to "pick up" the local dialect, which their parents do not.

Do you think this statement is true of both regional dialect and social dialect? When and how do you think people develop their social dialects?
(For background reading, see chapter 6 of Brown and Attardo, 2005.)

II   From a linguistic point of view, there are no good or bad varieties of a language. However, there is a social process called "language subordination" whereby some varieties are treated as having less value than others. Can you describe how this process works in any social situation you are familiar with?
(For background reading, see Lippi-Green, 1997.)

Further reading

Basic treatments
Crystal, D. (2003) *The Cambridge Encyclopedia of the English Language* (chapter 21) (2nd edition) Cambridge University Press
Spolsky, B. (1998) *Sociolinguistics* Oxford University Press
More detailed treatments
Holmes, J. (2008) *An Introduction to Sociolinguistics* (3rd edition) Pearson
Romaine, S. (2000) *Language in Society* (2nd edition) Oxford University Press
Speech style
Eckert, P. and J. Rickford (eds.) (2001) *Style and Sociolinguistic Variation* Cambridge University Press
Speech accommodation and register
Downes, W. (2001) "Register" In R. Mesthrie (ed.) *Concise Encyclopedia of Sociolinguistics* (259–262) Elsevier
Giles, H. (2001) "Speech accommodation" In R. Mesthrie (ed.) *Concise Encyclopedia of Sociolinguistics* (193–197) Elsevier

Slang and adolescent speech

Eble, C. (2004) "Slang" In E. Finegan and J. Rickford (eds.) *Language in the USA* (375–386) Cambridge University Press

Eckert, P. (2004) "Adolescent language" In E. Finegan and J. Rickford (eds.) *Language in the USA* (361–374) Cambridge University Press

African American English

Green, L. (2002) *African American English* Cambridge University Press

Smitherman, G. (2000) *talkin that talk* Routledge

Other references

Brown, S. and S. Attardo (2005) *Understanding Language Structure, Interaction and Variation* (2nd edition) University of Michigan Press

Eckert, P. (2000) *Linguistic Variation as Social Practice* Blackwell

Fought, C. (2003) *Chicano English in Context* Palgrave Macmillan

Labov, W. (2006) *The Social Stratification of English in New York City* (2nd edition) Cambridge University Press

Lippi-Green, R. (1997) *English with an Accent* Routledge

Mugglestone, L. (1995) *Talking Proper: The Rise of Accent as Social Symbol* Clarendon Press

Shibatani, M. (2001) "Honorifics" In R. Mesthrie (ed.) *Concise Encyclopedia of Sociolinguistics* (552–559) Elsevier

Trudgill, P. (1974) *The Social Differentiation of English in Norwich* Cambridge University Press

20 Language and culture

The Quakers rejected the use of *you* as a polite form of address, and preferred *thou*, which to them signaled intimacy and equality. By refusing to use *you* because they took it as a deferential form of address, the Quakers provoked hostility from others who regarded their behavior as a sign of contempt. The repercussions of such deviant usage were severe for some Quakers such as Richard Davis, who reported that when he addressed the lady of the house in which he worked as *thou*, "she took a stick and gave me such a blow upon my bare head, that made it swell and sore for a considerable time. She was so disturbed by it, that she swore she would kill me."

Romaine (2000)

The type of sociolinguistic variation described in the previous chapter is sometimes attributed to cultural differences. It is not unusual to find aspects of language identified as characteristic features of African American culture or European culture or Japanese culture. This approach to the study of language originates in the work of anthropologists who have used language as a source of information in the general study of "culture."

Culture

We use the term **culture** to refer to all the ideas and assumptions about the nature of things and people that we learn when we become members of social groups. It can be defined as "socially acquired knowledge." This is the kind of knowledge that, like our first language, we initially acquire without conscious awareness. We develop awareness of our knowledge, and hence of our culture, only after having developed language. The particular language we learn through the process of cultural transmission provides us, at least initially, with a ready-made system of categorizing the world around us and our experience of it.

With the words we acquire, we learn to recognize the types of category distinctions that are relevant in our social world. Very young children may not initially think of "dog" and "horse" as different types of entities and refer to both as *bow-wow*. As they develop a more elaborated conceptual system along with English as their first language, they learn to categorize distinct types of creatures as *a dog* or *a horse*. In native cultures of the Pacific, there were no horses and, not surprisingly, there were no words for them. In order to use words such as *dog* or *horse*, *rain* or *snow*, *father* or *uncle*, *week* or *weekend*, we must have a conceptual system that includes these people, things and ideas as distinct and identifiable categories.

Categories

Although there is a lot of variation among all the individual "dogs" in our experience, we can use the word *dog* to talk about any one of them as a member of the category. A **category** is a group with certain features in common and we can think of the vocabulary we learn as an inherited set of category labels. These are the words for referring to concepts that people in our social world have typically needed to talk about.

It is tempting to believe that there is a fixed relationship between the set of words we have learned (our categories) and the way external reality is organized. However, evidence from the world's languages would suggest that the organization of external reality actually varies to some extent according to the language being used to talk about it. Some languages may have lots of different words for types of "rain" or kinds of "coconut" and other languages may have only one or two. Although the Dani of New Guinea can see all colors of the spectrum, they only use names for two of them, equivalents of "black" and "white." The Inuit of Greenland have names for those two, plus red, green and yellow. English has names for those five colors, plus blue, brown, purple, pink, orange and gray. It seems that languages used by groups with more technology have more color terms. Observing this difference between the number of basic color terms in languages, we can say that there are conceptual distinctions that are **lexicalized** ("expressed as a single word") in one language and not in another.

Kinship terms

Some of the clearest examples of lexicalized categories are words used to refer to people who are members of the same family, or **kinship terms**. All languages have kinship terms (e.g. *brother, mother, grandmother*), but they don't all put family members into categories in the same way. In some languages, the equivalent of the word *father* is used not only for "male parent," but also for "male parent's brother." In English, we use the word *uncle* for this other type of individual. We have lexicalized the distinction between the two concepts. Yet, we also use the same word (*uncle*) for "female parent's brother." That distinction isn't lexicalized in English, but it is in other languages. In Watam (spoken in Papua New Guinea), the English word *uncle* would be translated as either *aes* (father's brother) or *akwae* (mother's brother). Speakers of Mopan Maya (in Belize, Central America) lexicalize a distinction based on a different conceptual arrangement. Each of the following words is (and is not) a translation of the English word *uncle*.

suku'un: older brother and parent's younger brother
tataa':   parent's older brother and grandfather

It would seem that distinctions in age among "uncles" is important in Mopan Mayan culture. Other distinctions among relatives can also be lexicalized differently in the world's languages. For example, in Norwegian, the distinction between "male parent's mother" (*farmor*) and "female parent's mother" (*mormor*) is lexicalized, but in English the word *grandmother* is generally used for both.

Time concepts

To take a more abstract example, when we learn a word such as *week* or *weekend*, we are inheriting a conceptual system that operates with amounts of time as common categories. Having words for units of time such as "two days" or "seven days" shows that we can think of time (i.e. something abstract) in amounts, using noun phrases, in the same way as "two people" or "seven books" (i.e. something physical). In another world view, time may not be treated in this way. In the Hopi language, spoken in Arizona, there were traditionally no terms equivalent to most of our time words and phrases (*two hours, thirty minutes*) because our terms express concepts from a culture operating on "clock time." Perhaps for a similar reason there was no term for a unit of seven days. There was no "week," nor was there a term for "Saturday and Sunday" combined as a unit of time. There was no "weekend."

Linguistic relativity

In these examples, we have treated differences in language use as evidence of different ways of talking about external reality. This is often discussed in terms of **linguistic relativity** because it seems that the structure of our language, with its predetermined categories, must have an influence on how we perceive the world. In its weak version, this idea simply captures the fact that we not only talk, but to a certain extent probably also think about the world of experience, using the categories provided by our language. Our first language seems to have a definite role in shaping "habitual thought," that is, the way we think about things as we go about our daily lives, without analyzing how we're thinking.

There is a stronger version of this idea, called **linguistic determinism**, which holds that "language determines thought." If language does indeed determine thought, then we will only be able to think in the categories provided by our language. For example, English speakers use one word for "snow," and generally see all that white stuff as one thing. In contrast, so the argument goes, Eskimos look out at all the white stuff and see it as many different things because they have lots of different words for "snow." So, the category system inherent in the language determines how the speaker interprets and articulates experience. We shall return to the topic of "snow," but the proposal just described provides a good example of an approach to analyzing the connection between language and culture that dates back to the eighteenth century.

The Sapir–Whorf hypothesis

The general analytic perspective we are considering is part of what became known as the **Sapir–Whorf hypothesis** during the middle of the twentieth century. At a time when American linguistics was still mainly carried out by scholars with strong backgrounds in anthropology, Edward Sapir and Benjamin Whorf produced arguments that the languages of Native Americans, such as the Hopi, led them to view the world differently from those who spoke European languages. We have already noted a difference between Hopi and English in the treatment of time. According to Whorf, the Hopi perceive the world differently from other tribes (including the English-speaking tribe) because their language leads them to do so. In the grammar of Hopi, there is a distinction between "animate" and "inanimate," and among the set of entities categorized as "animate" are clouds and stones. Whorf claimed that the Hopi believe that clouds and stones are living entities and that it is their language that leads them to believe this. English does not mark in its grammar that clouds and stones are "animate," so English speakers do not see the world in the same way as the Hopi. In Whorf's words, "We dissect nature along lines laid down by our native languages" (see Carroll, 1956).

There have been a number of arguments presented against this point of view. Following Sampson (1980), let us imagine a tribe with a language in which differences in sex are marked grammatically, so that the terms used for females, such as *girl* and *woman*, have special markings in the language. On close inspection, we find that these "feminine" markings are also used with the words for *stone* and *door*. Are we forced to conclude that this tribe believes that stones and doors are female entities in the same way as girls and women? This tribe is not an obscure group. They use the expressions *la femme* ("the woman"), *la pierre* ("the stone") and *la porte* ("the door"). It is the tribe that lives in France. Should we conclude that French speakers believe that stones and doors are "female" in the same way as women?

The problem with the conclusions invited in both the Hopi and French cases is that there is a confusion between linguistic classification ("animate," "feminine") and biological classification ("living," "female"). There is frequently a correspondence in languages between these classifications, but there does not have to be. Moreover, the linguistic forms do not force us to ignore biological distinctions. While the Hopi language has a particular linguistic classification for the word *stone*, it does not mean that Hopi truck drivers worry about killing living creatures if they run over some stones while driving.

Snow

Returning to "snow" in cold places, we should first replace "Eskimo" with more accurate terms for the people, Inuit, and their language, Inuktitut. According to Martin (1986), the Inuit of West Greenland have only two basic words for "snow" (*qanik*, "snow in the air," and *aput*, "snow on the ground"). From these two basic elements, they are able to create a large number of common expressions for different snow-related phenomena. Yet, there seems to be no compelling reason to suppose that those expressions are controlling vision or thought among their users. Some expressions will occur frequently in the context of habitual experiences, but it is the human who is thinking about the experience and determining what will be expressed, not the language.

English does lexicalize some conceptual distinctions in the area of "snow," with *sleet*, *slush* and *snowflake* as examples. However, English speakers can also create expressions, by manipulating their language, to refer to *fresh snow*, *powdery snow*, *spring snow* or *the dirty stuff that is piled up on the side of the street after the snow-plough has gone through*. These may be categories of snow for English speakers, but they are **non-lexicalized** ("not expressed as a single word"). English speakers can express category variation by making a distinction using lexicalized categories (*It's more like slush than snow outside*) and also by indicating special reference using non-lexicalized distinctions (*We decorated the windows with some fake plastic snow stuff*), but most of them have a very different view of "snow" from the average speaker of Inuktitut.

Just as speakers of Inuktitut, in their traditional way of life, developed a set of common expressions to talk about "snow," so the speakers of Tuvaluan (in the central Pacific) developed many expressions for different types of "coconut." In Hawai'i, the traditional language had a very large number of expressions for different kinds of "rain." Contemporary English seems to have a lot of expressions having to do with "money." Our languages reflect our concerns.

We inherit a language used to report knowledge, so we would expect that language to influence the organization of our knowledge in some way. However, we also inherit the ability to manipulate and be creative with that language in order to express our perceptions. When the Hopi borrowed the word *santi* ("Sunday") from English-speaking missionaries, they used it to refer to the period beginning with one *santi* and ending with the next *santi*, essentially developing their own concept of our "week." If thinking and perception were totally determined by language, then the concept of language change would be impossible. If a young Hopi girl had no word in her language for the object known to us as a *computer*, would she fail to perceive the object? Would she be unable to think about it? What the Hopi girl can do when she encounters a new entity is change her language to accommodate the need to refer to the new entity. The human manipulates the language, not the other way round.

Cognitive categories

As a way of analyzing cognition, or how people think, we can look at language structure for clues, not for causes. The fact that Hopi speakers inherit a language system in which clouds have "animate" as a feature may tell us something about a traditional belief system, or way of thinking, that is part of their culture and not ours. In the Yagua language, spoken in Peru, the set of entities with "animate" as a feature includes the moon, rocks and pineapples, as well as people. In the traditions of the Yagua, all these entities are treated as valued objects, so that their cultural interpretation of the feature "animate" may be closer to the concept "having special importance in life" rather than the concept "having life," as in the cultural interpretation of most English speakers.

Classifiers

We know about the classification of words in languages like Yagua because of grammatical markers called **classifiers** that indicate the type or "class" of noun involved. For example, in Swahili (spoken in East Africa), different prefixes are used as classifiers on nouns for humans (*wa-*), non-humans (*mi-*) and artifacts (*vi-*), as in *watoto* ("children"), *mimea* ("plants") and *visu* ("knives"). In fact, a conceptual distinction between raw materials (*miti*, "trees") and artifacts made from them (*viti*, "chairs") can be marked simply by the classifiers used.

In the Australian language Dyirbal, traditional uses of classifiers indicated that "men, kangaroos and boomerangs" were in one conceptual category while "women, fire and dangerous things" were in another. Exploring cultural beliefs (e.g. "The sun is the wife of the moon") can help us make sense of aspects of an unfamiliar world view and understand why the moon is classified among the first set and the sun among the second.

Classifiers are often used in connection with numbers to indicate the type of thing being counted. In the following Japanese examples, the classifiers are associated with objects conceptualized in terms of their shape as "long thin things" (*hon*), "flat thin things" (*mai*) or "small round things" (*ko*).

banana ni-hon ("two bananas")
syatu ni-mai ("two shirts")
ringo ni-ko ("two apples")

The closest English comes to using classifiers is when we talk about a "unit of" certain types of things. There is a distinction in English between things treated as **countable** (*shirt*, *word*, *chair*) and those treated as **non-countable** (*clothing*, *information*, *furniture*). It is ungrammatical in English to use *a/an* or the plural with non-countable nouns (i.e. **a clothing*, **an information*, **two furnitures*). To avoid these ungrammatical forms, we use classifier-type expressions such as "item of" or "piece of," as in *an item of clothing, a bit of information* and *two pieces of furniture*. The equivalent nouns in many other languages are treated as "countable," so the existence of a grammatical class of "non-countable entities" is evidence of a type of cognitive categorization underlying the expression of quantity in English.

Social categories

Words such as *uncle* or *grandmother*, discussed earlier, provide examples of **social categories**. These are categories of social organization that we can use to say how we are connected or related to others. We can provide technical definitions (e.g. "male parent's brother"), but in many situations a word such as *uncle* is used for a much larger number of people, including close friends, who are outside the class of individuals covered by the technical definition. The word *brother* is similarly used among many groups for someone who is not a family member. We can use these words as a means of social categorization, that is, marking individuals as members of a group defined by social connections.

Address terms

When a man on the street asks another, *Brother, can you spare a dollar?*, the word *brother* is being used as an **address term** (a word or phrase for the person being talked or written to). By claiming the kind of closeness in relationship associated with a family member, the speaker's choice of address term is an attempt to create solidarity (i.e. being the same in social status), perhaps leading to a willingness to hand over some cash. He could have begun his request with *Sir* instead, indicating an unequal relationship of power (i.e. being different in social status) and, since he is higher in status, perhaps *Sir* has the ability to hand over some cash.

More typically, an interaction based on an unequal relationship will feature address terms using a title (*Doctor*) or title plus last name (*Professor Buckingham*) for the one with higher status, and first name only for the one with lower status, as in: *Professor Buckingham, can I ask a question?* ~ *Yes, Jennifer, what is it?* More equal relationships have address terms that indicate similar status of the participants, such as first names or nicknames: *Bucky, ready for some more coffee?* ~ *Thanks, Jenny.*

In many languages, there is a choice between pronouns used for addressees who are socially close versus distant. This is known as the **T/V distinction**, as in the French pronouns *tu* (close) and *vous* (distant). A similar type of social categorization is found in German (*du/Sie*) and Spanish (*tú/Usted*). In each of these distinctions, as in older English usage (*thou/you*), the second form is used to indicate that the speakers do not really have a close relationship. Traditionally, these forms could be used to mark a power relationship. The higher status or more powerful speaker could use *tu* or *thou* to a lower-status addressee, but not vice versa, as the Quaker Richard Davis discovered to his detriment (described in this chapter's opening quotation). Lower-status individuals had to use the *vous* or *you* forms when addressing those of higher status. This usage is described as non-reciprocal, but the reciprocal use (both speakers using the same form) of the *tu* forms has generally increased in Europe among younger speakers, such as students, who may not know each other really well, but who find themselves in the same situation.

In English, people without special titles are addressed as *Mr.*, *Mrs.*, *Miss*, or *Ms.* Only the women's address terms include information about their social status. In fact, one of the most frequently used address terms for a woman indicates that she is the wife of a particular man (called "Frank Smith," for example), as in *Mrs. Smith*, and sometimes even *Mrs. Frank Smith*. When the original system was put in place, women were obviously identified socially through their relationship to a man, either as wife or daughter. These address terms continue to function as social category labels, identifying women, but not men, as married or not. A woman using *Ms.* as part of her address term is indicating that her social categorization is not based on her marital status. This type of observation leads us to a consideration of the most fundamental difference in social categorization, the one based on "gender."

Gender

We have already noted the difference between two uses of the word **gender** in Chapter 7. Biological (or "natural") gender is the distinction in sex between the "male" and "female" of each species. Grammatical gender is the distinction between "masculine" and "feminine," which is used to classify nouns in languages such as Spanish (*el sol*, *la luna*). A third use is for **social gender**, which is the distinction we make when we use words like "man" and "woman" to classify individuals in terms of their social roles.

Although the biological distinction ("male, female") underlies the social distinctions ("father, mother"), there is a great deal about the social roles of individuals as men or women that is unrelated to biology. It is in the sense of social gender, through the process of learning how to become a "boy" or a "girl," that we inherit a gendered culture. This process can be as simple as learning which category should wear pink versus blue, or as complex as understanding how one category was excluded (by having no vote) from the process of representative government for such a long time. Becoming a social gender also involves becoming familiar with gendered language use.

Gendered words

In Sidamo, spoken in Ethiopia, there are some words used only by men and some used only by women, so that the translation of "milk" would be *ado* by a man, but *gurda* by a woman. Many Native American languages, such as Gros Ventre (in Montana) and Koasati (in Louisiana), are reported to have had different versions used by men and women. In Japanese, when referring to themselves ("I"), men have traditionally used *boku* and women *watashi* or *atashi*. In Portuguese, saying "thank you" is *obrigado* if you're a man and *obrigada* if you're a woman.

These examples simply illustrate that there can be differences between the words used by men and women in a variety of languages. There are other examples, used to talk about men and women, which seem to imply that the words for men are "normal" and the words for women are "special additions." Pairs such as *hero–heroine* or *actor–actress* illustrate the derivation of terms for the woman's role from the man's. Marking this type of difference through gendered words has decreased in contemporary American English as *firemen* and *policemen* have become *firefighters* and *police officers*, but there is still a strong tendency to treat forms for the man (*his*) as the normal means of reference when speaking generally: *Each student is required to buy his own dictionary*. However, alternatives that include both genders (*his or her*), or avoid gendered usage (*their*) are becoming more common. Other terms, such as *career woman* and *working mother* (rarely "career man" or "working father") continue the pattern of special terms for women, not men.

When we reviewed social variation (Chapter 19), noting the differences between working-class and middle-class speech, we largely ignored gender differences. Yet, within each social class, there is substantial variation according to gender. Generally speaking, whenever there is a higher- versus lower-prestige variable (e.g. *talking/talkin'* or *I saw it/I seen it*), women are more likely to use the higher-prestige forms. The difference is most noticeable among middle-class speakers. In one study of double negatives (e.g. *I don't want none*) in lower-middle-class speech, substantially more men (32%) than women (1%) used the structure. This regular pattern of difference is sometimes explained in terms of women's socialization to be more careful, to be aware of social status, and to be more sensitive to how others may judge them. An alternative explanation appeals to the socialization of men to be strong, tough and independent. Forms which are non-standard or associated with working-class speech may be preferred by men because of their association with manual work, strength and toughness. And tough guys also have deep voices.

Gendered speech

In general, men have longer vocal tracts, larger larynxes and thicker vocal folds than women. The result is that men typically speak in a lower pitch range (80–200 Herz) than women (120–400 Herz). The term **pitch** is used to describe the effect of vibration in the vocal folds, with slower vibration making voices sound lower and rapid vibration making voices sound higher. Although "normal speaking" takes place with substantial overlap in the pitch ranges of men and women, there is a tendency to exaggerate the differences in many contexts in order to sound more "like a man" or more "like a woman."

Among women speaking contemporary American English, there is also generally more use of pitch movement, that is, more rising and falling intonation. The use of rising intonation (↑) at the end of statements (*It happened near San Diego* ↑ , *in southern California* ↑), the more frequent use of hedges (*sort of, kind of*) and tag questions (*It's kind of cold in here, isn't it?*) have all been identified as characteristic of women's speech. **Tag questions** are short questions consisting of an auxiliary (*don't, isn't*) and a pronoun (*it, you*), added to the end of a statement (*I hate it when it rains all day, don't you?*). They are used more often by women when expressing opinions. These features of women's speech all seem to be ways of inviting agreement with an idea rather than asserting it. Men tend to use more assertive forms and "strong" language (*It's too damn cold in here!*). Other researchers have pointed to a preference among women, in same-gender groups, for indirect speech acts (*Could I see that photo?*) rather than the direct speech acts (*Gimme that photo*) heard more often from men in same-gender groups.

It is important to pay attention to the concept of "same-gender" talk in describing features in the speech of men and women because much of our socialization takes place in such groups. By the time we are three years old, we have established a preference for talking to same-gender others. By the age of five, boys are actively excluding girls from their activities and commenting negatively on other boys who associate with girls. Throughout childhood, boys socialize in larger groups, often in competitive activities, establishing and maintaining hierarchical relationships (*I'm Spiderman and you have to follow me*). Girls socialize in smaller groups, more often in cooperative activities, establishing reciprocal relationships and exchanging roles (*You can be the doctor now and I'll be ill*). In many societies, this same-gender socialization is reinforced through separate educational experiences, creating young men and women who may interact with each other only rarely outside family settings. Not surprisingly, there are differences in the way each gender approaches interaction with the other.

Gendered interaction

Many of the features already identified in women's speech (e.g. frequent question-type forms) facilitate the exchange of turns, allowing others to speak, with the effect that interaction becomes a shared activity. Interaction among men appears to be organized in a more hierarchical way, with the right to speak or "having the floor" being treated as the goal. Men generally take longer turns at speaking and, in many social contexts (e.g. religious events), may be the only ones allowed to talk.

One effect of the different styles developed by men and women is that certain features become very salient in cross-gender interactions. For example, in same-gender discussions, there is little difference in the number of times speakers interrupt each other. However, in cross-gender interactions, men are much more likely to interrupt women, with 96 percent of the identified interruptions being attributed to men in one study involving American college students.

In same-gender conversations, women produce more back-channels as indicators of listening and paying attention. The term **back-channels** describes the use of words (*yeah*, *really?*) or sounds (*hmm*, *oh*) by listeners while someone else is speaking. Men not only produce fewer back-channels, but appear to treat them, when produced by others, as indications of agreement. In cross-gender interaction, the absence of back-channels from men tends to make women think the men are not paying attention to them. The more frequent production of back-channels by women leads men to think that the women are agreeing with what they're saying.

Other features have been identified as distinctive aspects of men's or women's ways of using language in interaction. In fact, the gendered nature of interactional styles has led some writers to describe conversations between men and women as a form of "cross-cultural communication." If we are to avoid miscommunication in this process, we must all be prepared to try to understand the impact of the cultures we inherit and, through the creativity with language that we are also given, to find new ways of articulating those cultures before we pass them on.

Study questions

1 What is one common definition of "culture" in the study of language?
2 What are kinship terms?
3 What is meant by "linguistic determinism"?
4 What are classifiers?
5 Why is this sentence ungrammatical? *She gave me a good advice.
6 Is the following sentence more likely to be spoken by a woman or a man, and why? *I think that golf on television is kind of boring, don't you?*

Tasks

A What is the difference between "cross-cultural," "intercultural" and "multicultural" communication?
B What is the "basic color term hierarchy"?
C We briefly considered a distinction that English makes between "countable" and "non-countable."
  (i) Can you assign the following words to three sets, labeled "countable," "non-countable" and "both countable and non-countable"?
  (ii) Which phrases referring to a "unit of" are typically used with the non-countable nouns (e.g. *a round of applause*)?

  applause, business, cash, chocolate, courage, crash, equipment, hair, lesson, luck, mistake, mountain, noise, paper, party, rain, research, rubbish, salmon, sand, shopping, tennis, theft, underwear

D According to Foley (1997), kinship terminology in Watam (a language spoken in Papua New Guinea) is rather different from English. The word *aes* is used for both father and father's brother while *aem* is used for both mother and mother's sister. The words *akwae* and *namkwae* are used for mother's brother and father's sister respectively.
  1 Using this information, can you complete the following comparative chart?
  2 What would be the problems involved in translating the English words *aunt* and *uncle* into Watam?
  3 How do English speakers make a distinction when they're talking about their father's brother versus their mother's brother or their father's sister versus their mother's sister?

English	Kinship category	Watam
mother	female parent	_____
_____	female parent's sister	_____
_____	male parent's sister	_____
_____	male parent	_____
_____	male parent's brother	_____
_____	female parent's brother	_____

E When a number is used with a noun in Ponapean (spoken in the western Pacific), an appropriate classifier is also used, as described in Lynch (1998). Some classifiers used as suffixes are *-men* ("animate things"), *-pwoat* ("long things"), *-mwut* ("heaps of things"), *-sop* ("stalks of things") and *-dip* ("slices of things"). Examples of numerals are *sili-* ("three") and *pah-* ("four"). Can you complete these noun phrases with appropriate endings?
Example: *pwutak reirei silimen* ("three tall boys")

(1) *sehu* _____ ("four stalks of sugarcane")
(2) *dipen mei* _____ ("four slices of breadfruit")
(3) *mwutin dippw* _____ ("four piles of grass")
(4) *nahi pwihk* _____ ("my three pigs")
(5) *tuhke* _____ ("a tree")

F How can we avoid "genderizing" when completing utterances such as these?

(1) *Everybody came in _____ own car.*
(2) *Someone called, but _____ didn't leave _____ name.*
(3) *A friend of mine told me _____ had met Brad Pitt in New Orleans.*
(4) *Every student must bring _____ dictionary to class.*
(5) *You won't be the first or last man or woman who gets _____ involved in a holiday romance.*
(6) *Nicole has a new baby and _____ cries a lot at night.*
(7) *My professor promised ____ would write me a letter of recommendation.*
(8) *I got an email from someone called Chris who said that _____ was looking forward to meeting me.*

Discussion topics/projects

I Why do you think there continue to be frequent references to the idea that "Eskimos have a hundred words for snow"? How would you try to convince someone who thinks this is a fact that it is best treated as a myth?
(For background reading, see chapter 19 of Pullum, 1991.)

II Is there a difference between "interruption" and "overlap" in conversation? What do you think is meant by the distinction between "report talk" and "rapport talk"? Should we distinguish between "fast-talking" and "slow-talking" styles rather than attribute certain features of interaction to men versus women? (For background reading, see chapter 7 of Tannen, 1990.)

Further reading

Basic treatments
Duranti, A. (2001) *Key Terms in Language and Culture* Blackwell
Kramsch, C. (1998) *Language and Culture* Oxford University Press
More detailed treatments
Duranti, A. (1997) *Linguistic Anthropology* Cambridge University Press
Foley, W. (1997) *Anthropological Linguistics* Blackwell
Culture
Kuper, A. (1999) *Culture: The Anthropologists' Account* Harvard University Press
Categories
Taylor, J. (2003) *Linguistic Categorization* (3rd edition) Oxford University Press
Linguistic relativity
Boroditsky, L. (2003) "Linguistic relativity" In L. Nadel (ed.) *Encyclopedia of Cognitive Science* (917–921) Nature Publishing Group
Cognitive categories
Ungerer, F. and H-J. Schmid (2006) *An Introduction to Cognitive Linguistics* (chapter 1) (2nd edition) Longman
Classifiers
Aikhenvald, A. (2000) *Classifiers* Oxford University Press
Social categories
Mesthrie, R., J. Swann, A. Deumert and W. Leap (2000) *Introducing Sociolinguistics* (chapter 3) John Benjamins
Developing social gender
Maccoby, E. (1998) *The Two Sexes* Harvard University Press
Gender and language
Coates, J. (2004) *Women, Men and Language* (3rd edition) Longman
Eckert, P. and S. McConnell-Ginet (2003) *Language and Gender* Cambridge University Press
Sources of examples
(Dyirbal) Lakoff, G. (1987) *Women, Fire and Dangerous Things* University of Chicago Press
(Hawaiian) Kent, H. (1986) *Treasury of Hawaiian Words in One Hundred and One Categories* University of Hawai'i Press
(Hopi) Malotki, E. (1983) *Hopi Time* Walter de Gruyter
(Inuit) Martin, L. (1986) "Eskimo words for snow: a case study in the genesis and decay of an anthropological example" *American Anthropologist* 88: 418–423

(Japanese) Frawley, W. (1992) *Linguistic Semantics* Lawrence Erlbaum

(Mopan Maya) Danziger, E. (2001) *Relatively Speaking* Oxford University Press

(Ponapean) Lynch, J. (1998) *Pacific Languages* University of Hawai'i Press

(Sidamo) Hudson, G. (2000) *Essential Introductory Linguistics* Blackwell

(Swahili) Hinnebusch, T. (1987) "Swahili" In T. Shopen (ed.) *Languages and Their Status* (209–294) University of Pennsylvania Press

(Tuvaluan) Finegan, E. and N. Besnier (1989) *Language: Its Structure and Use* Harcourt Brace Jovanovich

(Watam) Foley, W. (1997) *Anthropological Linguistics* Blackwell

Other references

Carroll, J. (ed.) (1956) *Language, Thought and Reality: Selected Writings of Benjamin Lee Whorf* MIT Press

Pullum, G. (1991) *The Great Eskimo Vocabulary Hoax* University of Chicago Press

Sampson, G. (1980) *Schools of Linguistics* Stanford University Press

Tannen, D. (1990) *You Just Don't Understand* William Morrow

Glossary

AAVE: African American Vernacular English

accent: aspects of pronunciation that identify where a speaker is from, in contrast to **dialect**

acoustic phonetics: the study of the physical properties of speech as sound waves

acquisition: the gradual development of ability in a first or second language by using it naturally in communicative situations

acronym: a new word formed from the initial letters of other words (e.g. *NASA*)

active voice: the form of the verb used to say what the **subject** does (e.g. *He stole it*) in contrast to the **passive voice**

address term: a word or phrase for the person being talked or written to

adjective (Adj): a word such as *happy* or *strange* used with a noun to provide more information

adverb (Adv): a word such as *slowly* or *really* used with a verb or adjective to provide more information

affective factors: emotional reactions such as self-consciousness or negative feelings that may influence learning

affix: a **bound morpheme** such as *un-* or *-ed* added to a word (e.g. *undressed*)

affricate: a **consonant** produced by stopping then releasing the airflow through a narrow opening (e.g. the first and last sounds in *church*)

African American English (AAE): a social dialect used by many African Americans in different regions of the USA

African American Vernacular English (AAVE): the casual speech style used by many African Americans as a **vernacular**

agent: the **semantic role** of the noun phrase identifying the one who performs the action of the verb in an event (*The boy kicked the ball*)

agrammatic speech: the type of speech without grammatical markers, often associated with **Broca's aphasia**

agreement: the grammatical connection between two parts of a sentence, as in the connection between a **subject** (*Cathy*) and the form of a verb (*loves chocolate*)

allomorph: one of a closely related set of **morphs**

allophone: one of a closely related set of speech sounds or **phones**

alphabet (alphabetic writing): a way of writing in which one symbol represents one sound segment

alternate sign language: a system of hand signals used in a specific context where speech cannot be used (by people who can speak), in contrast to a **primary sign language**

alveolar: a **consonant** produced with the front part of the tongue on the **alveolar ridge** (e.g. the first and last sounds in _dot_)

alveolar ridge: the rough bony ridge immediately behind the upper front teeth

Ameslan (or ASL): American Sign Language

analogy: a process of forming a new word to be similar in some way to an existing word

anaphora (anaphoric expressions): use of pronouns (_it_) and noun phrases with _the_ (_the puppy_) to refer back to something already mentioned

anomia: a language disorder in which it is difficult to find words, often associated with **Wernicke's aphasia**

antecedent: the first mention of someone or something later referred to via **anaphora**

antonymy: the **lexical relation** in which words have opposite meanings (_"Shallow" is an antonym of "deep"_)

aphasia: an impairment of language function due to localized brain damage that leads to difficulty in understanding and/or producing language

applied linguistics: the study of a large range of practical issues involving language in general and **second language learning** in particular

arbitrariness: a property of language describing the fact that there is no natural connection between a linguistic form and its meaning

arcuate fasciculus: a bundle of nerve fibers connecting **Broca's area** and **Wernicke's area** in the left hemisphere of the brain

article (Art): a word such as _a_, _an_ or _the_ used with a noun

articulatory parameters: the four key aspects of visual information used in the description of signs (**shape**, **orientation**, **location** and **movement**)

articulatory phonetics: the study of how speech sounds are produced

ASL (or Ameslan): American Sign Language

aspiration: a puff of air that sometimes accompanies the pronunciation of a **stop**

assimilation: the process whereby a feature of one sound becomes part of another during speech production

associative meaning: the type of meaning that people might connect with the use of words (e.g. _needle_ = "painful") that is not part of **conceptual meaning**

audiolingual method: a mid-twentieth-century approach to language teaching, with repetitive drills used to develop fluent spoken language as a set of habits

auditory phonetics: the study of the perception of speech sounds by the ear, also called "perceptual phonetics"

auxiliary verb (Aux): a verb such as _will_ used with another verb

babbling: the use of syllable sequences (_ba-ba_) and combinations (_ma-ga_) by young children in their first year

back-channels: the use of words (_yeah_) and sounds (_hmm_) by listeners while someone else is speaking

backformation: the process of reducing a word such as a noun to a shorter version and using it as a new word such as a verb (e.g. _babysit_ from _babysitter_)

background knowledge: information that is not in a text, but is used from memory by a reader to understand the text

beats: **gestures** involving short quick movements of the hands or fingers that go along with the rhythm of talk

bidialectal: being capable of speaking two **dialects**

bilabial: a **consonant** produced by using both lips (e.g. the first and last sounds in _pub_)

bilingual: a term used to describe a native speaker of two languages or a country with two official languages, in contrast to **monolingual**

bilingualism: the state of having two languages

blending: the process of combining the beginning of one word and the end of another word to form a new word (e.g. _brunch_ from _breakfast_ and _lunch_)

borrowing: the process of taking words from other languages

bound morpheme: a **morpheme** such as _un-_ or _-ed_ that cannot stand alone and must be attached to another form (e.g. _undressed_)

broadening: a semantic change in which a word is used with a more general meaning (e.g. _foda_ (animal fodder) → _food_ (any kind)), in contrast to **narrowing**

Broca's aphasia: a language disorder in which speech production is typically reduced, distorted, slow and missing grammatical markers

Broca's area: a part of the brain in the left hemisphere involved in speech production

calque: a type of **borrowing** in which each element of a word is translated into the borrowing language (e.g. _gratte-ciel_ "scrape-sky" for _skyscraper_)

caregiver speech: speech addressed to young children by the adult(s) or older children who are looking after them

category: a group with certain features in common

characters: forms used in Chinese writing

classifiers: grammatical markers that indicate the type or "class" of a **noun**

clipping: the process of reducing a word of more than one syllable to a shorter form (e.g. _ad_ from _advertisement_)

closed syllable: a **syllable** that ends with a **consonant** or **coda**

coarticulation: the process of making one sound virtually at the same time as the next sound

coda: the part of a syllable after the **vowel**

cognates: words in different languages that have a similar form and meaning (e.g. English _friend_ and German _Freund_)

cognitive category: a **category** used in the organization of how we think

coherence: the connections that create a meaningful interpretation of texts

cohesion: the ties and connections that exist within texts

cohesive ties: the individual connections between words and phrases in a text

co-hyponyms: words in **hyponymy** that share the same **superordinate** (_"Daffodil" and "rose" are co-hyponyms of "flower"_)

coinage: the invention of new words (e.g. _xerox_)

collocation: a relationship between words that frequently occur together (e.g. _salt and pepper_)

communication strategy: a way of overcoming a gap between communicative intent and a limited ability to express that intent, as part of **strategic competence**

communicative approaches: approaches to language teaching that are based on learning through using language rather than learning about language

communicative competence: the general ability to use language accurately, appropriately and flexibly

communicative signals: behavior used intentionally to provide information

comparative reconstruction: the creation of the original form of an ancestor language on the basis of comparable forms in languages that are descendants

complementizer (C): a word such as *that* introducing a **complement phrase**

complement phrase (CP): a structure such as *that Mary helped George* used to complete a construction beginning with a structure such as *Cathy knew*

completion point: in conversation, the end of a **turn**, usually marked by a pause at the end of a phrase or sentence

compounding: the process of combining two (or more) words to form a new word (e.g. *waterbed*)

conceptual meaning: the basic components of meaning conveyed by the literal use of words

conduction aphasia: a language disorder associated with damage to the **arcuate fasciculus** in which repeating words or phrases is difficult

conjunction: a word such as *and* or *because* used to make connections between words, phrases and sentences

consonant: a speech sound produced by restricting the airflow in some way

consonantal alphabet: a way of writing in which each symbol represents a consonant sound

consonant cluster: two or more **consonants** in sequence

constituent analysis: a grammatical analysis of how small constituents (or components) go together to form larger constituents in sentences

context: either the **physical context** or the **linguistic context** (**co-text**) in which words are used

convergence: adopting a speech style that attempts to reduce social distance by using forms that are similar to those used by the person being talked to, as a type of **speech accommodation**, in contrast to **divergence**

conversation analysis: the study of turn-taking in conversation

conversion: the process of changing the function of a word, such as a noun to a verb, as a way of forming new words, also known as "category change" or "functional shift" (e.g. *vacation* in *They're vacationing in Florida*)

cooing: the earliest use of speech-like sounds by an infant in the first few months

co-operative principle: an underlying assumption of conversation that you will "make your conversational contribution such as is required, at the stage at which it occurs, by the accepted purpose or direction of the talk exchange in which you are engaged"

corpus linguistics: the study of language in use by analyzing the occurrence and frequency of forms in a large collection of texts typically stored in a computer

co-text: the set of other words used in the same phrase or sentence, also called the **linguistic context**

countable: type of noun that can be used in English with *a/an* and the plural (e.g. *a cup, two cups*), in contrast to **non-countable**

covert prestige: the status of a speech style or feature as having positive value, but which is "hidden" or not valued similarly among the larger community, in contrast to **overt prestige**

creole: a variety of a language that developed from a **pidgin** and is used as a first language by a population of native speakers

creolization: the process of development from a **pidgin** to a **creole**, in contrast to **decreolization**

critical period: the time from birth to puberty during which normal first language acquisition can take place

cultural transmission: the process whereby knowledge of a language is passed from one generation to the next

culture: socially acquired knowledge

cuneiform: a way of writing created by pressing a wedge-shaped implement into soft clay

decreolization: the process whereby a **creole** is used with fewer distinct creole features as it becomes more like a standard variety, in contrast to **creolization**

deep structure: the underlying structure of sentences as represented by **phrase structure rules**

deictics: **gestures** used to point at things or people

deixis (deictic expressions): using words such as *this* or *here* as a way of "pointing" with language

dental: a **consonant** produced with the tongue tip behind the upper front teeth (e.g. the first sound in *that*)

derivation: the process of forming new words by adding **affixes**

derivational morpheme: a **bound morpheme** such as -*ish* used to make new words or words of a different grammatical category (e.g. *boyish*), in contrast to an **inflectional morpheme**

descriptive approach: an approach to grammar that is based on a description of the structures actually used in a language, not what should be used, in contrast to the **prescriptive approach**

diachronic variation: differences resulting from change over a period of time, in contrast to **synchronic variation**

dialect: aspects of the grammar, vocabulary and pronunciation of a variety of a language, in contrast to **accent**

dialect boundary: a line representing a set of **isoglosses**, used to separate one dialect area from another

dialect continuum: the gradual merging of one regional variety of a language into another

dialectology: the study of **dialects**

dichotic listening: an experiment in which a listener hears two different sounds simultaneously, each through a different earphone

diglossia: a situation where there is a "high" or special variety of a language used in formal situations (e.g. Classical Arabic), and a "low" variety used locally and informally (e.g. Lebanese Arabic)

digraph: a combination of letters used in writing for a single sound (e.g. "ph" for /f/)

diphthong: a sound formed by combining two **vowel** sounds (e.g. b*oy*)

direct speech act: an action in which the form used (e.g. interrogative) directly matches the function (e.g. question) performed by a speaker with an utterance, in contrast to an **indirect speech act**

discourse analysis: the study of language beyond the sentence, in text and conversation

displacement: a property of language that allows users to talk about things and events not present in the immediate environment

divergence: adopting a speech style that emphasizes social distance by using forms that are different from those used by the person being talked to, as a form of **speech accommodation**, in contrast to **convergence**

duality: a property of language whereby linguistic forms have two simultaneous levels of sound production and meaning, also called "double articulation"

Early Modern English: the form of English in use between 1500 and 1700

elision: the process of leaving out a sound segment in the pronunciation of a word

emblems: non-verbal signals such as "thumbs up" (= things are good) that function like fixed phrases with conventional interpretations

epenthesis: a sound change involving the addition of a sound to a word (e.g. *timr* → *timber*)

eponym: a word derived from the name of a person or place (e.g. *sandwich*)

etymology: the study of the origin and history of words

experiencer: the **semantic role** of the noun phrase identifying the entity that has the feeling, perception or state described by the verb (e.g. *The boy feels sad*)

external change: influences from the outside that cause changes in a language, in contrast to **internal change**

face: a person's public self-image as described in the study of **politeness**

face-saving act: saying something that reduces a possible threat to another person's self-image

face-threatening act: saying something that represents a threat to another person's self-image

filled pause: a break in the flow of speech, using sounds such as *em* and *er*

finger-spelling: a system of hand configurations used to represent the letters of the alphabet in **sign language**

fixed reference: a property of a communication system whereby each signal is fixed as relating to one particular object or occasion

flap: a sound produced with the tongue tip briefly touching the **alveolar ridge**

foreigner talk: a way of using a language with non-native speakers that is simpler in structure and vocabulary

fossilization: the process whereby an **interlanguage**, containing many non-**L2** features, stops developing toward more accurate forms of the **L2**

free morpheme: a **morpheme** that can stand by itself as a single word

fricative: a **consonant** produced by almost blocking the airflow (e.g. the first and last sounds in *five*)

functional morpheme: a **free morpheme** that is used as a function word, such as a conjunction (*and*) or a preposition (*in*)

gender: a term used in three ways: (1) a biological distinction between male and female, also called **natural gender**; (2) a distinction between classes of nouns as masculine, feminine (or neuter), also called **grammatical gender**; (3) a distinction between the social roles of men and women, also called **social gender**

generative grammar: a set of rules defining the possible sentences in a language

gestures: use of the hands, typically while speaking

glides: sounds produced with the tongue in motion to or from a vowel sound, also called "semi-vowels" or "approximants" (e.g. the first sounds in _wet_, _yes_)

glottal: a sound produced in the space between the **vocal folds** (e.g. the first sound in _hat_)

glottal stop: a sound produced when the air passing through the **glottis** is stopped completely then released

glottis: the space between the **vocal folds**

goal: the **semantic role** of the noun phrase identifying where an entity moves to (e.g. _The boy walked to the window_)

gradable antonyms: words with opposite meanings along a scale (e.g. _big–small_)

grammar: the analysis of the structure of phrases and sentences

grammar–translation method: the traditional form of language teaching, with vocabulary lists and sets of grammar rules

grammatical competence: the ability to use words and structures accurately as part of **communicative competence**

grammatical gender: a grammatical category designating the class of a noun as masculine or feminine (or neuter), in contrast to other types of **gender**

hedge: a word or phrase used to indicate that you are not really sure that what you are saying is sufficiently correct or complete

hierarchical organization: the analysis of constituents in a sentence showing which constituents are higher than and contain other constituents

holophrastic (utterance): a single form functioning as a phrase or sentence in the early speech of young children

homonyms: two words with the same form that are unrelated in meaning (e.g. _mole_ (on skin) – _mole_ (small animal))

homophones: two or more words with different forms and the same pronunciation (e.g. _to–too–two_)

hypocorism: a word-formation process in which a longer word is reduced to a shorter form with _-y_ or _-ie_ at the end (e.g. _telly_, _movie_)

hyponymy: the **lexical relation** in which the meaning of one word is included in the meaning of another (e.g. _"Daffodil" is a hyponym of "flower"_)

iconics: **gestures** that seem to echo or imitate the meaning of what is said

ideogram (ideographic writing): a way of writing in which each symbol represents a concept

idiolect: the personal **dialect** of an individual speaker

implicature: an additional meaning conveyed by a speaker adhering to the **co-operative principle**

indirect speech act: an action in which the form used (e.g. interrogative) does not directly match the function (e.g. request) performed by a speaker with an utterance, in contrast to a **direct speech act**

inference: additional information used by a listener/reader to create a connection between what is said and what must be meant

infix: a **morpheme** that is inserted in the middle of a word (e.g. _-rn-_ in _srnal_)

inflectional morpheme: a **bound morpheme** used to indicate the grammatical function of a word, also called an "inflection" (e.g. _dogs_, _walked_)

informative signals: behavior that provides information, usually unintentionally

innateness hypothesis: the idea that humans are genetically equipped to acquire language

input: the language that an acquirer/learner is exposed to, in contrast to **output**

instrument: the **semantic role** of the noun phrase identifying the entity that is used to perform the action of the verb (e.g. *The boy cut the rope with a razor*)

instrumental motivation: the desire to learn an **L2**, not to join the community of L2-users, but to achieve some other goal, in contrast to **integrative motivation**

integrative motivation: the desire to learn an **L2** in order to take part in the social life of the community of L2-users, in contrast to **instrumental motivation**

interdental: a **consonant** produced with the tongue tip between the upper and lower teeth (e.g. the first sound in *that*)

interlanguage: the interim system of **L2** learners, which has some features of the **L1** and **L2** plus some that are independent of the **L1** and the **L2**

internal change: change in a language that is not caused by outside influence, in contrast to **external change**

isogloss: a line on a map separating two areas in which a particular linguistic feature is significantly different, used in the study of **dialect**

jargon: special technical vocabulary associated with a specific activity or topic as part of a **register**

kinship terms: words used to refer to people who are members of the same family that indicate their relationship with other members

L1: first language, acquired as a child

L2: second language

labeled and bracketed sentences: a type of analysis in which constituents in a sentence are marked off by brackets with labels describing each type of constituent

labiodental: a **consonant** produced with the upper teeth and the lower lip (e.g. the first sounds in *very funny*)

language planning: choosing and developing an official language or languages for use in government and education

larynx: the part of the throat that contains the **vocal folds**, also called the voice box

lateralization (lateralized): divided into a left side and a right side, with control of functions on one side or the other (used in describing the human brain)

learning: the conscious process of accumulating knowledge, in contrast to **acquisition**

lexicalized: expressed as a single word, in contrast to **non-lexicalized**

lexical morpheme: a **free morpheme** that is a content word such as a noun or verb

lexical relations: the relationships of meaning, such as **synonymy**, between words

lexical rules: rules stating which words can be used for constituents generated by **phrase structure rules**

lexifier (language): the main source (language) of words in a **pidgin**

linguistic context: the set of other words used in the same phrase or sentence, also called **co-text**

linguistic determinism: the idea that we can only think in the categories provided by our language, in contrast to **linguistic relativity**

linguistic geography: the study of language variation based on where different varieties of the language are used

linguistic relativity: the idea that, to some extent, we think about the world using categories provided by our language, in contrast to **linguistic determinism**

linguistic variable: a feature of language use that distinguishes one group of speakers from another

liquid: a sound produced by letting air flow around the sides of the tongue (e.g. the first sound in *lip*)

loan-translation: a type of **borrowing** in which each element of a word is translated into the borrowing language, also called **calque**

localization view: the belief that specific aspects of linguistic ability have specific locations in the brain

location (in semantics): the **semantic role** of the noun phrase identifying where an entity is (e.g. *The boy is sitting in the classroom*)

location (in sign language): an **articulatory parameter** of ASL identifying the place where hands are positioned in relation to the head and upper body of the signer

logogram (logographic writing): a way of writing in which each symbol represents a word

majority principle: in **comparative reconstruction**, the choice of the form that occurs more often than any other form in the set of descendant languages

malapropism: a speech error in which one word is used instead of another with a similar beginning, end and number of syllables (e.g. *medication* used instead of "meditation")

manner maxim: the assumption in conversation that you will "be clear, brief and orderly"

maxim: one of four assumptions in conversation connected to the **co-operative principle**

metathesis: a sound change involving the reversal in position of two sounds (e.g. *hros* → *horse*)

metonymy: a word used in place of another with which it is closely connected in everyday experience (e.g. *He drank the whole bottle* (= the liquid))

Middle English: the form of English in use between 1100 and 1500

minimal pair (set): two (or more) words that are identical in form except for a contrast in one **phoneme** in the same position in each word (e.g. *bad*, *mad*)

Modern English: the form of English in use since 1700

monolingual: having, or being able to use, only one language, in contrast to **bilingual**

morph: an actual form used as part of a word, representing one version of a **morpheme**

morpheme: a minimal unit of meaning or grammatical function

morphology: the analysis of the structure of words

most natural development principle: in **comparative reconstruction**, the choice of older versus newer forms on the basis of commonly observed types of sound change

motor cortex: a part of the brain that controls muscle movement

movement: an **articulatory parameter** in **ASL** describing the type of motion used in forming signs

movement rules: rules that are used to move constituents in structures derived from **phrase structure rules**. They have a special rewrite arrow: ⇒

narrowing: a semantic change in which a word is used with a less general meaning (e.g. *mete* (any type of food) → *meat* (only animal flesh)), in contrast to **broadening**

nasal: a sound produced through the nose (e.g. the first sounds in *my name*)

nasalization: pronunciation of a sound with air flowing through the nose, typically before a **nasal** consonant

natural gender: a distinction based on the biological categories of male, female or neither, in contrast to other types of **gender**

negative face: the need to be independent and free from imposition, in contrast to **positive face**

negative transfer: the use of a feature from the **L1** (that is really different from the **L2**) while performing in the **L2**, in contrast to **positive transfer**

negotiated input: **L2** material that an acquirer/learner is exposed to when active attention is drawn to that material during interaction in the **L2**

neologism: a new word

neurolinguistics: the study of the relationship between language and the brain

non-countable: type of noun that is not used in English with *a/an* or the plural (e.g. *a furniture, *two furnitures), in contrast to **countable**

non-gradable antonyms: words which are direct opposites (e.g. *alive–dead*)

non-lexicalized: not expressed as a single word, in contrast to **lexicalized**

NORMS: "non-mobile, older, rural, male speakers" selected as informants in dialect surveys

noun (N): a word such as *boy, bicycle* or *freedom* used to describe a person, thing or idea

noun phrase (NP): a phrase such as *the boy* or *an old bicycle*, containing a **noun** plus other constituents

nucleus: the **vowel** in a **syllable**

number: the grammatical category of **nouns** as singular or plural

Old English: the form of English in use before 1100

one-word stage: the period in **L1** acquisition when children can produce single terms for objects

onomatopoeia (onomatopoeic): words containing sounds similar to the noises they describe (e.g. *bang, cuckoo*)

onset: the part of the **syllable** before the **vowel**

open syllable: a **syllable** that ends with a **vowel** (or **nucleus**) and has no **coda**

oralism: a method designed to teach deaf students to speak and read lips rather than use **sign language**

orientation: the way the hand is positioned as an **articulatory parameter** of ASL

orthography: the spelling system of a language

output: the language produced by an acquirer/learner, in contrast to **input**

overextension: in **L1** acquisition, using a word to refer to more objects than is usual in the language (*ball* used to refer to the moon)

overgeneralization: in **L1** acquisition, using an **inflectional morpheme** on more words than is usual in the language (e.g. *two foots*)

overt prestige: status that is generally recognized as "better" or more positively valued in the larger community, in contrast to **covert prestige**

palate: the hard part of the roof of the mouth

palatal: a **consonant** produced by raising the tongue to the **palate**, also called "alveo-palatal" (e.g. the first sounds in *ship* and *yacht*)

passive voice: the form of the verb used to say what happens to the **subject** (e.g. *The car **was stolen***) in contrast to **active voice**

person: the grammatical category distinguishing first person (involving the speaker, *me*), second person (involving the hearer, *you*) and third person (involving any others, *she*, *them*)

person deixis: using words such as *him* or *them* as a way of "pointing" to a person with language

pharyngeal: a sound produced in the **pharynx**

pharynx: the area inside the throat above the **larynx**

philology: the study of language history and change

phone: a physically produced speech sound, representing one version of a **phoneme**

phoneme: the smallest meaning-distinguishing sound unit in the abstract representation of the sounds of a language

phonetic alphabet: a set of symbols, each one representing a distinct sound segment

phonetics: the study of the characteristics of speech sounds

phonology: the study of the systems and patterns of speech sounds in languages

phonotactics: constraints on the permissible combination of sounds in a language

phrase structure rules: rules stating that the structure of a phrase of a specific type consists of one or more constituents in a particular order

physical context: the situation, time or place in which words are used

pictogram (pictographic writing): a way of writing in which a picture/drawing of an object is used to represent the object

pidgin: a variety of a language that developed for a practical purpose such as trade, but which has no native speakers, in contrast to a **creole**

pitch: the effect of vibration in the **vocal folds**, making voices sound lower, higher, rising or falling

politeness: showing awareness and consideration of another person's public self-image

polysemy: a word having two or more related meanings (e.g. *foot*, of person, of bed, of mountain)

positive face: the need to be connected, to belong, to be a member of a group, in contrast to **negative face**

positive transfer: the use of a feature from the **L1** that is similar to the **L2** while performing in the **L2**, in contrast to **negative transfer**

post-creole continuum: the range of varieties that evolves in communities where a **creole** is spoken, usually as a result of **decreolization**

postvocalic: used after a vowel

pragmatics: the study of speaker meaning and how more is communicated than is said

prefix: a **bound morpheme** added to the beginning of a word (e.g. *unhappy*)

preposition (Prep): a word such as *in* or *with* used with a **noun phrase**

preposition phrase (PP): a phrase such as *with a dog*, consisting of a **preposition** plus a **noun phrase**

prescriptive approach: an approach to grammar that has rules for the proper use of the language, traditionally based on Latin grammar, in contrast to the **descriptive approach**

prestige: higher status

presupposition: an assumption by a speaker/ writer about what is true or already known by the listener/reader

primary sign language: a sign language that is the first language of a group of people who are typically deaf and do not use a spoken language (e.g. **ASL**), in contrast to an **alternate sign language**

primes: the sets of features that form contrasting elements within the **articulatory parameters** of ASL

productivity: a property of language that allows users to create new expressions, also called "creativity" or "open-endedness"

pronoun (Pro): a word such as *it* or *them* used in place of a **noun phrase**

proper noun (PN): a noun such as *Cathy*, with an initial capital letter, used as the name of someone or something

prothesis: a sound change involving the addition of a sound to the beginning of a word (e.g. *spiritus → espíritu*)

Proto-Indo-European: the hypothesized original form of a language that was the source of many languages in India and Europe

prototype: the most characteristic instance of a category (e.g. *"Robin" is the prototype of "bird"*)

quality maxim: the assumption in conversation that you will "not say that which you believe to be false or for which you lack adequate evidence"

quantity maxim: the assumption in conversation that you will "make your contribution as informative as is required, but not more, or less, than is required"

rebus writing: a way of writing in which a pictorial representation of an object is used to indicate the sound of the word for that object

recursion: the repeated application of a rule in generating structures

reduplication: the process of repeating all or part of a form

reference: an act by which a speaker/writer uses language to enable a listener/reader to identify someone or something

reflexivity: a special property of human language that allows language to be used to think and talk about language itself

register: a conventional way of using language that is appropriate in a specific situation, occupation or topic, characterized by the use of special **jargon**

relation maxim: the assumption in conversation that you will "be relevant"

reversives: **antonyms** in which the meaning of one is the reverse action of the other (e.g. *dress–undress*)

rhyme: the part of the **syllable** containing the **vowel** plus any following **consonant(s)**, also called "rime"

right ear advantage: the fact that humans typically hear speech sounds more readily via the right ear

Sapir–Whorf hypothesis: the general idea that differences in language structure cause people to view the world differently, from the names of two American linguists, Edward Sapir and Benjamin Whorf

schema: a conventional knowledge structure in memory for specific things, such as a supermarket (food is displayed on shelves, arranged in aisles, etc.)

schwa: a mid central vowel /ə/, often used in an unstressed **syllable** (e.g. *afford, oven*)

script: a conventional knowledge structure in memory for the series of actions involved in events such as "Going to the dentist"

second language (L2) learning: the process of developing ability in another language, after **L1** acquisition

segment: an individual sound used in language

semantic features: basic elements such as "human," included as plus (+ human) or minus (−human), used in an analysis of the components of word meaning

semantic role: the part played by a **noun phrase**, such as **agent**, in the event described by the sentence

semantics: the study of the meaning of words, phrases and sentences

shape: the configuration of the hand(s) as an **articulatory parameter** of **ASL**

Signed English: using English sentences with signs instead of words, also called Manually Coded English or MCE

Sign language (or Sign): a communication system using the hands (with the face and other parts of the body)

slang: words or phrases used instead of more conventional forms by those who are typically outside established higher status groups (e.g. *bucks* for *dollars*)

slip of the ear: a processing error in which one word or phrase is heard as another, as in hearing *great ape* when the utterance was "gray tape"

slip of the tongue: a speech error in which a sound or word is produced in the wrong place, as in *black bloxes* (instead of "black boxes")

social category: a **category** in which group members are defined by social connections

social dialect: a variety of a language with features that differ according to the social status (e.g. middle class or working class) of the speaker

social gender: a distinction between individuals in terms of their social roles as women and men, in contrast to other types of **gender**

social marker: a linguistic feature that marks the speaker as a member of a particular social group

social variable: a factor such as working class or middle class that is used to identify one group of speakers as different from another

sociolect: social dialect, a variety of a language that is strongly associated with one social group (e.g. working-class speech)

sociolinguistic competence: the ability to use language appropriately according to the social context as part of **communicative competence**

sociolinguistics: the study of the relationship between language and society

sound loss: a sound change in which a particular sound is no longer used in a language (e.g. the velar fricative [x], in Scottish *loch*, but not in Modern English)

source: the **semantic role** of the noun phrase identifying where an entity moves from (e.g. *The boy ran from the house*)

spatial deixis: using words such as *here* or *there* as a way of "pointing" to a location with language

speech accommodation: modifying speech style toward (**convergence**) or away from (**divergence**) the perceived style of the person being talked to

speech act: an action such as "promising" performed by a speaker with an utterance, either as a **direct speech act** or an **indirect speech act**

speech community: a group of people who share a set of norms and expectations regarding the use of language

speech style: a way of speaking that is either formal/careful or informal/casual

spoonerism: a slip of the tongue in which two parts of words or two words are switched, as in *a dog of bag food* (for "a bag of dog food")

standard language: the variety of a language treated as the official language and used in public broadcasting, publishing and education

stem: the base form to which **affixes** are attached in the formation of words

stop: a **consonant** produced by stopping the airflow, then letting it go, also called "plosive" (e.g. the first and last sounds in *cat*)

strategic competence: the ability to use language to organize effective messages and to overcome potential communication problems as part of **communicative competence**

structural ambiguity: a situation in which a single phrase or sentence has two (or more) different underlying structures and interpretations

structural analysis: the investigation of the distribution of grammatical forms in a language

style-shifting: changing **speech style** from formal to informal or vice versa

subject: the grammatical function of the **noun phrase** typically used to refer to someone or something performing the action of the **verb** (e.g. *The boy stole it*)

suffix: a **bound morpheme** added to the end of a word (e.g. *fainted, illness*)

superordinate: the higher-level term in **hyponymy** (e.g. *flower–daffodil*)

surface structure: the structure of individual sentences after the application of **movement rules** to **deep structure**

syllabic writing (syllabary): a way of writing in which each symbol represents a **syllable**

syllable: a unit of sound consisting of a vowel and optional consonants before or after the vowel

synchronic variation: differences in language form found in different places at the same time, in contrast to **diachronic variation**

synonymy: the **lexical relation** in which two or more words have very closely related meanings (e.g. *"Conceal" is a synonym of "hide"*)

syntax (syntactic structures): (the analysis of) the structure of phrases and sentences

taboo terms: words or phrases that are avoided in formal speech, but are used in swearing, for example (e.g. *fuck*)

tag questions: short questions consisting of an **auxiliary** (e.g. *don't*) and a **pronoun** (e.g. *you*), added to the end of a statement (e.g. *I hate it when it rains all day, **don't you?***)

task-based learning: using activities involving information exchange and problem solving as a way of developing ability in language

telegraphic speech: strings of words (**lexical morphemes** without **inflectional morphemes**) in phrases (*daddy go bye-bye*) produced by two-year-old children

temporal deixis: using words such as *now* or *tomorrow* as a way of "pointing" to a time with language tense: the grammatical category distinguishing forms of the **verb** as present tense and past tense

theme: the **semantic role** of the noun phrase used to identify the entity involved in or affected by the action of the verb in an event (e.g. *The boy kicked the ball*)

tip of the tongue phenomenon: the experience of knowing a word, but being unable to access it and bring it to the surface in order to say it

traditional grammar: the description of the structure of phrases and sentences based on established categories used in the analysis of Latin and Greek

transfer: using sounds, expressions and structures from the **L1** while performing in an **L2**

tree diagram: a diagram with branches showing the **hierarchical organization** of structures

turn: in conversation, the unit of talk by one speaker, ended by the beginning of the next speaker's unit of talk

turn-taking: the way in which each speaker takes a **turn** in conversation

T/V distinction: the difference between pronouns such as *tu* (socially close) and *vous* (socially distant) in French, used as **address terms**

two-word stage: a period beginning at around 18–20 months when children produce two terms together as an utterance (*baby chair*)

uvula: the small appendage at the end of the **velum**

uvular: a sound produced with the back of the tongue near the **uvula**

velar: a **consonant** produced by raising the back of the tongue to the **velum** (e.g. the first and last sounds in *geek*)

velum: the soft area at the back of the roof of the mouth, also called the "soft palate"

verb (V): a word such as *go, drown* or *know* used to describe an action, event or state

verb phrase (VP): a phrase such as *saw a dog*, containing a **verb** and other constituents

vernacular: a social dialect with low prestige spoken by a lower-status group, with marked differences from the **standard language**

vocal folds (or cords): thin strips of muscle in the **larynx** which can be open, in **voiceless sounds**, or close together, creating vibration in **voiced sounds**

voiced sounds: speech sounds produced with vibration of the **vocal folds**

voiceless sounds: speech sounds produced without vibration of the **vocal folds**

vowel: a sound produced through the **vocal folds** without constriction of the airflow in the mouth

Wernicke's aphasia: a language disorder in which comprehension is typically slow while speech is fluent, but vague and missing content words

Wernicke's area: a part of the brain in the left hemisphere involved in language comprehension

writing: the symbolic representation of language through the use of graphic signs

References

Adams, V. (2001) *Complex Words in English* Pearson

Adamson, S. (2000) "A lovely little example" In O. Fischer, A. Rosenbach and D. Stein (eds.)
Pathways of Change: Grammaticalization in English (39–66) John Benjamins

Aikhenvald, A. (2000) *Classifiers* Oxford University Press

Aitchison, J. (2000) *The Seeds of Speech* (Canto edition) Cambridge University Press
(2001) *Language Change: Progress or Decay?* (3rd edition) Cambridge University Press
(2003) *Words in the Mind* (3rd edition) Blackwell
(2008) *The Articulate Mammal* (5th edition) Routledge

Allan, K. (1986) *Linguistic Meaning* Routledge

Allen, J. (2000) *Middle Egyptian: An Introduction to the Language and Culture of Hieroglyphs*
Cambridge University Press

Allport, G. (1983) "Language and cognition" In R. Harris (ed.) *Approaches to Language* (80–94)
Pergamon Press

Anderson, S. (2004) *Doctor Dolittle's Delusion* Yale University Press

Apel, K. and J. Masterson (2001) *Beyond Baby Talk* Three Rivers Press

Ashby, M. and J. Maidment (2005) *Introducing Phonetic Science* Cambridge University Press

Austin, P. (ed.) (2008) *One Thousand Languages* University of California Press

Baker, M. (2001) *The Atoms of Language: The Mind's Hidden Rules of Grammar* Basic Books

Barber, C., J. Beal and P. Shaw (2009) *The English Language: A Historical Introduction* (2nd
edition) Cambridge University Press

Barbour, S. and P. Stevenson (1990) *Variation in German* Cambridge University Press

Bass, A., E. Gilland and R. Baker (2008) "Evolutionary origins for social vocalization in a
vertebrate hindbrain-spinal compartment" *Science* 321 (July 18): 417–421

Bauer, L. (2003) *Introducing Linguistic Morphology* (2nd edition) Edinburgh University Press

Beaken, M. (1996) *The Making of Language* Edinburgh University Press

Bloom, P. (2002) *How Children Learn the Meaning of Words* MIT Press

Bond, Z. (1999) *Slips of the Ear* Academic Press

Booij, G. (2007) *The Grammar of Words: An Introduction to Morphology* (2nd edition) Oxford
University Press

Boroditsky, L. (2003) "Linguistic relativity" In L. Nadel (ed.) *Encyclopedia of Cognitive Science*
(917–921) Nature Publishing Group

Braine, M. (1971) "The acquisition of language in infant and child" In C. Reed (ed.) *The Learning of Language* Appleton-Century-Crofts

Brinton, L. (2000) *The Structure of Modern English* John Benjamins

Brown, G. (1990) *Listening to Spoken English* Longman

(1998) "Context creation in discourse understanding" In K. Malmkjær and J. Williams (eds.) *Context in Language Learning and Language Understanding* (171–192) Cambridge University Press

Brown, G. and G. Yule (1983) *Discourse Analysis* Cambridge University Press

Brown, K. and J. Miller (1991) *Syntax: A Linguistic Introduction to Sentence Structure* (2nd edition) Routledge

Brown, P. and S. Levinson (1987) *Politeness: Some Universals in Language Use* Cambridge University Press

Brown, R. (1973) *A First Language* Harvard University Press

Brown, S. and S. Attardo (2005) *Understanding Language Structure, Interaction, and Variation* (2nd edition) University of Michigan Press

Bruner, J. (1983) *Child's Talk: Learning to Use Language* Norton

Bryson, B. (1994) *Made in America* William Morrow

Buckingham, H. and A. Kertesz (1976) *Neologistic Jargon Aphasia* Swets and Zeitlinger

Burling, R. (2005) *The Talking Ape* Oxford University Press

Burridge, K. (2004) *Blooming English* Cambridge University Press

Cameron, D. (1995) *Verbal Hygiene* Routledge

(2001) *Working with Spoken Discourse* Sage

Campbell, L. (2004) *Historical Linguistics: An Introduction* (2nd edition) MIT Press

Cannon, G. (1990) *The Life and Mind of Oriental Jones* Cambridge University Press

Caplan, D. (1996) *Language: Structure, Processing and Disorders* MIT Press

Carlin, G. (1997) *Braindroppings* Hyperion

Carnie, A. (2002) *Syntax* Blackwell

Carroll, J. (ed.) (1956) *Language, Thought and Reality: Selected Writings of Benjamin Lee Whorf* MIT Press

Carstairs-McCarthy, A. (2002) *An Introduction to English Morphology* Edinburgh University Press

Catford, J. (2002) *A Practical Introduction to Phonetics* Oxford University Press

Cazden, C. (1972) *Child Language and Education* Holt

Celce-Murcia, M. and D. Larsen-Freeman (1999) *The Grammar Book* (2nd edition) Heinle and Heinle

Chambers, J. and P. Trudgill (1998) *Dialectology* (2nd edition) Cambridge University Press

Chapman, S. (2005) *Paul Grice: Philosopher and Linguist* Palgrave Macmillan

Cheney, D. and R. Seyfarth (1990) *How Monkeys See the World* University of Chicago Press

Clark, E. (1993) *The Lexicon in Acquisition* Cambridge University Press

(2009) *First Language Acquisition* (2nd edition) Cambridge University Press

Coates, J. (2004) *Women, Men and Language* (3rd edition) Longman

Coates, R. (1999) *Word Structure* Routledge

Comrie, B. (ed.) (1987) *The World's Major Languages* Oxford University Press

Cook, G. (2003) *Applied Linguistics* Oxford University Press

Cook, V. (2004) *The English Writing System* Hodder Arnold

Corballis, M. (2002) *From Hand to Mouth* Princeton University Press

Coulmas, F. (2003) *Writing Systems* Cambridge University Press

Coupland, D. (1991) *Generation X: Tales for an Accelerated Culture* St. Martin's Press

Cruse, A. (2004) *Meaning in Language* (2nd edition) Oxford University Press

Cruttenden, A. (2008) *Gimson's Pronunciation of English* (7th edition) Arnold

Crystal, D. (2003) *The Cambridge Encyclopedia of the English Language* (2nd edition) Cambridge University Press

(2008) *A Dictionary of Linguistics and Phonetics* (6th edition) Blackwell

Curtiss, S. (1977) *Genie: A Psycholinguistic Study of a Modern-day Wild Child* Academic Press

Cutting, J. (2008) *Pragmatics and Discourse* (2nd edition) Routledge

Damasio, A. (1994) *Descartes' Error* Putnam

Daniels, P. and W. Bright (1996) *The World's Writing Systems* Oxford University Press

Danziger, E. (2001) *Relatively Speaking* Oxford University Press

Darwin, C. (1871) *The Descent of Man, and Selection in Relation to Sex* John Murray

Davenport, M. and S. Hannahs (2005) *Introducing Phonetics and Phonology* (2nd edition) Hodder Arnold

Davies, W. (1987) *Egyptian Hieroglyphics* British Museum/University of California Press

Deacon, T. (1997) *The Symbolic Species* W. W. Norton

Denning, K., B. Kessler and W. Leben (2007) *English Vocabulary Elements* (2nd edition) Oxford University Press

Downes, W. (2001) "Register" In R. Mesthrie (ed.) *Concise Encyclopedia of Sociolinguistics* (259–262) Elsevier

Downing, B. and J. Fuller (1984) "Cultural contact and the Expansion of the Hmong Lexicon" Unpublished manuscript, Department of Linguistics, University of Minnesota

Duanmu, S. (2008) *Syllable Structure* Oxford University Press

Duranti, A. (1997) *Linguistic Anthropology* Cambridge University Press

(2001) *Key Terms in Language and Culture* Blackwell

Eble, C. (2004) "Slang" In E. Finegan and J. Rickford (eds.) *Language in the USA* (375–386) Cambridge University Press

Eckert, P. (2000) *Linguistic Variation as Social Practice* Blackwell

(2004) "Adolescent language" In E. Finegan and J. Rickford (eds.) *Language in the USA* (361–374) Cambridge University Press

Eckert, P. and S. McConnell-Ginet (2003) *Language and Gender* Cambridge University Press

Eckert, P. and J. Rickford (eds.) (2001) *Style and Sociolinguistic Variation* Cambridge University Press

Ekman, P. (1999) "Emotional and conversational nonverbal signals" In L. Messing and R. Campbell (eds.) *Gesture, Speech and Sign* (45–55) Oxford University Press

Ellis, R. (1997) *Second Language Acquisition* Oxford University Press

Espy, W. (1975) *An Almanac of Words at Play* Clarkson Potter

Ethnologue (2005) (15th edition) SIL International

Fabb, N. (1998) "Compounding" In A. Spencer and A. Zwicky (eds.) *The Handbook of Morphology* (66–83) Blackwell

Fant, L. (1977) *Sign Language* Joyce Media

Faulkner, W. (1929) *The Sound and the Fury* Jonathan Cape

Finegan, E. and N. Besnier (1989) *Language: Its Structure and Use* Harcourt Brace Jovanovich

Finegan, E. and J. Rickford (eds.) (2004) *Language in the USA* Cambridge University Press

Flaherty, A. (2004) *The Midnight Disease* Houghton Mifflin

Foley, W. (1997) *Anthropological Linguistics* Blackwell

Fought, C. (2003) *Chicano English in Context* Palgrave Macmillan

Frawley, W. (1992) *Linguistic Semantics* Lawrence Erlbaum

Friend, T. (2004) *Animal Talk* Simon and Schuster

Fromkin, V., R. Rodman and N. Hyams (2007) *An Introduction to Language* (8th edition) Thomson Heinle

Gardner, R., B. Gardner and T. Van Cantfort (eds.) (1989) *Teaching Sign Language to Chimpanzees* State University of New York Press

Gass, S. and L. Selinker (2001) *Second Language Acquisition: An Introductory Course* (2nd edition) Lawrence Erlbaum

Geschwind, N. (1991) "Specializations of the human brain" In W. Wang (ed.) *The Emergence of Language* (72–87) W. H. Freeman

Gibson, K. and T. Ingold (eds.) (1993) *Tools, Language and Cognition in Human Evolution* Cambridge University Press

Giles, H. (2001) "Speech accommodation" In R. Mesthrie (ed.) *Concise Encyclopedia of Sociolinguistics* (193–197) Elsevier

Glassner, J. (2003) *The Invention of Cuneiform* Johns Hopkins University Press

Gleason, H. (1955) *Workbook in Descriptive Linguistics* Holt

Goldin-Meadow, S. (2003) *Hearing Gesture* Harvard University Press

Goodglass, H., E. Kaplan and B. Barresi (2001) *The Assessment of Aphasia and Related Disorders* (3rd edition) Lippincott, Williams and Wilkins

Green, L. (2002) *African American English* Cambridge University Press

Grice, P. (1975) "Logic and conversation" In P. Cole and J. Morgan (eds.) *Syntax and Semantics 3: Speech Acts* (41–58) Academic Press

(1989) *Studies in the Way of Words* Harvard University Press

Griffen, D. (2001) *Animal Minds* University of Chicago Press

Grundy, P. (2008) *Doing Pragmatics* (3nd edition) Hodder

Guiora, A., B. Beit-Hallahmi, R. Brannon, C. Dull and T. Scovel (1972) "The effects of experimentally induced change in ego states on pronunciation ability in a second language: an exploratory study" *Comprehensive Psychiatry* 13: 5–23.

Handbook of the International Phonetic Association (1999) Cambridge University Press

Hardcastle, W. and N. Hewlett (1999) *Coarticulation: Theory, Data and Techniques* Cambridge University Press

Hauser, M. (1996) *The Evolution of Communication* MIT Press

Have, P. (2007) *Doing Conversation Analysis* (2nd edition) Sage

Hayes, C. (1951) *The Ape in Our House* Harper

Heilman, K. (2002) *Matter of Mind* Oxford University Press

Hess, E. (2008) *Nim Chimpsky: The Chimp Who Would Be Human* Bantam Books

Hinnebusch, T. (1987) "Swahili" In T. Shopen (ed.) *Languages and Their Status* (209–294) University of Pennsylvania Press

Hockett, C. (1960) "The origin of speech" *Scientific American* 203: 89–96

Holmes, J. (2008) *An Introduction to Sociolinguistics* (3rd edition) Pearson

Huang, Y. (2000) *Anaphora: A Cross-Linguistic Approach* Oxford University Press

Huddleston, R. and G. Pullum (2005) *A Student's Introduction to English Grammar* Cambridge University Press

Hudson, G. (2000) *Essential Introductory Linguistics* Blackwell

Hudson, R. (1998) *English Grammar* Routledge

Hugdahl, K. and R. Davidson (2004) *The Asymmetrical Brain* MIT Press

Hughes, A., P. Trudgill and D. Watt (2005) *English Accents and Dialects* Hodder Arnold

Humphries, T. and C. Padden (2003) *Learning American Sign Language* (2nd edition) Allyn and Bacon

Hurford, J. (1994) *Grammar: A Student's Guide* Cambridge University Press

Hurford, J., B. Heasley and M. Smith (2007) *Semantics: A Coursebook* (2nd edition) Cambridge University Press

Ingram, J. (2007) *Neurolinguistics* Cambridge University Press

Inoue, K. (1979) "Japanese" In T. Shopen (ed.) *Languages and Their Speakers* (241–300) Winthrop Publishers

Janson, T. (2002) *Speak: A Short History of Languages* Oxford University Press

Jeffery, L. (1990) *The Local Scripts of Archaic Greece* Clarendon Press

Jeffries, L. (2006) *Discovering Language* Palgrave Macmillan

Jensen, H. (1969) *Sign, Symbol and Script* (translated by G. Unwin) (3rd edition) Putnam's

Jespersen, O. (1922) *Language. Its Nature, Development and Origin* Macmillan

Johannson, S. (2005) *Origins of Language* John Benjamins

Johnson, K. (2003) *Acoustic and Auditory Phonetics* (2nd edition) Blackwell

Johnston, T. and A. Schembri (2007) *Australian Sign Language: An Introduction to Sign Language Linguistics* Cambridge University Press

Jones, D., P. Roach, J. Hartman and J. Setter (2006) *Cambridge English Pronouncing Dictionary* (17th edition) Cambridge University Press

Jones, S. (2002) *Antonymy* Routledge

Jusczyk, P. (1997) *The Discovery of Spoken Language* MIT Press

Kellerman, E., T. Ammerlan, T. Bongaerts and N. Poulisse (1990) "System and hierarchy in L2 compensatory strategies" In R. Scarcella, E. Anderson and S. Krashen (eds.)

Developing Communicative Competence in a Second Language (163–178) Newbury House

Kellogg, W. and L. Kellogg (1933) *The Ape and the Child* McGraw-Hill

Kendon, A. (1988) *Sign Languages of Aboriginal Australia* Cambridge University Press
(2004) *Gesture* Cambridge University Press

Kenneally, C. (2007) *The First Word* Viking Press

Kent, H. (1986) *Treasury of Hawaiian Words in One Hundred and One Categories* University of Hawai'i Press

Kramsch, C. (1998) *Language and Culture* Oxford University Press

Kreidler, C. (2004) *The Pronunciation of English* (2nd edition) Blackwell

Kretzschmar, W. (2004) "Regional dialects" In E. Finegan and J. Rickford (eds.) *Language in the USA* (39–57) Cambridge University Press

Kroeger, P. (2005) *Analyzing Grammar* Cambridge University Press

Kuper, A. (1999) *Culture: The Anthropologist's Account* Harvard University Press

Labov, W. (2001) *Principles of Linguistic Change* volume 2: *Social Factors* Blackwell
(2006) *The Social Stratification of English in New York City* (2nd edition) Cambridge University Press

Ladefoged, P. (2006) *A Course in Phonetics* (5th edition) Thomson

Lakoff, G. (1987) *Women, Fire and Dangerous Things* University of Chicago Press

Lakoff, R. (1990) *Talking Power* Basic Books

Language Files (2007) (10th edition) Ohio State University Press

Lerer, S. (2007) *Inventing English: A Portable History of the Language* Columbia University Press

Lesser, R. and L. Milroy (1993) *Linguistics and Aphasia* Longman

Levinson, S. (1983) *Pragmatics* Cambridge University Press

Lewis, G. (2000) *Turkish Grammar* (2nd edition) Oxford University Press

Lieber, R. (2004) *Morphology and Lexical Semantics* Cambridge University Press

Lieberman, P. (1998) *Eve Spoke: Human Language and Human Evolution* W. W. Norton

Lightbown, P. and N. Spada (2006) *How Languages Are Learned* (3rd edition) Oxford University Press

Lippi-Green, R. (1997) *English with an Accent* Routledge

Loritz, D. (1999) *How the Brain Evolved Language* Oxford University Press

Lucas, C. and C. Valli (2004) "American Sign Language" In E. Finegan and J. Rickford (eds.) *Language in the USA* (230–244) Cambridge University Press

Lum, D. (1990) *Pass On, No Pass Back!* Bamboo Ridge Press

Lust, B. (2006) *Child Language* Cambridge University Press

Lynch, J. (1998) *Pacific Languages* University of Hawai'i Press

Maccoby, E. (1998) *The Two Sexes* Harvard University Press

Mackay, D. (1970) *A Flock of Words* Harcourt

MacNeilage, P. (1998) "The frame/content theory of evolution of speech production" *Behavioral and Brain Sciences* 21: 499–546

Malmkjær, K. and J. Williams (eds.) (1998) *Context in Language Learning and Language Understanding* Cambridge University Press

Malotki, E. (1983) *Hopi Time* Walter de Gruyter

Man, J. (2000) *Alpha Beta* John Wiley

Martin, L. (1986) "'Eskimo words for snow': a case study in the genesis and decay of an anthropological example" *American Anthropologist* 88: 418–423

McMahon, A. (1994) *Understanding Language Change* Cambridge University Press

   (2002) *An Introduction to English Phonology* Oxford University Press

McNeill, D. (1966) "Developmental psycholinguistics" In F. Smith and G. Miller (eds.) *The Genesis of Language* (15–84) MIT Press

   (1992) *Hand and Mind* University of Chicago Press

Merrifield, W., C. Naish, C. Rensch and G. Story (2003) *Laboratory Manual for Morphology and Syntax* (7th edition) Summer Institute of Linguistics

Mesthrie, R., J. Swann, A. Deumert and W. Leap (2000) *Introducing Sociolinguistics* John Benjamins

Meyer, C. (2002) *English Corpus Linguistics* Cambridge University Press

Miller, J. (2008) *An Introduction to English Syntax* (2nd edition) Edinburgh University Press

Minkova, D. and R. Stockwell (2009) *English Words: History and Structure* (2nd edition) Cambridge University Press

Mithen, S. (2006) *The Singing Neanderthals* Harvard University Press

Morenberg, M. (2003) *Doing Grammar* (3rd edition) Oxford University Press

Mosel, U. and E. Hovdhaugen (1992) *Samoan Reference Grammar* Scandinavian University Press

Moskowitz, B. (1991) "The acquisition of language" In W. Wang (ed.) *The Emergence of Language* (131–149) W. H. Freeman

Mugglestone, L. (1995) *Talking Proper: The Rise of Accent as Social Symbol* Clarendon Press

Murphy, M. (2003) *Semantic Relations and the Lexicon* Cambridge University Press

Myers-Scotton, C. (2006) *Multiple Voices* Blackwell

Napoli, D. (2003) *Language Matters* Oxford University Press

Nichols, P. (2004) "Creole languages: forging new identities" In E. Finegan and J. Rickford (eds.) *Language in the USA* (133–152) Cambridge University Press

Obler, L. and K. Gjerlow (1999) *Language and the Brain* Cambridge University Press

Odden, D. (2005) *Introducing Phonology* Cambridge University Press

O'Grady, W. (1997) *Syntactic Development* University of Chicago Press

   (2005) *How Children Learn Language* Cambridge University Press

O'Grady, W., J. Archibald, M. Aronoff and J. Rees-Miller (2005) *Contemporary Linguistics* (5th edition) Bedford/St. Martin's Press

Oller, D. (2000) *The Emergence of the Speech Capacity* Lawrence Erlbaum

Overstreet, M. (1999) *Whales, Candlelight and Stuff Like That: General Extenders in English Discourse* Oxford University Press

Paltridge, B. (2006) *Discourse Analysis* Continuum

Patterson, F. and E. Linden (1981) *The Education of Koko* Holt

Payne, T. (2006) *Exploring Language Structure* Cambridge University Press

Peccei, J. (1999) *Pragmatics* Routledge

Penfield, W. and L. Roberts (1959) *Speech and Brain Mechanisms* Princeton University Press

Pica, T., L. Holliday, N. Lewis, D. Berducci and J. Newman (1991) "Language learning through interaction: what role does gender play?" *Studies in Second Language Acquisition* 11: 63–90

Pinker, S. (1994) *The Language Instinct* William Morrow

(1999) *Words and Rules* HarperCollins

(2007) *The Stuff of Thought* Viking

Plag, I. (2003) *Word-formation in English* Cambridge University Press

Poulisse, N. (1999) *Slips of the Tongue* John Benjamins

Premack, A. and D. Premack (1991) "Teaching language to an ape" In W. Wang (ed.) *The Emergence of Language* (16–27) W. H. Freeman

Psathas, G. (1995) *Conversation Analysis* Sage

Pullum, G. (1991) *The Great Eskimo Vocabulary Hoax* University of Chicago Press

Pullum, G. and W. Ladusaw (1996) *Phonetic Symbol Guide* (2nd edition) University of Chicago Press

Quirk, R., S. Greenbaum, G. Leech and J. Svartvik (1985) *A Comprehensive Grammar of the English Language* Longman

Radford, A. (2004) *English Syntax* Cambridge University Press

Radford, A., M. Atkinson, D. Britain, H. Clahsen and A. Spencer (2009) *Linguistics: An Introduction* (2nd edition) Cambridge University Press

Renkema, J. (2004) *Introduction to Discourse Studies* (2nd edition) John Benjamins

Richards, J. and T. Rodgers (2001) *Approaches and Methods in Language Teaching* (2nd edition) Cambridge University Press

Rimpau, J., R. Gardner and B. Gardner (1989) "Expression of person, place and instrument in ASL utterances of children and chimpanzees" In R. Gardner, B. Gardner and T. van Cantfort (eds.) *Teaching Sign Language to Chimpanzees* (240–268) State University of New York Press

Rissanen, M. (2008) "From 'quickly' to 'fairly': on the history of *rather*" *English Language and Linguistics* 12: 345–359

Roach, P. (2000) *English Phonetics and Phonology* (3rd edition) Cambridge University Press

(2001) *Phonetics* Oxford University Press

Robinson, A. (2007) *The Story of Writing* (2nd edition) Thames and Hudson

Rogers, H. (2005) *Writing Systems: A Linguistic Approach* Blackwell

Rogers, L. and G. Kaplan (2000) *Songs, Roars and Rituals* Harvard University Press

Romaine, S. (1988) *Pidgin and Creole Languages* Longman

(2000) *Language in Society* (2nd edition) Oxford University Press

Ross, J. (1967) *Constraints on Variables in Syntax* Indiana University Linguistics Club

Rumbaugh, D. (ed.) (1977) *Language Learning by a Chimpanzee: The LANA Project* Academic Press

Rymer, R. (1993) *Genie* HarperCollins

Sacks, O. (1989) *Seeing Voices* University of California Press

Saeed, J. (2003) *Semantics* (2nd edition) Blackwell

Sakoda, K. and J. Siegel (2003) *Pidgin Grammar* Bess Press

Sampson, G. (1980) *Schools of Linguistics* Stanford University Press

   (2005) *The "Language Instinct" Debate* (Revised edition) Continuum

Sanford, A. and S. Garrod (1981) *Understanding Written Language* Wiley

Sankoff, G. and S. Laberge (1974) "On the acquisition of native speakers by a language" In
     D. DeCamp and I. Hancock (eds.) *Pidgins and Creoles* (73–84) Georgetown University Press

Savage-Rumbaugh, S. and R. Lewin (1994) *Kanzi* John Wiley

Saville-Troike, M. (2006) *Introducing Second Language Acquisition* Cambridge University Press

Schiffrin, D. (1987) *Discourse Markers* Cambridge University Press

Schendl, H. (2001) *Historical Linguistics* Oxford University Press

Schmandt-Besserat, D. (1996) *How Writing Came About* University of Texas Press

Sedaris, D. (2000) *Me Talk Pretty One Day* Little Brown

Seinfeld, J. (1993) *Seinlanguage* Bantam Books

Shibatani, M. (2001) "Honorifics" In R. Mesthrie (ed.) *Concise Encyclopedia of Sociolinguistics*
     (552–559) Elsevier

Siegel, J. (2008) *The Emergence of Pidgin and Creole Languages* Oxford University Press

Sihler, A. (2000) *Language History: An Introduction* John Benjamins

Sinclair, J. (2003) *Reading Concordances* Pearson

Singleton, D. and L. Ryan (2004) *Language Acquisition: The Age Factor* (2nd edition)
     Multilingual Matters

Smitherman, G. (2000) *talkin that talk: African American Language and Culture* Routledge

Sperber, D. and D. Wilson (1995) *Relevance* (2nd edition) Blackwell

Spolsky, B. (1998) *Sociolinguistics* Oxford University Press

Springer, S. and G. Deutsch (2001) *Left Brain, Right Brain* (6th edition) W. H. Freeman

Stewart, D., E. Stewart and J. Little (2006) *American Sign Language the Easy Way* (2nd edition)
     Barron's Educational

Stokoe, W. (1960) *Sign Language Structure: An Outline of the Visual Communication Systems of*
     the American Deaf Studies in Linguistics, Occasional Papers 8 University of Buffalo

   (2001) *Language in Hand* Gallaudet University Press

Stubbs, M. (2001) *Words and Phrases* Blackwell

Sutton-Spence, R. and B. Woll (1999) *The Linguistics of British Sign Language* Cambridge
     University Press

Swan, M. (2005) *Grammar* Oxford University Press

Tallermann, M. (2005) *Understanding Syntax* (2nd edition) Hodder Arnold

Tannen, D. (1984) *Conversational Style* Ablex

   (1990) *You Just Don't Understand* William Morrow

Taylor, J. (2003) *Linguistic Categorization* (3rd edition) Oxford University Press

Terrace, H. (1979) *Nim: A Chimpanzee Who Learned Sign Language* Knopf

Thomas, J. (1995) *Meaning in Interaction* Longman

Thomas, L. (1993) *Beginning Syntax* Blackwell

Tomasello, M. (2003) *Constructing a Language* Harvard University Press

Tonouchi, L. (2001) *Da Word* Bamboo Ridge Press

Trudgill, P. (1974) *The Social Differentiation of English in Norwich* Cambridge University Press
    (1983) *On Dialect* Blackwell
    (2000) *Sociolinguistics* (4th edition) Penguin Books

Trudgill, P. and J. Hannah (2008) *International English* (5th edition) Hodder

Umiker-Sebeok, D-J. and T. Sebeok (eds.) (1987) *Monastic Sign Languages* Mouton de Gruyter

Ungerer, F. and H-J. Schmid (2006) *An Introduction to Cognitive Linguistics* (2nd edition) Pearson

Ur, P. (1988) *Grammar Practice Activities* Cambridge University Press

Valian, V. (1999) "Input and language acquisition" In W. Ritchie and T. Bhatia (eds.) *Handbook of Child Language Acquisition* (497–530) Academic Press

Valli, C., C. Lucas and K. Mulrooney (2005) *Linguistics of American Sign Language: An Introduction* (4th edition) Gallaudet University Press

van Dijk, T. (1996) "Discourse, power and access" In C. Caldas-Coulthard and M. Coulthard (eds.) *Texts and Practices: Readings in Critical Discourse Analysis* (84–104) Routledge

VanPatten, B. (2003) *From Input to Output: A Teacher's Guide to Second Language Acquisition* McGraw-Hill

Verschueren, J. (1999) *Understanding Pragmatics* Arnold

Vise, D. and M. Malseed (2005) *The Google Story* Delacorte Press

von Frisch, K. (1993) *The Dance Language and Orientation of Bees* Harvard University Press

Wardhaugh, R. (2006) *An Introduction to Sociolinguistics* (5th edition) Blackwell

Watts, R. (2003) *Politeness* Cambridge University Press

Weir, R. (1966) "Questions on the learning of phonology" In F. Smith and G. Miller (eds.) *The Genesis of Language* (153–168) MIT Press

Widdowson, H. (1978) *Teaching Language as Communication* Oxford University Press
    (2007) *Discourse Analysis* Oxford University Press

Wiley, T. (2004) "Language planning, language policy and the English-Only movement" In E. Finegan and J. Rickford (eds.) *Language in the USA* (319–338) Cambridge University Press

Wolfram, W. and B. Ward (eds.) (2006) *American Voices: How Dialects Differ from Coast to Coast* Blackwell

Woodard, R. (2003) *The Cambridge Encyclopedia of the World's Ancient Languages* Cambridge University Press

Yip, M. and S. Matthews (2007) *The Bilingual Child* Cambridge University Press

Yu, A. (2007) *A Natural History of Infixation* Oxford University Press

Yule, G. (1996) *Pragmatics* Oxford University Press
    (1998) *Explaining English Grammar* Oxford University Press

Index

Technical terms and page references where definitions can be found are indicated by **bold** type.